"BEYOND THE RAINBOW: AN IN-DEPTH GUIDE TO UNDERSTANDING LGBTAI LIVES"

Navigating Sexual Orientation, Gender Identity, Discrimination, Mental Health, And More

Jamie Anderson

Independently Published

ISBN (Print): 9798390582237

Printed in the United States of America

Design Layout by:

Gracen Regal Services

gracenregalservices@gmail.com

+2349135950469

TABLE OF CONTENTS

INTRODUCTION

The Lesbian, Gay, Bisexual, Transgender, Asexual, and Intersex (LGBTAI) community has been gaining increasing visibility and acceptance in recent years. However, many people still struggle to fully understand and accept this diverse group of individuals. This book aims to provide a comprehensive overview of the various identities and experiences within the LGBTAI community.

In this book, we will explore topics such as sexual orientation, gender identity, intersexuality, asexuality, coming out, discrimination and violence, mental health, allies, relationships, parenting, faith, workplace and education, health, culture, activism, intersectionality, religion, mental health, international contexts, disability, and the criminal justice system. Each chapter will delve into the specific nuances and challenges faced by different members of the LGBTAI community.

Through this book, we hope to provide readers with a greater understanding of the diverse experiences and perspectives within the LGBTAI community. Whether you are a member of the community yourself or an ally seeking to educate yourself and better support your loved ones, this book is intended to be a valuable resource.

It is our hope that this book will promote greater acceptance and inclusion of the LGBTAI community, and contribute to a more compassionate and just society for all.

<u>ONE</u>
Sexual Orientation

A person's sexual orientation describes the gender(s) they feel a romantic or sexual attraction toward. In contrast to popular belief, there is a lot more nuance to sexual orientation than being either heterosexual (attracted to people of the same gender) or homosexual (attracted to people of the opposite gender). Within the LGBTAI community, many different sexual identities coexist.

- **Lesbian:** A woman who is attracted to other women
- **Gay:** A man who is attracted to other men
- **Bisexual:** An individual who is attracted to both men and women, or to individuals of multiple genders
- **Pansexual:** An individual who is attracted to people regardless of their gender identity
- **Asexual:** An individual who experiences little or no sexual attraction to others
- **Demisexual:** An individual who experiences sexual attraction only after forming a deep emotional connection with another person
- **Polysexual:** Refers to individuals who are attracted to multiple genders, but not necessarily all genders.

To be clear, sexual orientation is not the same thing as gender identity or biological sex. Whereas one's sexual orientation describes the people to whom one is attracted, one's gender identity describes the gender with which one identifies. The term "biological sex" is used to describe an individual's innate sexual characteristics. A more accepting and affirming world can be created for people of all identities if the differences between sexual orientation, gender identity, and biological sex are recognized and respected.

While discussions of sexual orientation typically center on a person's attraction to people of one or the other gender, it's important to keep in mind that there are many different ways in which people can feel sexual. People whose sexual orientation or gender identity does not conform to mainstream standards may self-identify as queer. Others may self-identify as questioning to express uncertainty about or curiosity about their sexual orientation.

Keep in mind that a person's sexual orientation can shift at any time. Some people may view their sexuality as an immutable part of who they are, but others may notice that their attraction to particular partners or their desires change over time. Many things can cause this, including maturation and the introduction of novel perspectives and identities.

Homophobia and transphobia, two terms for the same phenomenon, refer to discrimination and prejudice against people who do not identify as heterosexual. Many people continue to experience discrimination, violence, and harassment because of their sexual orientation or gender identity, despite advances towards greater acceptance and inclusion. Dismantling preconceived notions and prejudices about people of different sexual orientations is an essential part of building a more accepting and welcoming society. The belief that transgender people are mentally ill is just one example of how these misconceptions manifest; others include the idea that all gay men are effeminate or that being bisexual is just a passing phase.

Acceptance and understanding can also be aided by learning more about them. We can better understand the needs and challenges of people of non-heterosexual orientations, as well as the ways in which society can work to create a more equitable and supportive environment, if we learn from their experiences and perspectives. The idea that one's sexual orientation can be altered at will is widely held but incorrect. Nonetheless, studies have shown repeatedly that one's sexual orientation is not something that can be changed. Instead, it is something fundamental to a person's identity that develops over time and is influenced by both internal and external factors.

Although much remains to be discovered, studies have pointed to genetic, hormonal, and developmental factors as possible culprits in sexual orientation. Some research suggests that sexual orientation may be influenced by one's genetic makeup, and that the brains of people with different sexual orientations may be structured differently. Despite the fact that one's sexual orientation cannot be changed, many people who do not identify as heterosexual may have difficulty accepting themselves or fear being judged negatively by others. This is often the case for people whose families or communities are less tolerant of alternative sexual identities. Access to mental health care and social support networks should be made available to those who may be experiencing such difficulties.

Recognizing the intersections of identities is also crucial to grasping sexual orientation. Some people who don't identify as heterosexual may also feel a strong sense of solidarity with other marginalized groups, such as people of color, people with disabilities, the poor, and the homeless. Intersecting and compounding identities can lead to one-of-a-kind encounters with discrimination and marginalization.

Recognizing the influence of social and political factors in forming opinions about sexual orientation is also crucial. Access to basic rights and resources, such as healthcare, education, and employment, can be severely hampered by laws and policies that criminalize or discriminate against people with non-heterosexual orientations.

In addition, there can be significant differences in the reception of people of different sexual orientations depending on where they live. Non-heterosexual orientations are celebrated and embraced in some parts of the world, while they are criminalized and shunned in others. The richness and complexity of the human experience can be better understood when we consider the wide range of cultural and social attitudes towards sexual orientation. It's worth noting that people of non-heterosexual orientations are not immune to attraction changes over time. Some people consider themselves to be bisexual or pansexual, meaning they have romantic interests in both sexes. Some people may say they are asexual because they don't feel sexual attraction to anyone. Some people may also say they are "questioning" or "queer," indicating that they are unsure of or still experimenting with their sexual orientation.

The effects of stigma and discrimination on the mental health of people of non-heterosexual orientations must also be acknowledged. Discrimination and rejection based on sexual orientation has been linked to an increased risk of mental health issues like depression, anxiety, and substance abuse, as shown in study after study. This highlights the need for inclusive spaces that welcome people of all sexual orientations and gender identities.

Recognizing that one's sexual orientation is a private matter is also crucial. Coming out as gay or lesbian to family, friends, and coworkers can be an emotionally trying time for many people. This may be especially true for those who are forced to endure the harsh social and legal consequences of their non-heterosexual orientation. Coming out and being open about one's sexual orientation is also not a one-and-done deal; rather, it's an ongoing procedure. It is possible that people will have to face discrimination or misunderstanding based on their sexual orientation in a variety of settings and communities. Therefore, it is crucial to establish communities and safe havens where people of various sexual orientations can feel accepted and secure.

Recognizing the variety within non-heterosexual communities is also critical to a complete comprehension of sexual orientation. For instance, the experiences and viewpoints of lesbian, gay, and bisexual people may vary by race, ethnicity, and gender identity. The experiences of people who label themselves as pansexual or asexual may also vary from those of lesbian, gay, or bisexual people. More acceptance and tolerance can be fostered by raising awareness of the many identities that make up non-heterosexual communities.

Furthermore, one's sexual orientation is not something one can decide to change. People's sexual preferences have nothing to do with their own free will, despite common belief to the contrary. Instead, a person's sexual orientation is a fundamental part of who they are and cannot be altered through therapy or other conversion methods. Efforts to alter a person's sexual orientation are frowned upon by the medical and mental health communities at large, where they are seen as unethical and even harmful.

Furthermore, people of non-heterosexual orientations may encounter additional difficulties and barriers when trying to gain access to healthcare. For instance, they may experience bias or incomprehension from medical staff, resulting in inadequate or delayed treatment. The need for healthcare facilities that welcome people of all sexual orientations and gender identities is highlighted.

Recognizing the significance of intersectionality is also crucial to grasping sexual orientation. People of non-heterosexual orientations, for instance, who also identify with other oppressed groups may experience multiple layers of discrimination and oppression. People from underrepresented groups may also be members of racial or ethnic minorities, have disabilities, or come from disadvantaged socioeconomic backgrounds. Greater awareness and understanding of the unique challenges faced by people of non-heterosexual orientations can be fostered through an increased focus on the intersections of identity.

Furthermore, acknowledging that sexual orientation is not binary but rather can exist on a spectrum is crucial. There are many terms that people may use to describe their sexual orientation, including demisexual, asexual, and queer, in addition to the more commonly known orientations of lesbian, gay, bisexual, and pansexual. It's crucial to treat everyone with dignity and acceptance, regardless of their sexual orientation, and to avoid making assumptions based on stereotypes or bias.

It's important to note that a person's sexual orientation, gender identity, and biological sex are all separate but interrelated facets of their identity. A person's sexual orientation refers to the gender or genders to which they are attracted, while their gender identity refers to their own sense of gender, which may or may not coincide with their biological gender. The biological sex refers to the differences between a male and female body. It's also crucial to understand that sexual orientation and gender identity aren't always the same thing. A transgender man, for instance, may feel attracted to people of any gender, while a cisgender woman may feel only attracted to people who share her gender. The influence of social and cultural factors on an individual's sexual orientation should also be taken into account. It is clear that biological, psychological, and environmental factors all play a role in shaping sexual attraction and identity, though research into the precise causes of sexual orientation is ongoing.

Studies have shown that people with non-heterosexual orientations are more likely to have a close family member who shares that orientation. This finding suggests that genetics may play a role in sexual orientation. Prenatal hormones may play a role, too, in shaping sexual preferences. It's important to remember, though, that biology isn't the only factor in deciding a person's sexual orientation. Individuals' understanding and expression of sexual orientation may be influenced by environmental and social factors such as cultural attitudes towards non-heterosexual orientations, family acceptance, and availability of resources and support.

Also, people of non-heterosexual orientations may have very different experiences depending on their own culture and society. Non-heterosexual orientations face discrimination, violence, and other forms of harm in many parts of the world because of the stigma and criminalization associated with them. It's possible that non-heterosexual orientations receive more attention and resources in settings where they're more widely celebrated and accepted. The identities of people with non-heterosexual orientations, such as their race, ethnicity, religion, and ability status, can further complicate their experiences. The theory of intersectionality draws attention to the ways in which multiple facets of an individual's identity interact to shape their exposure to oppression and privilege.

"Double Minority" describes the unique forms of discrimination and marginalization that some people who identify as both LGBTQ+ and a member of a marginalized racial or ethnic group may experience. As a result of their sexual orientation, people with disabilities may have a harder time gaining access to the resources and support they need.

Understanding sexual orientation also necessitates a persistent dedication to combating oppressive systems that have a negative impact on the LGBTQ+ community. This involves working to dismantle harmful stereotypes and beliefs that keep discrimination and bias alive, as well as advocating for policies and practices that advance equality and inclusion.

Recognizing that some people's sexual orientation may shift over time is also crucial. A person's identity and sense of self can shift in response to their life experiences, cultural norms, and other factors. Some people, for instance, may identify as heterosexual at a young age but change their orientation to bisexuality or pansexuality as they learn more about the people they find attractive. In a similar vein, some people may label themselves as gay or lesbian in their younger years, but shift to bisexual or queer in their later years as they learn more about the nuances of their attraction and identity. It's also crucial to acknowledge the fact that some people have trouble accepting and/or expressing their sexual orientation, especially in societies where this is frowned upon and even criminalized. This can make people feel unworthy of help and create barriers to receiving services and assistance.

Therefore, it is essential to commit to ongoing education and advocacy efforts, as well as to creating safe and supportive environments for individuals to explore and express their identity, in order to promote greater understanding and acceptance of diverse sexual orientations. As part of this effort, we must combat the harmful stereotypes and biases that contribute to discrimination and marginalization, and we must also ensure that people have access to healthcare, mental health resources, and social support networks.

Recognizing the range of identities held by people who identify as LGBTQ+ is also crucial to gaining insight into sexual orientation. There are many identities that can be discussed alongside those of lesbian, gay, bisexual, and pansexual people. These identities can range from asexual to aromantic to demisexual and beyond. There is a wide range of identities and life experiences within the LGBTQ+ community, all of which should be respected.

Furthermore, in order to comprehend sexual orientation, one must acknowledge and combat the effects of systemic oppression and discrimination against people who do not identify as heterosexual. Many members of the LGBTQ+ community continue to face violence, harassment, and discrimination on a daily basis, and it is important to recognize the legacy of anti-LGBTQ+ laws, policies, and social norms.

It's crucial to acknowledge the multifaceted nature of oppression and discrimination, including the ways in which people who identify as LGBTQ+ may also be targeted for prejudice on the basis of their race, ethnicity, religion, or disability. Combating these interrelated oppressions calls for intersectional activism and advocacy, as well as an openness to hearing and prioritizing the voices of those on the margins of the LGBTQ+ community.

TWO
LGBTAI History

*T*he history of the LGBTAI movement is a story of struggle, perseverance, and progress. It is a movement that has been shaped by the activism and sacrifices of countless individuals who fought for the right to love, live, and express themselves freely. The modern LGBTAI movement can be traced back to the Stonewall riots in 1969. The riots, which took place in New York City, were a response to police harassment and discrimination against the LGBTAI community. The riots marked a turning point in the movement, as it galvanized the community to demand equal rights and dignity.

Throughout the 1970s, LGBTAI activists worked tirelessly to raise awareness about discrimination and to promote social acceptance. They organized protests, marches, and rallies, and lobbied lawmakers to pass laws that protected the rights of LGBTAI individuals. In the 1980s, the LGBTAI movement faced a new challenge with the emergence of the AIDS epidemic. Many LGBTAI activists focused their efforts on raising awareness about the disease and fighting for access to treatment and care for those who were affected. The epidemic also highlighted the discrimination and stigma that many LGBTAI individuals faced, and the need for greater societal acceptance and understanding. The 1990s and 2000s saw significant progress in terms of legal rights and protections for LGBTAI individuals. In 1996, the Defense of Marriage Act was passed, which defined marriage as a union between a man and a woman. However, this law was later overturned by the Supreme Court in 2015, in the landmark case Obergefell v. Hodges, which legalized same-sex marriage nationwide.

In recent years, the LGBTAI movement has continued to evolve and expand to include a wider range of identities and experiences. The fight for transgender rights, in particular, has gained greater visibility and momentum. In 2021, President Joe Biden signed an executive order that extended anti-discrimination protections to LGBTAI individuals, including those who are transgender. Despite the progress that has been made, the LGBTAI community still faces significant challenges and discrimination. It is important for everyone to continue to educate themselves about the history of the LGBTAI movement, and to support efforts to promote equality and justice for all.

The history of the LGBTAI movement is also marked by the contributions of key figures who helped to advance the cause of equality and justice. One such figure is Harvey Milk, who became the first openly gay person to be elected to public office in California in 1977. Milk was a vocal advocate for LGBTAI rights and worked tirelessly to promote social acceptance and political representation for the community. Another important figure in LGBTAI history is Marsha P. Johnson, an African American transgender woman and activist who played a key role in the Stonewall riots. Johnson was a fierce advocate for transgender rights and was instrumental in founding the Street Transvestite Action Revolutionaries (STAR), an organization that provided support and resources to transgender individuals.

The LGBTAI movement has also been shaped by the contributions of countless other activists, allies, and community members. Through their activism, they have challenged discrimination, fought for legal rights, and worked to create a more inclusive and accepting society. Despite the progress that has been made, the LGBTAI community still faces significant challenges and discrimination. Transgender individuals, in particular, continue to face high levels of violence and discrimination, and are often marginalized within the broader LGBTAI community. LGBTAI youth also continue to face high rates of homelessness and suicide.

In order to continue making progress towards equality and justice for all, it is important for individuals to educate themselves about the history of the LGBTAI movement and to actively support efforts to promote social acceptance and political representation for the community. This includes advocating for policies that protect the rights of LGBTAI individuals, supporting organizations that provide resources and support to the community, and standing in solidarity with marginalized individuals within the LGBTAI community. In addition to legal and social challenges, the LGBTAI community also faces disparities in healthcare and access to resources. For example, LGBTAI individuals are at a higher risk for certain health issues, such as mental health disorders and substance abuse, due to societal stigma and discrimination. Furthermore, transgender individuals often face significant barriers to accessing appropriate healthcare, including gender-affirming medical care.

The fight for LGBTAI equality and justice is ongoing, and it is important for individuals to recognize the intersectionality of the movement. This includes recognizing the unique experiences and challenges faced by individuals who hold multiple marginalized identities, such as LGBTAI people of color or LGBTAI individuals with disabilities.

One important aspect of the LGBTAI movement is the creation and cultivation of safe spaces for the community. These spaces can include community centers, advocacy organizations, and social groups, and provide LGBTAI individuals with a sense of belonging and support. Safe spaces can also serve as a platform for organizing and advocacy, and can help to amplify the voices of marginalized individuals within the community. The history of the LGBTAI movement is one of resilience, perseverance, and progress. While significant strides have been made in terms of legal rights and social acceptance, the community still faces significant challenges and barriers. It is important for individuals to continue to educate themselves about the history of the LGBTAI movement, and to actively support efforts to promote equality and justice for all members of the community.

One important aspect of the evolution of the LGBTAI movement has been the growing recognition of the importance of intersectionality. This means recognizing that individuals may hold multiple marginalized identities, and that these identities can intersect and compound to create unique experiences of discrimination and oppression. For example, an LGBTAI person of color may face discrimination based on both their sexual orientation or gender identity, as well as their race or ethnicity. As a result, many advocacy organizations and movements within the LGBTAI community have made a concerted effort to address intersectionality and to center the experiences of marginalized individuals within the community. This includes initiatives aimed at promoting racial justice, disability rights, and economic equality, among others.

Another important aspect of the evolution of the LGBTAI movement has been the increasing visibility of transgender individuals and issues. While the movement has historically focused primarily on LGBTAI individuals, there has been a growing recognition of the unique challenges faced by transgender individuals and a push to promote greater inclusion and acceptance for this population. This includes advocacy for gender-affirming medical care, legal recognition of gender identity, and greater representation of transgender individuals in media and politics. While there is still much work to be done to ensure that transgender individuals are fully included and supported within the LGBTAI community, progress has been made in recent years, and there is growing recognition of the unique challenges and experiences faced by this population. The evolution of the LGBTAI movement has been marked by a growing recognition of the importance of intersectionality and a focus on promoting greater inclusion and acceptance for all members of the community. While there is still much work to be done, the progress that has been made thus far is a testament to the resilience and perseverance of the

LGBTAI community, and serves as a source of inspiration and motivation for continued advocacy and activism.

In recent years, the LGBTAI movement has also made significant strides in terms of legal rights and protections. In 2015, the United States Supreme Court legalized same-sex marriage nationwide, a historic victory for the LGBTAI community. This landmark decision represented a major step forward in terms of legal recognition and equality, and helped to set a precedent for similar victories around the world. In addition to legal victories, the LGBTAI movement has also seen progress in terms of social acceptance and representation. There has been a growing recognition of the importance of representation in media and popular culture, and a push for greater visibility of LGBTAI individuals in film, television, and other forms of entertainment.

This increased visibility has helped to promote greater acceptance and understanding of LGBTAI issues, and has provided a platform for LGBTAI individuals to share their stories and experiences. It has also helped to promote a sense of community and belonging among LGBTAI individuals, and has served as a source of inspiration and empowerment for individuals who may be struggling with issues related to their sexual orientation or gender identity. Despite the progress that has been made, the LGBTAI community still faces significant challenges and discrimination. This includes ongoing discrimination in areas such as employment, housing, and healthcare, as well as ongoing efforts to roll back legal protections and rights. Additionally, there are still many individuals who do not fully understand or accept the experiences of LGBTAI individuals, which can contribute to feelings of isolation, alienation, and shame.

In order to continue making progress towards greater equality and justice for all members of the LGBTAI community, it is important for individuals to remain engaged and active in advocacy efforts. This includes supporting organizations that provide resources and support to the community, advocating for policies that protect the rights of LGBTAI individuals, and continuing to educate oneself and others about the experiences and challenges faced by the community. With continued advocacy and action, it is possible to build a more inclusive and accepting society for all.

One important aspect of advancing the rights and acceptance of the LGBTAI community is the role of allies. Allies are individuals who do not identify as LGBTAI themselves but support the community and its goals for equality and justice. Allies can play an important role in promoting greater understanding and acceptance of LGBTAI individuals, challenging discrimination and prejudice, and advocating for policies that protect the rights of the community. There are a number of ways that individuals can become effective allies to the LGBTAI community. This includes educating oneself about the experiences and challenges faced by LGBTAI individuals, and actively working to challenge discrimination and prejudice in one's own life and community. It also includes advocating for policies that promote greater equality and protection for the community, such as employment nondiscrimination laws or transgender-inclusive healthcare policies.

Another important aspect of allyship is listening to and amplifying the voices of marginalized individuals within the community. This means centering the experiences and perspectives of individuals who hold multiple marginalized identities, such as LGBTAI people of color or LGBTAI individuals with disabilities. It also means acknowledging and addressing the ways in which allyship can sometimes inadvertently contribute to further marginalization or exclusion, and being open to feedback and critique from within the community. Another important aspect of the LGBTAI movement is the concept of intersectionality. Intersectionality refers to the interconnected nature of social identities, and the ways in which systems of oppression can intersect and compound to create unique experiences of discrimination and marginalization. For example, an LGBTAI person of color may face different and more complex forms of discrimination and marginalization than an LGBTAI person who is white.

Understanding and addressing intersectionality is crucial for creating a more inclusive and just movement. This means recognizing and addressing the ways in which various forms of oppression intersect, and working to create a movement that is truly inclusive and representative of all members of the LGBTAI community. It also means acknowledging and addressing the ways in which privilege and power dynamics can operate within the movement itself, and being open to feedback and critique from marginalized individuals. Another important aspect of the LGBTAI movement is the recognition of the diversity and complexity of individual experiences. While there are common experiences and challenges faced by many LGBTAI individuals, each person's experience is unique and shaped by a variety of factors, including race, ethnicity, culture, religion, disability, socioeconomic status, and more. It is important to recognize and celebrate this diversity, and to work to create a movement that is inclusive and welcoming to all individuals, regardless of their background or identity.

One important issue that the LGBTAI movement continues to face is the persistence of discrimination and violence against LGBTAI individuals.

Despite legal protections and greater societal acceptance, many LGBTAI individuals still face discrimination and harassment in their daily lives, and are at greater risk of violence and hate crimes. This includes discrimination and violence directed towards transgender and gender non-conforming individuals, who face particularly high levels of violence and marginalization. To address these ongoing challenges, the LGBTAI movement continues to work towards greater legal protections and societal acceptance. This includes advocating for policies that protect the rights of LGBTAI individuals, such as employment nondiscrimination laws, transgender-inclusive healthcare policies, and protections against hate crimes. It also includes challenging societal norms and attitudes that contribute to discrimination and marginalization, and promoting greater understanding and acceptance of LGBTAI individuals.

Another important issue facing the LGBTAI movement is the ongoing struggle for representation and visibility. While there have been significant gains in terms of media representation and visibility for LGBTAI individuals, there is still a need for greater representation and visibility for all members of the community. This includes representation for individuals who hold multiple marginalized identities, such as LGBTAI people of color or LGBTAI individuals with disabilities, as well as representation in areas such as politics, business, and other areas of public life. Another important issue facing the LGBTAI movement is the ongoing struggle for healthcare access and equity. LGBTAI individuals have historically faced significant barriers to accessing healthcare, including discrimination and stigma from healthcare providers, lack of insurance coverage for necessary services, and inadequate medical research and treatment options. To address these challenges, the LGBTAI movement has advocated for greater access to healthcare services and coverage, as well as increased research and funding for LGBTAI-specific health issues. This includes advocating for policies that ensure insurance coverage for necessary healthcare services, such as gender-affirming surgeries for transgender individuals, and working to address the lack of research and understanding around LGBTAI-specific health issues, such as HIV/AIDS and mental health. Additionally, the LGBTAI movement has increasingly recognized the importance of community support and resources in promoting health and well-being. This includes efforts to create community-based healthcare models, such as LGBTQ+ health centers and clinics that are sensitive to the unique needs and experiences of LGBTAI individuals.

In recent years, the LGBTAI movement has also increasingly focused on issues of intersectionality and coalition-building, recognizing the ways in which various forms of oppression intersect and the importance of working in solidarity with other marginalized communities. This includes efforts to build alliances with other social justice movements, such as the Black Lives Matter and immigrant rights movements, and to center the voices and experiences of LGBTAI individuals who hold multiple marginalized identities.

Another important issue facing the LGBTAI movement is the ongoing struggle for education and inclusion in schools and educational institutions. LGBTAI youth have historically faced significant barriers to accessing education, including harassment and discrimination from peers and teachers, lack of supportive resources and policies, and exclusion from curricula and educational materials. To address these challenges, the LGBTAI movement has advocated for greater education and inclusion for LGBTAI students, as well as increased research and funding for LGBTAI-inclusive education. This includes advocating for policies that ensure safe and supportive school environments for LGBTAI students, such as anti-bullying and nondiscrimination policies, and working to address the lack of representation and inclusion of LGBTAI individuals in curricula and educational materials. Additionally, the LGBTAI movement has increasingly recognized the importance of providing supportive resources and services for LGBTAI youth, both within and outside of educational institutions. This includes efforts to create safe spaces for LGBTAI youth, such as LGBTQ+ youth centers and support groups, and to provide access to mental health services and resources.

In recent years, the LGBTAI movement has also increasingly focused on issues of representation and diversity in educational institutions, recognizing the importance of centering the voices and experiences of LGBTAI individuals from diverse backgrounds and communities. This includes efforts to increase representation of LGBTAI individuals in educational leadership positions and to promote intersectional approaches to LGBTAI-inclusive education.

Another important issue facing the LGBTAI movement is the ongoing struggle for economic justice and equality. LGBTAI individuals have historically faced significant barriers to accessing employment, housing, and other economic opportunities, including discrimination and stigma from employers and landlords, lack of legal protections, and economic disparities based on sexual orientation, gender identity, race, and other factors. To address these challenges, the LGBTAI movement has advocated for greater economic justice and equality for LGBTAI individuals, as well as increased research and funding for LGBTAI-specific economic issues. This includes advocating for policies that ensure equal employment opportunities and nondiscrimination protections for LGBTAI individuals, as well as working to address the economic disparities that impact LGBTAI communities, such as poverty and homelessness. Additionally, the LGBTAI movement has increasingly recognized the importance of community support and resources in promoting economic well-being and stability for LGBTAI individuals. This includes efforts to create community-based economic models, such as LGBTQ+ businesses and cooperatives, that are sensitive to the unique needs and experiences of LGBTAI individuals.

In recent years, the LGBTAI movement has also increasingly focused on issues of intersectionality and coalition-building in the fight for economic justice, recognizing the ways in which various forms of oppression intersect and the importance of working in solidarity with other marginalized communities. This includes efforts to build alliances with other social justice movements, such as the labor and environmental justice movements, and to center the voices and experiences of LGBTAI individuals who hold multiple marginalized identities.

Another important issue facing the LGBTAI movement is the ongoing struggle for healthcare access and equity. LGBTAI individuals have historically faced significant barriers to accessing healthcare, including discrimination and stigma from healthcare providers, lack of healthcare coverage and resources, and inadequate or inappropriate healthcare services for LGBTAI individuals. To address these challenges, the LGBTAI movement has advocated for greater healthcare access and equity for LGBTAI individuals, as well as increased research and funding for LGBTAI-specific healthcare issues. This includes advocating for policies that ensure equal healthcare access and nondiscrimination protections for LGBTAI individuals, as well as working to address the healthcare disparities that impact LGBTAI communities, such as higher rates of certain health conditions and inadequate or inappropriate healthcare services. Additionally, the LGBTAI movement has increasingly recognized the importance of community support and resources in promoting healthcare access and equity for LGBTAI individuals. This includes efforts to create community-based healthcare models, such as LGBTQ+ clinics and health centers that are sensitive to the unique needs and experiences of LGBTAI individuals.

The LGBTAI movement has also increasingly focused in recent years, on issues of intersectionality and coalition-building in the fight for healthcare access and equity, recognizing the ways in which various forms of oppression intersect and the importance of working in solidarity with other marginalized communities. This includes efforts to build alliances with other social justice movements, such as the disability and reproductive justice movements, and to center the voices and experiences of LGBTAI individuals who hold multiple marginalized identities. Another important issue facing the LGBTAI movement is the ongoing struggle for safety and protection, particularly in the face of violence and discrimination. LGBTAI individuals have historically faced high rates of violence, hate crimes, and discrimination, including harassment, assault, and even murder based on their sexual orientation, gender identity, or expression. To address these challenges, the LGBTAI movement has advocated for greater safety and protection for LGBTAI individuals, as well as increased research and funding for LGBTAI-specific violence prevention and response efforts. This includes advocating for policies that ensure equal protection under the law and increased support for victims of violence and discrimination.

Additionally, the LGBTAI movement has increasingly recognized the importance of community support and resources in promoting safety and protection for LGBTAI individuals. This includes efforts to create community-based safety models, such as LGBTQ+ neighborhood watch programs and crisis hotlines that are sensitive to the unique needs and experiences of LGBTAI individuals.

In recent years, the LGBTAI movement has also increasingly focused on issues of intersectionality and coalition-building in the fight for safety and protection, recognizing the ways in which various forms of oppression intersect and the importance of working in solidarity with other marginalized communities. This includes efforts to build alliances with other social justice movements, such as the racial justice and immigrant rights movements, and to center the voices and experiences of LGBTAI individuals who hold multiple marginalized identities. Another important issue facing the LGBTAI movement is the ongoing struggle for representation and visibility in various areas of society. LGBTAI individuals have historically been marginalized and underrepresented in many areas of public life, including media, politics, and education. To address these challenges, the LGBTAI movement has advocated for greater representation and visibility for LGBTAI individuals, as well as increased education and awareness of LGBTAI issues. This includes advocating for policies that promote equal representation of LGBTAI individuals in media and political positions, as well as efforts to increase LGBTAI representation in education and healthcare settings. Additionally, the LGBTAI movement has increasingly recognized the importance of intersectionality and coalition-building in the fight for representation and visibility, recognizing the ways in which various forms of oppression intersect and the importance of working in solidarity with other marginalized communities. This includes efforts to build alliances with other social justice movements, such as the feminist and disability rights movements, and to center the voices and experiences of LGBTAI individuals who hold multiple marginalized identities.

In recent years, the LGBTAI movement has also focused on promoting positive representation and visibility of LGBTAI individuals, recognizing the impact that media and cultural representations can have on public attitudes and perceptions of LGBTAI individuals. This includes efforts to promote accurate and positive representations of LGBTAI individuals in media, literature, and other cultural productions, as well as to increase education and awareness of LGBTAI issues in schools and other educational settings. Another important issue facing the LGBTAI movement is the ongoing struggle for healthcare access and equity. LGBTAI individuals have historically faced significant barriers to healthcare access, including discrimination, lack of insurance coverage, and lack of culturally competent care. To address these challenges, the LGBTAI movement has advocated for greater healthcare access and equity for LGBTAI individuals, as well as increased education and awareness of LGBTAI-specific health needs. This includes advocating for policies that promote equal access to healthcare for LGBTAI individuals, as well as efforts to increase LGBTAI representation in healthcare settings and improve cultural competency training for healthcare providers. Additionally, the LGBTAI movement has increasingly recognized the importance of intersectionality and coalition-building in the fight for healthcare access and equity, recognizing the ways in which various forms of oppression intersect and the importance of working in solidarity with other marginalized communities. This includes efforts to build alliances with other social justice movements, such as the disability rights and reproductive justice movements, and to center the voices and experiences of LGBTAI individuals who hold multiple marginalized identities.

In recent years, the LGBTAI movement has also focused on promoting research and funding for LGBTAI-specific healthcare needs, recognizing the unique health risks and challenges faced by LGBTAI individuals. This includes efforts to increase research and funding for LGBTAI-specific health issues, such as HIV/AIDS, mental health, and substance abuse, as well as to increase education and awareness of LGBTAI-specific health needs among healthcare providers and the general public. Another important issue facing the LGBTAI movement is the ongoing fight for trans rights and inclusion. Transgender individuals have historically faced significant discrimination and marginalization, and have been particularly vulnerable to violence and harassment. To address these challenges, the LGBTAI movement has increasingly focused on promoting trans rights and inclusion, recognizing the importance of centering the voices and experiences of transgender individuals in the fight for LGBTQ+ rights. This includes advocating for policies that promote equal rights and protections for transgender individuals, such as legal recognition of gender identity, access to healthcare and education, and protection from discrimination and violence. Additionally, the LGBTAI movement has increasingly recognized the importance of intersectionality and coalition-building in the fight for trans rights and inclusion, recognizing the ways in which various forms of oppression intersect and the importance of working in solidarity with other marginalized communities. This includes efforts to build alliances with other social justice movements, such as the racial justice and disability rights movements, and to center the voices and experiences of transgender individuals who hold multiple marginalized identities.

In recent years, the LGBTAI movement has also focused on promoting positive and inclusive representations of transgender individuals in media and culture, recognizing the impact that media and cultural representations can have on public attitudes and perceptions of transgender individuals. This includes efforts to promote accurate and positive representations of transgender individuals in media, literature, and other cultural productions, as well as to increase education and awareness of transgender issues in schools and other educational settings.

Overall, the LGBTAI movement continues to work towards greater trans rights and inclusion, through ongoing advocacy, education, and activism. By promoting equal rights and protections for transgender individuals and working to address systemic barriers to inclusion, the movement strives to create a more just and inclusive society for all members of the LGBTAI community.

Another important issue facing the LGBTAI movement is the ongoing fight for global LGBTQ+ rights. While significant progress has been made in many countries, LGBTQ+ individuals continue to face persecution, discrimination, and violence in many parts of the world, including in countries where homosexuality is still illegal. To address these challenges, the LGBTAI movement has increasingly focused on promoting global LGBTQ+ rights, recognizing the importance of international solidarity and advocacy in the fight for LGBTQ+ equality. This includes advocating for policies that promote equal rights and protections for LGBTQ+ individuals around the world, such as legal recognition of same-sex relationships, protection from discrimination and violence, and access to healthcare and education. Additionally, the LGBTAI movement has worked to build alliances with LGBTQ+ activists and organizations around the world, and to support their efforts to promote LGBTQ+ rights and inclusion in their own countries. This includes providing financial and logistical support, sharing resources and expertise, and working to elevate the voices and experiences of LGBTQ+ individuals around the world.

In recent years, the LGBTAI movement has also increasingly focused on promoting LGBTQ+ rights in the context of global human rights and social justice movements, recognizing the ways in which various forms of oppression intersect and the importance of working in solidarity with other marginalized communities. This includes efforts to build alliances with other social justice movements, such as the environmental and labor movements, and to center the voices and experiences of LGBTQ+ individuals who hold multiple marginalized identities.

Another important issue facing the LGBTAI movement is the ongoing fight for LGBTQ+ youth rights and inclusion. LGBTQ+ youth face unique challenges, including bullying, harassment, and discrimination, which can have serious consequences for their mental health and well-being. To address these challenges, the LGBTAI movement has increasingly focused on promoting LGBTQ+ youth rights and inclusion, recognizing the importance of supporting and empowering LGBTQ+ youth to lead fulfilling and successful lives. This includes advocating for policies and programs that promote equal rights and protections for LGBTQ+ youth, such as anti-bullying laws and policies, access to LGBTQ+ affirming healthcare and education, and protection from conversion therapy. Additionally, the LGBTAI movement has worked to build supportive communities and networks for LGBTQ+ youth, including through LGBTQ+ youth organizations, mentorship programs, and peer support groups. These initiatives provide a vital source of support and resources for LGBTQ+ youth, and help to promote their well-being and resilience in the face of discrimination and marginalization.

In recent years, the LGBTAI movement has also increasingly focused on promoting positive and inclusive representations of LGBTQ+ youth in media and culture, recognizing the impact that media and cultural representations can have on public attitudes and perceptions of LGBTQ+ youth. This includes efforts to promote accurate and positive representations of LGBTQ+ youth in media, literature, and other cultural productions, as well as to increase education and awareness of LGBTQ+ youth issues in schools and other educational settings.

Another important area of focus for the LGBTAI movement is intersectionality, which recognizes the ways in which various forms of oppression, such as racism, sexism, ableism, and transphobia, intersect and compound to create unique challenges and barriers for individuals who hold multiple marginalized identities. The LGBTAI movement has increasingly recognized the importance of centering the voices and experiences of LGBTQ+ individuals who hold multiple marginalized identities, such as LGBTQ+ people of color, LGBTQ+ individuals with disabilities, and transgender and gender nonconforming individuals. This includes working to address the unique challenges and barriers faced by these communities, such as discrimination, violence, and systemic barriers to inclusion. To address these challenges, the LGBTAI movement has worked to build alliances with other social justice movements, such as the Black Lives Matter movement and the disability rights movement, recognizing the importance of working in solidarity with other marginalized communities to promote greater social justice and equity for all.

One of the key challenges facing the LGBTAI movement today is the ongoing fight for transgender rights and inclusion. Transgender individuals continue to face high levels of discrimination, harassment, and violence, both in the United States and around the world. This includes barriers to healthcare, employment, housing, and education, as well as high rates of suicide and homelessness. To address these challenges, the LGBTAI movement has increasingly focused on promoting transgender rights and inclusion, recognizing the importance of centering the voices and experiences of transgender and gender nonconforming individuals. This includes advocating for policies and programs that promote equal rights and protections for transgender individuals, such as access to healthcare and gender-affirming treatments, protections from discrimination in employment and housing, and access to inclusive education.

Additionally, the LGBTAI movement has worked to build supportive communities and networks for transgender and gender nonconforming individuals, including through transgender and gender nonconforming organizations, peer support groups, and mentorship programs. These initiatives provide a vital source of support and resources for transgender individuals, and help to promote their well-being and resilience in the face of discrimination and marginalization.

In recent years, the LGBTAI movement has also increasingly focused on promoting positive and inclusive representations of transgender and gender nonconforming individuals in media and culture, recognizing the impact that media and cultural representations can have on public attitudes and perceptions of transgender individuals. This includes efforts to promote accurate and positive representations of transgender individuals in media, literature, and other cultural productions, as well as to increase education and awareness of transgender issues in schools and other educational settings.

Another area of focus for the LGBTAI movement is promoting greater inclusion and visibility for LGBTQ+ individuals in the workplace. LGBTQ+ individuals continue to face significant challenges in the workplace, including discrimination, harassment, and unequal treatment. To address these challenges, the LGBTAI movement has worked to promote workplace diversity and inclusion, encouraging employers to adopt inclusive policies and practices that support LGBTQ+ employees. This includes efforts to promote nondiscrimination policies, provide inclusive benefits such as healthcare coverage for same-sex partners, and provide resources and training to promote greater awareness and understanding of LGBTQ+ issues in the workplace.

Additionally, the LGBTAI movement has worked to promote LGBTQ+ entrepreneurship and economic empowerment, recognizing the importance of creating opportunities for LGBTQ+ individuals to succeed and thrive in the workplace. This includes initiatives to provide funding and support for LGBTQ+-owned businesses, as well as efforts to promote entrepreneurship and leadership development among LGBTQ+ individuals. The LGBTAI movement has a rich history of activism and advocacy for equal rights and protections for LGBTQ+ individuals. Over the years, the movement has made significant progress in terms of legal rights and societal acceptance, including the legalization of same-sex marriage, the repeal of "Don't Ask, Don't Tell", and increased representation in media and popular culture.

However, the movement continues to face ongoing challenges, including discrimination, harassment, and violence towards transgender individuals, and unequal treatment and barriers to inclusion in the workplace. To address these challenges, the LGBTAI movement has increasingly focused on promoting transgender rights and inclusion, workplace diversity and inclusion, and greater visibility and representation of LGBTQ+ individuals in media and popular culture.

Overall, the LGBTAI movement strives to create a more just and inclusive society for all members of the LGBTQ+ community, through ongoing advocacy, education, and activism.

THREE
Gender Identity

*U*nderstanding Gender Identity is an important component of understanding the LGBTQ+ community. Gender identity refers to an individual's internal sense of their gender, which may or may not align with the sex they were assigned at birth. It's important to recognize that sex assigned at birth is not the same as gender identity, and that gender identity is a deeply personal and individual experience.

Transgender individuals are those who identify with a gender that is different from the sex assigned to them at birth. This may involve transitioning socially, medically, or legally to align their gender expression and identity with their true sense of self. Nonbinary individuals may identify as neither exclusively male nor exclusively female, and may experience their gender as a spectrum or fluid concept. Genderqueer individuals may identify with a nontraditional gender identity that does not fit within the traditional binary categories of male and female. It's important to recognize and respect the diversity of gender identities and expressions within the LGBTQ+ community. This means creating inclusive and affirming spaces that recognize the validity and importance of all gender identities. It also means challenging the harmful societal norms and stereotypes that perpetuate binary gender roles and reinforce gender-based discrimination.

Furthermore, understanding gender identity requires recognizing and challenging the systemic oppression and discrimination that many transgender, nonbinary, and genderqueer individuals face. This includes the barriers to accessing healthcare, employment, and other essential resources, as well as the violence and harassment that many face in their daily lives. It's also important to note that gender identity is not a choice, but an intrinsic aspect of an individual's sense of self. For many transgender, nonbinary, and genderqueer individuals, the journey towards accepting and embracing their gender identity can be a complex and difficult process. This may involve grappling with feelings of shame, fear, and uncertainty, as well as navigating the social, cultural, and legal barriers to living authentically.

In addition, it's important to recognize that gender identity is not the same as sexual orientation. While gender identity refers to an individual's internal sense of their gender, sexual orientation refers to an individual's romantic and/or sexual attraction to others. While the two may intersect for some individuals, they are distinct aspects of a person's identity and should be treated as such.

Understanding gender identity also requires recognizing the impact of intersectionality on the experiences of transgender, nonbinary, and genderqueer individuals. This means recognizing the ways in which gender identity intersects with other aspects of an individual's identity, such as race, ethnicity, class, and disability, and how this can shape their experiences of discrimination and oppression.

Ultimately, understanding gender identity requires a commitment to inclusivity, empathy, and respect. This means listening to and learning from the experiences of transgender, nonbinary, and genderqueer individuals, and working to create a society that values and celebrates the full diversity of gender identities and expressions. By doing so, we can build a more equitable and just world for all. It's also important to recognize the impact that societal norms and expectations can have on an individual's gender identity. Traditional gender roles and stereotypes often reinforce binary and heteronormative views of gender, which can lead to marginalization and exclusion for individuals who do not fit these narrow categories.

As such, it's crucial for individuals, communities, and institutions to challenge and disrupt these harmful norms and actively work towards creating a more inclusive and affirming environment for all gender identities. This can involve everything from using gender-neutral language and pronouns to providing access to gender-affirming healthcare and legal protections.

Moreover, it's important to recognize that the experiences of transgender, nonbinary, and genderqueer individuals are not monolithic, and that each person's journey towards understanding and expressing their gender identity is unique. As such, it's important to approach these conversations with openness, curiosity, and a willingness to learn from diverse perspectives and experiences.

Understanding gender identity is an ongoing process that requires both individual reflection and collective action. By creating spaces and opportunities for dialogue and learning, we can work towards a future where all individuals are free to express and celebrate their gender identities without fear of discrimination or violence. It's also important to acknowledge that the journey towards understanding and accepting one's gender identity is not always a linear or easy process. Many transgender, nonbinary, and genderqueer individuals face significant challenges in accessing supportive resources, such as mental health services, gender-affirming healthcare, and legal protections.

For example, transgender individuals may face barriers to obtaining legal recognition of their gender, such as through changes to their name and gender marker on government-issued identification documents. This can create significant difficulties in accessing basic services, such as healthcare and housing, and may also expose individuals to discrimination and violence. Additionally, transgender and gender non-conforming individuals face high rates of discrimination and violence, including harassment, physical assault, and homicide. This underscores the urgent need for greater societal recognition and protection of transgender and gender non-conforming individuals.

In order to better support transgender, nonbinary, and genderqueer individuals, it's important to advocate for policies and programs that affirm and protect gender diversity. This may include creating more gender-inclusive spaces, improving access to gender-affirming healthcare, and ensuring legal protections against discrimination and violence. It's also important to recognize that gender identity is not necessarily tied to one's biological sex or physical appearance. Many transgender and gender non-conforming individuals may not conform to traditional societal expectations for how they should present themselves based on their assigned sex at birth.

For example, a person assigned male at birth may identify as a woman and choose to present themselves in a more feminine manner, such as by wearing dresses or makeup. Conversely, a person assigned female at birth may identify as nonbinary and choose to present themselves in a more androgynous manner, such as by wearing clothing traditionally associated with both men and women. It's also important to recognize that gender identity is not a choice. Rather, it is an inherent aspect of one's identity that may be discovered or realized over time. As such, it's important to avoid stigmatizing or pathologizing individuals based on their gender identity.

Furthermore, it's important to recognize the intersectional nature of gender identity, particularly in relation to other aspects of identity such as race, ethnicity, class, and ability. Transgender and gender non-conforming individuals who hold marginalized identities may face compounded discrimination and marginalization, making it even more crucial to center their experiences and needs in conversations around gender identity.

Another important aspect of understanding gender identity is recognizing the importance of using individuals' preferred pronouns and names. For many transgender and nonbinary individuals, using their correct pronouns and name is a crucial aspect of affirming their gender identity and sense of self. It's important to recognize that misgendering or deadnaming (using someone's birth name instead of their chosen name) can be incredibly hurtful and invalidating.

Additionally, it's important to understand the various challenges that transgender and gender non-conforming individuals may face, such as discrimination in employment, housing, and healthcare. Many individuals also experience higher rates of violence and harassment, particularly trans women of color.

It's crucial to advocate for policies and systems that support and affirm transgender and gender non-conforming individuals, such as legal recognition of gender identity and inclusive healthcare policies. By working towards creating a more affirming and supportive society, we can ensure that all individuals are able to live their lives authentically and without fear of discrimination or marginalization.

Another important topic to discuss in understanding gender identity is the experience of gender dysphoria. Gender dysphoria refers to the distress or discomfort an individual may feel as a result of the disconnect between their gender identity and their assigned sex at birth. This can manifest in various ways, including discomfort with one's body, social discomfort or anxiety, and a general sense of dissatisfaction or discomfort with one's assigned gender. It's important to recognize that gender dysphoria is a legitimate medical condition recognized by major medical organizations, including the American Psychological Association and the World Professional Association for Transgender Health. Access to gender-affirming healthcare, such as hormone therapy or gender confirmation surgery, can be crucial in alleviating gender dysphoria and improving overall well-being for transgender individuals.

However, it's also important to recognize that not all transgender individuals experience gender dysphoria, and that the experience of gender is highly individual and nuanced. It's important to approach the topic of gender identity with empathy, respect, and a willingness to learn about and affirm individuals' unique experiences and identities. Another important aspect of understanding gender identity is recognizing the impact that societal norms and expectations can have on individuals' experiences of gender. Gender roles, expectations, and stereotypes can be pervasive and deeply ingrained in society, influencing everything from childhood development to career opportunities.

For transgender and gender non-conforming individuals, societal expectations around gender can lead to discrimination, harassment, and exclusion. This can manifest in various ways, including employment discrimination, lack of access to healthcare, and social exclusion or stigma. It's important to recognize that creating a more inclusive and affirming society for transgender and gender non-conforming individuals requires not just individual acceptance and support, but also systemic change. This can include advocating for policies that protect the rights of transgender individuals, such as legal recognition of gender identity, anti-discrimination laws, and access to healthcare.

It's important to recognize that individuals' experiences of gender are complex and nuanced, and may not fit neatly into traditional binary conceptions of gender. Nonbinary, genderqueer, and other gender non-conforming individuals may have unique experiences and needs that require different forms of support and recognition. It's also important to note that the journey of exploring and understanding one's gender identity can be complex and difficult. For many individuals, it can involve a process of questioning, self-discovery, and self-acceptance.

For transgender individuals, this journey may include undergoing medical procedures such as hormone therapy or gender-affirming surgeries. However, it's important to recognize that not all transgender individuals choose to undergo these procedures, and that medical transition is not the only way to affirm one's gender identity. Additionally, it's important to understand that gender identity is not a mental disorder or illness. However, transgender individuals may experience mental health challenges related to societal stigma and discrimination, and may benefit from access to mental health resources and support.

Understanding gender identity also requires recognizing and respecting individuals' preferred pronouns and names. This may involve using gender-neutral pronouns such as they/them or ze/zir, or using a transgender individual's chosen name rather than their birth name. It's also important to note that understanding gender identity requires an intersectional approach that recognizes the ways in which gender identity intersects with other aspects of identity such as race, ethnicity, class, and ability. Transgender individuals who belong to marginalized communities may face additional challenges and barriers to accessing healthcare, education, and employment opportunities.

Moreover, it's important to understand that gender identity is not a binary or fixed concept. Many individuals may identify as nonbinary, meaning that they do not identify as exclusively male or female, or they may identify as a combination of multiple genders. It's crucial to respect and honor the diversity of gender identities and expressions, and to create spaces that are inclusive and affirming for all individuals.

Understanding gender identity can also involve understanding the history and experiences of transgender and gender nonconforming individuals. This includes recognizing the contributions of transgender individuals to society, as well as acknowledging the discrimination and violence that transgender individuals face on a daily basis. Additionally, it's important to recognize the impact that societal norms and expectations around gender have on individuals. For example, many individuals may feel pressured to conform to traditional gender roles and expressions, even if those roles and expressions don't align with their true identity. This can lead to feelings of discomfort, anxiety, and even depression.

Understanding gender identity also involves recognizing the importance of language and terminology. Using correct pronouns and language that reflects an individual's gender identity is crucial in creating a safe and inclusive environment. It's also important to avoid assumptions about an individual's gender identity based on their appearance or other characteristics.

It's also important to recognize the intersectionality of gender identity with other aspects of a person's identity, such as race, ethnicity, disability, and socioeconomic status. These intersections can compound experiences of discrimination and marginalization, and it's important to understand how different forms of oppression can intersect to create unique experiences for individuals.

Another aspect of understanding gender identity is recognizing the various challenges that transgender and gender nonconforming individuals may face in accessing healthcare, including discrimination, lack of access to gender-affirming care, and lack of understanding from healthcare providers. This can lead to significant health disparities, such as higher rates of mental health concerns and HIV infection, among transgender individuals. To address these challenges, healthcare providers must receive proper education and training on gender-affirming care and must create safe and inclusive environments for all patients. Additionally, policies must be put in place to ensure that transgender and gender nonconforming individuals have access to affordable, gender-affirming healthcare.

It's important to understand the experiences of individuals who identify as nonbinary, meaning they do not exclusively identify as male or female. Nonbinary individuals often face unique challenges, such as a lack of legal recognition and a lack of understanding and visibility in society. Additionally, there is a need for more research on the experiences and health disparities of nonbinary individuals. It's also important to recognize that gender identity is a personal and deeply felt sense of self, and individuals should be able to express and identify their gender in the way that feels most authentic to them. This includes respecting individuals' preferred pronouns and using inclusive language. In addition to understanding gender identity on an individual level, it's important to recognize the larger societal and cultural factors that shape our understanding of gender. This includes examining how gender roles and expectations are constructed and perpetuated, and how they intersect with other aspects of identity such as race, class, and sexuality.

By understanding gender identity in all its complexity, we can work towards creating a more inclusive and equitable society for all individuals, regardless of their gender identity. This involves advocating for legal protections, challenging harmful stereotypes and discrimination, and creating inclusive environments in our communities, schools, and workplaces. It's also important to note that while gender identity and sexual orientation are distinct concepts, they are often intertwined in personal experiences and societal understandings. For example, individuals who identify as transgender or nonbinary may also identify as gay, lesbian, or bisexual, and may face additional challenges as a result of their intersecting identities.

Furthermore, it's crucial to recognize that the language and concepts around gender and sexual orientation are constantly evolving, and individuals may use different terminology to describe themselves and their experiences. It's important to be open to learning about new terminology and to respect individuals' self-identification.

FOUR
Intersex

Intersex is a term used to describe individuals who are born with variations in their sex characteristics that do not fit typical male or female classifications. Intersex variations can include differences in chromosomes, hormones, genitals, or internal reproductive organs.

Unfortunately, intersex individuals have historically been subject to medical procedures and social stigmatization aimed at forcing them into binary sex classifications. Intersex infants have often been subjected to non-consensual surgeries to alter their genitals in order to conform to typical male or female appearances. These practices, known as intersex genital mutilation, can have long-lasting physical and psychological effects on individuals. It is important to recognize and support intersex individuals in their right to bodily autonomy and self-determination. This includes promoting awareness and understanding of intersex variations, and advocating for policies that protect the rights of intersex individuals. It also involves rejecting harmful and inaccurate stereotypes and promoting the diversity of gender and sex variations in society.

Intersex individuals face unique challenges, including the need for specialized medical care and the risk of discrimination and marginalization. It is essential that healthcare providers, educators, and policymakers receive education and training on intersex issues to ensure that intersex individuals are treated with respect, dignity, and compassion. By recognizing and supporting the intersex community, we can promote a more inclusive and accepting society for all LGBTAI individuals.

In recent years, there has been a growing recognition of the importance of intersex rights and the need for better healthcare options for intersex individuals. Many intersex individuals have experienced significant trauma and discrimination in medical settings due to the lack of understanding and acceptance of intersex variations.

There are also ongoing efforts to increase visibility and representation of intersex individuals in media and society, and to ensure that intersex people are not subjected to non-consensual medical interventions or surgeries that are often performed without their informed consent.

One of the challenges in understanding intersex is the complexity and diversity of intersex variations. Intersex is not a single, uniform category, but rather a broad spectrum of variations in sex characteristics that can occur for a variety of reasons. Some intersex variations may be visible at birth, while others may not become apparent until later in life. It is important to recognize that intersex is not a disorder or medical condition that needs to be fixed, but rather a natural variation in human biology. Intersex individuals have the right to self-determination and to make informed decisions about their own bodies and healthcare.

To better understand intersex, it is essential to listen to and learn from intersex individuals and their experiences. This includes recognizing and respecting the diversity of intersex identities and experiences, and working to create a more supportive and affirming society for intersex individuals. As society continues to evolve and become more inclusive, it is important to continue the conversation and increase awareness about intersex and the unique challenges faced by intersex individuals. By working together to promote understanding and acceptance, we can create a world that is more compassionate and equitable for all individuals, regardless of their sex characteristics.

In addition to the challenges faced by intersex individuals, it is also important to recognize the diversity of experiences within the intersex community. Some intersex individuals may experience medical interventions at a young age in order to conform to societal expectations of binary gender, while others may not realize they are intersex until later in life. It is also important to recognize the intersectionality of intersex identities with other marginalized identities, such as race, ethnicity, religion, and disability. For example, intersex individuals of color may face additional discrimination and barriers to healthcare access. It is essential to support and advocate for intersex individuals' right to self-determination and bodily autonomy, including the right to choose or refuse medical interventions. Education and awareness about intersex issues can also help to combat harmful and stigmatizing attitudes and promote greater understanding and acceptance.

Another important aspect to consider in understanding intersex is the role of medicalization and pathologization. Historically, intersex traits were often seen as medical conditions that required intervention, rather than a natural variation of human diversity. This approach has led to harmful practices such as non-consensual surgeries and hormone therapies that aim to alter intersex bodies to fit within societal norms of binary gender.

More recently, there has been a movement towards a more affirming and supportive approach that prioritizes informed consent and patient autonomy. This approach seeks to provide intersex individuals with accurate information about their bodies and medical options, while also recognizing their right to make decisions about their own bodies. It is also important to recognize that intersex individuals may not always identify as LGBTQ+ and that their identities should be respected and validated regardless of their sexual orientation or gender identity. Furthermore, while intersex individuals share some common experiences, their experiences may also vary widely, and it is important to avoid making generalizations or assumptions about their lives. It is important to understand that intersex is not a disorder or a medical condition that needs to be "fixed". Rather, it is a natural variation in human anatomy and biology that has always existed. Many intersex individuals do not experience any negative health effects and do not require medical intervention.

However, some intersex individuals may face challenges related to their intersex status, including discrimination, stigma, and the pressure to conform to binary gender norms. Intersex individuals may also face medical interventions, such as surgeries or hormone treatments, without their informed consent, which can have negative physical and psychological consequences.

Recognizing and supporting intersex individuals means acknowledging and respecting their autonomy and bodily integrity, and working towards ending harmful practices such as non-consensual surgeries or treatments. It also means creating a society that is inclusive and supportive of intersex individuals, where they can live as their authentic selves without fear of discrimination or prejudice.

Intersex individuals have often faced stigmatization, discrimination, and mistreatment, both medically and socially. In many cultures, intersex individuals were often forced to undergo surgeries and medical interventions without their consent to conform to binary gender norms, leading to lifelong physical and psychological consequences. However, in recent years, there has been a growing recognition of the importance of respecting intersex individuals' bodily autonomy and right to self-determination. It is crucial to understand that intersex is a natural variation of human anatomy and is not a disorder or a medical condition that needs to be "fixed." Intersex individuals deserve the same respect, dignity, and rights as all other members of society. Supporting intersex individuals means recognizing and acknowledging their existence, understanding their unique needs and experiences, and advocating for their rights and well-being.

The medical community also has a responsibility to provide intersex individuals with appropriate and compassionate care that respects their autonomy and promotes their physical and mental health. This includes providing access to accurate and unbiased information, counseling, and support, as well as refraining from non-consensual surgeries and other interventions that are not medically necessary or in the individual's best interest. In addition, it's important to recognize that intersex individuals are not a monolithic group and that there is a wide range of intersex variations. Some intersex variations are more visible, such as differences in external genitalia, while others are internal and may not be apparent until puberty or later in life.

Historically, intersex individuals have faced significant stigma, discrimination, and mistreatment. Many have undergone unnecessary and harmful medical interventions in an attempt to conform to societal norms of binary sex. These interventions can include genital surgeries and hormone treatments that can have lasting physical and emotional effects.

It's important to recognize the importance of bodily autonomy for intersex individuals and to support their right to make decisions about their own bodies. This can involve advocating for changes in medical practice and policy to ensure that intersex individuals are not subjected to non-consensual medical interventions. It can also involve working to create a more inclusive and accepting society that values and respects the diversity of human bodies and identities.

Intersex individuals have often been subjected to discrimination and harmful medical interventions, such as genital mutilation and hormone treatments, in an attempt to "normalize" their bodies. This approach is now widely considered to be unethical and unnecessary, and the intersex community is advocating for greater recognition of their rights and experiences. It is important to understand that intersex is a natural variation of human biology and that intersex individuals are not abnormal or in need of "fixing." Rather, they deserve respect and support for who they are, and medical interventions should only be pursued if they are medically necessary and consensually agreed upon by the individual and their healthcare provider.

As with other aspects of the LGBTQIA+ community, it is important for society to become more educated about intersex individuals and their experiences in order to promote greater acceptance and inclusivity. This includes providing accurate information about intersex conditions and advocating for the rights of intersex individuals to self-determination and bodily autonomy. Intersex individuals have historically faced stigma and discrimination, which can have a significant impact on their mental health and wellbeing. It is important to recognize and support intersex individuals by acknowledging their experiences and advocating for their rights.

One key issue for intersex individuals is the medicalization of their bodies. Many intersex individuals are subjected to unnecessary surgeries and medical interventions aimed at "normalizing" their bodies, often without their consent. These procedures can cause physical and emotional harm, and they are often based on outdated notions of gender and sexuality.

It is also important to understand that being intersex is not a binary issue. Intersex individuals can have a range of differences in their physical characteristics and reproductive systems, and there is no one "correct" way for intersex bodies to look or function. Intersex individuals deserve to be respected and valued for who they are, and they should not be forced into conforming to narrow ideas of what is "normal" or "natural." By understanding and supporting intersex individuals, we can work towards a more inclusive and just society for all.

It is important to recognize that intersex is not a disorder or condition that needs to be fixed. Instead, it is simply a natural variation in human biology. Unfortunately, many intersex individuals have historically been subjected to non-consensual surgeries and other harmful medical interventions aimed at "normalizing" their bodies. These procedures can have lifelong physical, emotional, and psychological consequences. It is also important for society to recognize and support intersex individuals in a way that respects their autonomy and human rights. This includes providing access to accurate information and resources, as well as promoting policies and legislation that protect intersex individuals from discrimination and harmful medical practices.

In recent years, there has been a growing movement to raise awareness about intersex issues and advocate for intersex rights. This includes efforts to promote intersex visibility in the media and public discourse, as well as initiatives aimed at improving medical care for intersex individuals and ensuring that their voices are heard in discussions about their own bodies and health.

By understanding and supporting intersex individuals, we can work towards creating a more inclusive and compassionate society that values and celebrates the diversity of human experiences and identities. It's important to note that intersex individuals have historically been subjected to harmful and unnecessary medical procedures, such as genital surgeries and hormone therapies, in order to conform to societal norms around binary sex. These practices have often been carried out without the individual's consent and have had long-term physical and psychological consequences.

Therefore, it is crucial to support intersex individuals in affirming their identities and bodies, and to advocate for their rights and bodily autonomy. This includes respecting their right to choose whether or not to undergo medical interventions, as well as providing them with access to comprehensive healthcare that addresses their unique needs. It's important to note that being intersex is not the same as being transgender or having a different sexual orientation. Intersex individuals can identify as any gender and have any sexual orientation, just like anyone else. However, because intersex individuals are born with bodies that don't fit typical binary sex classifications, they may face unique challenges related to their gender and sexuality.

Historically, intersex individuals have been subjected to medical interventions without their consent in an attempt to "normalize" their bodies. These interventions, such as genital surgeries and hormone treatments, have caused physical and psychological harm to many intersex individuals. It's important to recognize and support intersex individuals in their right to bodily autonomy and self-determination.

In recent years, there has been a growing movement to raise awareness about intersex issues and advocate for intersex rights. This includes advocating for an end to non-consensual medical interventions, promoting intersex-inclusive language and policies, and supporting intersex individuals in their journey to self-discovery and self-acceptance. It is important to note that intersex individuals have faced a significant amount of discrimination and stigma due to their physical differences. This can lead to a range of physical and emotional difficulties, including difficulty finding appropriate medical care, body dysmorphia, and depression. It is crucial for society to become more educated about intersex conditions and provide support for those who identify as intersex. It is also worth mentioning that there is a movement to change the term "intersex" to "variations in sex characteristics" (VSC) to reflect the diversity of physical differences that exist within this group. This change in terminology is meant to reduce stigma and promote inclusivity. It is important to recognize and support intersex individuals. Intersex people have historically been subjected to forced surgeries and medical treatments to conform their bodies to societal norms. These surgeries are often performed on infants and children without their consent and can lead to physical and psychological harm.

Intersex advocates have been working to raise awareness about intersex issues and promote the rights of intersex individuals. This includes advocating for informed consent for medical treatments, ending the practice of non-consensual surgeries on intersex infants and children, and ensuring intersex people have access to appropriate healthcare and support.

Understanding and accepting intersex individuals is an important part of creating a more inclusive and equitable society. By recognizing and valuing diversity in all its forms, we can work towards creating a world where everyone feels seen, heard, and respected.

FIVE
Asexuality

Asexuality is a sexual orientation characterized by a lack of sexual attraction towards anyone. People who identify as asexual may still experience romantic attraction and engage in romantic relationships, but they do not experience sexual attraction. It's important to note that asexuality is not the same as celibacy, which is a deliberate choice to abstain from sexual activity. Asexuality is an inherent aspect of a person's identity and is not something that can be changed or "fixed."

Asexuality is often misunderstood and even stigmatized in society. Some people assume that asexuality is simply a lack of sexual experience or a medical condition that can be treated. However, asexuality is a valid sexual orientation, just like heterosexuality, homosexuality, or bisexuality. It's important to understand that asexual people are not "broken" or "incomplete" because they do not experience sexual attraction.

One common misconception about asexuality is that asexual people are not capable of feeling love or forming meaningful relationships. This is not true. Asexual people can and do experience romantic attraction and may engage in romantic relationships. However, it's important to note that not all asexual people are interested in romantic relationships, just as not all non-asexual people are interested in romantic relationships.

Another misconception about asexuality is that asexual people are prudish or have no interest in sex. While asexual people do not experience sexual attraction, they may still engage in sexual activity for various reasons, such as to please a partner or to explore their own sexuality. It's also important to note that asexual people may have a range of attitudes towards sex, from indifference to aversion.

It's important to understand the differences between asexuality and other sexual orientations. For example, asexual people may sometimes be confused with people who identify as demisexual, which means they only experience sexual attraction after developing a deep emotional connection with someone. Additionally, some asexual people may also identify as aromantic, meaning they do not experience romantic attraction. It's also important to note that asexual people may still face discrimination and prejudice in society. They may feel pressured to conform to societal expectations of sexual attraction and relationships, or they may be misunderstood and dismissed by others who don't understand their experiences. Asexual individuals may also face challenges in finding and maintaining romantic relationships, as their lack of sexual attraction can be a barrier for some potential partners.

One important aspect of understanding asexuality is recognizing that asexuality is a spectrum. Just as there are varying degrees of sexual attraction for people who identify as heterosexual, homosexual, or bisexual, there is also a range of experiences for asexual individuals. Some asexual people may experience little to no sexual attraction, while others may experience it occasionally or in specific circumstances.

Asexuality is also not a monolithic experience. It can intersect with other aspects of a person's identity, such as gender, race, and disability. For example, asexual people who are also members of marginalized communities may face unique challenges and experiences related to their asexuality. It's also important to note that asexuality is not a mental disorder or a pathology. While some asexual individuals may experience distress or difficulties related to their asexuality, this is often due to the societal pressures and expectations they face, rather than a problem with their identity itself.

One way to support asexual individuals is to increase education and awareness about asexuality. This can include including asexuality in discussions about sexual orientation and diversity, as well as providing resources and support for asexual individuals and their allies. Educating ourselves about asexuality can also help us to be better allies and advocates for asexual individuals, and to challenge harmful myths and stereotypes about asexuality. Another important aspect of supporting asexual individuals is to respect their boundaries and choices. This means not pressuring them into sexual activity or relationships, and respecting their decision to not engage in sexual activity or romantic relationships if that is their preference. It also means not assuming that asexual individuals are interested in sexual or romantic relationships with others, and instead allowing them to define their own identity and experiences.

Creating inclusive spaces for asexual individuals is also important. This can include creating spaces where asexual individuals can connect with others who share their experiences, such as online communities or in-person support groups. It can also include creating safe and welcoming spaces for asexual individuals in broader LGBTQ+ communities, and ensuring that asexual individuals are included in conversations and advocacy efforts related to sexual and gender diversity.

One of the key challenges that asexual individuals face is the pressure to conform to societal norms and expectations around sexual attraction and relationships. Asexuality is still relatively unknown or misunderstood by many people, which can lead to a lack of acceptance or even hostility towards asexual individuals. This can make it difficult for asexual individuals to feel comfortable and accepted in social and dating situations, and can lead to feelings of isolation and alienation.

Another challenge that asexual individuals may face is the assumption that their lack of sexual attraction means that they are not interested in romantic relationships or intimacy. However, many asexual individuals do experience romantic attraction and desire for intimacy, even if they do not experience sexual attraction. It's important to recognize and respect these experiences, and to avoid assuming that all asexual individuals have the same preferences or desires.

Asexual individuals may also face challenges in accessing healthcare, particularly around issues related to sexual and reproductive health. Many healthcare providers may not be familiar with asexuality, which can lead to misunderstandings or inadequate care. It's important for healthcare providers to be educated about asexuality and to provide a safe and welcoming environment for asexual individuals to discuss their health concerns.

One way to further support asexual individuals is to address and challenge the harmful stereotypes and misconceptions that are often associated with asexuality. For example, some people may assume that asexual individuals are simply repressed or have a low sex drive, rather than recognizing asexuality as a valid sexual orientation. Others may assume that asexual individuals are somehow broken or incomplete, which can lead to feelings of shame or inadequacy. It's important to challenge these stereotypes and to recognize asexuality as a legitimate and valuable aspect of human diversity. This can involve sharing stories and experiences of asexual individuals, as well as providing accurate information about asexuality and its range of experiences. It can also involve creating opportunities for asexual individuals to connect with each other and with allies, in order to build a sense of community and support.

Another important way to support asexual individuals is to advocate for their inclusion and representation in broader social and political discussions about sexuality and human relationships. This means recognizing asexual individuals as part of the broader LGBTQ+ community and ensuring that their voices and perspectives are heard and valued in discussions about sexual and gender diversity. It also means advocating for policies and practices that respect the autonomy and dignity of all individuals, regardless of their sexual orientation. Another important aspect of supporting asexual individuals is to recognize and address the ways in which asexuality intersects with other aspects of identity, such as race, gender, and disability. Asexual individuals who belong to marginalized communities may face additional challenges and barriers, such as racism, transphobia, and ableism, which can compound the difficulties they face as asexual individuals. It's important to recognize and address these intersectional challenges in order to create a more inclusive and equitable society.

For example, asexual individuals who belong to racial or ethnic minority groups may face challenges related to cultural stereotypes and expectations around sexuality and gender roles. They may also face racism and discrimination in broader society, which can compound the challenges they face as asexual individuals. Similarly, asexual individuals who identify as transgender or gender non-conforming may face additional challenges related to gender identity and expression, which can intersect with their experiences of asexuality.

Addressing these intersectional challenges requires a commitment to understanding and addressing the ways in which multiple forms of oppression and discrimination intersect and compound each other. This can involve creating safe and welcoming spaces for asexual individuals who belong to marginalized communities, as well as advocating for policies and practices that promote equity and justice for all individuals, regardless of their identities.

Another important aspect of supporting asexual individuals is to recognize and address the ways in which asexual individuals may face discrimination or marginalization within LGBTQ+ communities. While asexual individuals are often included under the broader umbrella of LGBTQ+, they may still face stigma or misunderstanding from other members of the community who prioritize sexual attraction as a defining aspect of queer identity. This can lead to feelings of exclusion or alienation from LGBTQ+ spaces and communities. It's important to recognize and address these issues in order to create a more inclusive and welcoming LGBTQ+ community. This can involve advocating for asexuality to be recognized as a legitimate sexual orientation within LGBTQ+ spaces and organizations, as well as creating spaces and events specifically for asexual individuals within broader LGBTQ+ communities. It can also involve educating other members of the community about asexuality and its unique experiences and challenges.

Another important aspect of supporting asexual individuals is to recognize the diversity and complexity of asexual experiences. Asexuality is a broad and varied spectrum, and individuals may experience a range of different feelings and desires related to sexuality and intimacy. It's important to recognize and respect the individual choices and boundaries of asexual individuals, and to avoid making assumptions or generalizations about their experiences.

One way to support asexual individuals is to provide resources and information about asexuality and its range of experiences. This can involve sharing stories and experiences of asexual individuals, as well as providing accurate information about asexuality and its intersection with other aspects of identity. It can also involve creating opportunities for asexual individuals to connect with each other and with allies, in order to build a sense of community and support. Another way to further support asexual individuals is to address the ways in which asexuality intersects with mental health and well-being. Asexual individuals may face additional challenges related to mental health and well-being, such as feelings of isolation or anxiety related to their experiences of asexuality, or pressure from society or intimate partners to conform to norms of sexual attraction and behavior.

It's important to recognize and address these mental health challenges in order to promote the well-being of asexual individuals. This can involve providing access to mental health resources and support, as well as promoting a more accepting and inclusive culture around asexuality. Another important way to support asexual individuals is to advocate for their representation in media and popular culture. Asexual individuals are often underrepresented or misrepresented in media and popular culture, which can contribute to feelings of isolation or invisibility. By promoting accurate and positive representation of asexual individuals in media and popular culture, we can help to increase understanding and acceptance of asexuality in broader society.

Another important aspect of supporting asexual individuals is to address the ways in which asexual identities intersect with other aspects of identity, such as race, gender, and disability. Asexual individuals may face unique challenges related to their intersecting identities, such as the intersection of asexuality with experiences of racism or ableism. It's important to recognize and address these intersectional challenges in order to create a more inclusive and equitable society for asexual individuals. This can involve promoting intersectional awareness and understanding, as well as advocating for policies and practices that address the unique needs and challenges of asexual individuals who may also face other forms of marginalization or discrimination.

Another important way to support asexual individuals is to promote allyship and activism within broader communities. Allies can play a critical role in supporting asexual individuals by advocating for their inclusion and recognition, challenging discrimination and prejudice, and promoting understanding and awareness of asexuality. This can involve engaging in activism and advocacy efforts aimed at promoting asexual rights and visibility, as well as participating in education and awareness initiatives to promote understanding of asexual identities and experiences. By building a strong network of allies and advocates, we can create a more supportive and inclusive society for asexual individuals. It's also important to recognize that asexuality is a valid and natural variation of human sexuality, and not a disorder or something that needs to be "fixed." Asexual individuals should not be pathologized or stigmatized, but rather respected and accepted for who they are.

However, despite increasing awareness and acceptance of asexuality, asexual individuals may still face discrimination and prejudice in many areas of life, including in intimate relationships, employment, healthcare, and legal protections. It's important to advocate for policies and practices that promote equality and inclusion for asexual individuals, such as anti-discrimination laws and inclusive healthcare policies.

Additionally, research on asexuality is still relatively limited, and there is much to be learned about the experiences and needs of asexual individuals. Increased research and understanding of asexuality can help to promote greater acceptance and inclusion of asexual individuals, as well as inform the development of policies and practices that meet the unique needs of asexual individuals. It's important to recognize that asexuality is not a static identity, but rather a fluid and diverse experience that can vary across different contexts and over time. Some asexual individuals may experience occasional or situational sexual attraction, while others may experience romantic attraction or desire for emotional intimacy without sexual attraction. It's also important to recognize that asexuality can intersect with other sexual orientations and identities, such as aromanticism or demisexuality. Aromantic individuals do not experience romantic attraction, while demisexual individuals experience sexual attraction only after developing a strong emotional bond with another person.

Therefore, supporting asexual individuals also means recognizing and respecting the diversity and complexity of asexual identities and experiences. This can involve creating safe and inclusive spaces for individuals to explore and express their identities, as well as promoting education and awareness about the diversity of asexual experiences.

In addition, it's important to recognize that asexual individuals can still have fulfilling and meaningful relationships, both romantic and platonic. Asexual individuals may have different needs and expectations in their relationships, but these relationships can still be characterized by intimacy, emotional connection, and mutual respect. Another important aspect of supporting asexual individuals is to recognize and address the impact of asexuality on mental health and well-being. Asexual individuals may experience feelings of isolation, shame, or invalidation due to a lack of understanding or acceptance of their identity.

It's important to provide a supportive and affirming environment for asexual individuals to explore and express their identities, as well as access mental health resources if needed. This can involve promoting access to therapy or counseling that is sensitive to asexual experiences, as well as providing social support and community resources that help to counter feelings of isolation or invalidation. In addition, it's important to recognize the role of stigmatization and discrimination in contributing to negative mental health outcomes among asexual individuals. Asexual individuals may face discrimination or marginalization in many areas of life, such as in the workplace or in healthcare settings, which can contribute to feelings of shame or low self-worth.

Therefore, supporting asexual individuals also means advocating for policies and practices that promote equality and inclusion, as well as challenging discrimination and prejudice when it occurs. Another important aspect of supporting asexual individuals is recognizing the intersectionality of their experiences. Asexual individuals may also experience discrimination and marginalization based on other aspects of their identity, such as race, ethnicity, gender identity, or disability. It's important to acknowledge the unique challenges that asexual individuals from marginalized communities may face, and to work towards creating inclusive and affirming spaces that recognize and celebrate diversity.

Furthermore, asexual individuals may also experience challenges related to navigating sexual and romantic relationships in a society that places a high value on sexual attraction and intimacy. Asexual individuals may feel pressure to conform to societal norms around sex and relationships, which can contribute to feelings of invalidation or shame.

It's important to recognize that asexual individuals have the right to autonomy and agency in their relationships and to communicate their needs and boundaries to their partners. By promoting education and awareness about asexuality and advocating for the right to bodily autonomy, we can help to create a society that respects and supports asexual individuals in their choices around intimacy and relationships. Another important aspect of supporting asexual individuals is recognizing the diversity within the asexual community. Asexual individuals may experience their sexuality and romantic orientation in different ways and may identify with different labels within the asexual spectrum.

Some asexual individuals may experience romantic attraction but not sexual attraction (known as romantic asexuals or aromantic heterosexuals), while others may experience both romantic and sexual attraction to varying degrees (known as gray-asexuals or demisexuals). There are also asexual individuals who experience sexual attraction but have no desire to act on it (known as celibate asexuals). It's important to recognize and respect the diversity of experiences and identities within the asexual community, and to avoid making assumptions about individuals based on a single label or category.

In addition, it's important to recognize that asexual individuals may also experience fluidity or changes in their sexual and romantic orientations over time. It's important to support individuals in their self-exploration and to create spaces where they can express themselves without fear of judgment or invalidation. One important way to support asexual individuals is by creating safe and inclusive spaces where they can express themselves without fear of judgment or discrimination. This can be done through the promotion of education and awareness about asexuality, as well as by creating social and community networks that allow asexual individuals to connect with others who share similar experiences and identities. It's also important to recognize the role of mental health in the well-being of asexual individuals. Asexual individuals may experience feelings of isolation, shame, or invalidation due to societal expectations around sexuality and relationships, and may benefit from access to mental health resources and support.

In addition, asexual individuals may face unique challenges in accessing healthcare services that are sensitive and responsive to their needs. It's important for healthcare providers to recognize the diversity of sexual orientations and identities, and to create inclusive and affirming environments that respect the autonomy and dignity of all patients.

Another important aspect of supporting asexual individuals is recognizing the intersectionality of their identities. Asexual individuals may also identify as members of other marginalized communities, such as people of color, individuals with disabilities, or members of the LGBTQ+ community. These intersecting identities can result in unique challenges and experiences of discrimination and marginalization.

It's important to recognize and address these intersecting forms of discrimination, and to work towards creating inclusive and affirming spaces that support the diverse experiences and identities of asexual individuals. In addition, promoting awareness and education about asexuality can help to combat the harmful myths and stereotypes that exist about asexual individuals. By challenging these harmful beliefs, we can create a more understanding and accepting society that celebrates the diversity of human sexuality and relationships. One additional way to support asexual individuals is to advocate for increased representation and visibility of asexuality in mainstream media and popular culture. Asexual individuals are often underrepresented or portrayed inaccurately in mainstream media, which can perpetuate harmful myths and stereotypes about their experiences and identities.

By advocating for increased representation and visibility of asexuality in media and popular culture, we can help to raise awareness and understanding of asexuality, and promote more positive and inclusive representations of asexual individuals.

An important way to support asexual individuals is to work towards creating policies and laws that protect their rights and ensure their equal treatment under the law. Asexual individuals may face discrimination in areas such as employment, healthcare, and housing, and it's important to work towards creating policies and laws that address these forms of discrimination and promote equality for all individuals, regardless of their sexual orientation or identity. Another important way to support asexual individuals is to create safe and inclusive spaces where they can connect with others who share similar experiences and identities. This can include creating online communities or in-person support groups, providing access to resources and information about asexuality, and promoting events and activities that celebrate asexual identities and experiences.

Creating these safe and inclusive spaces can help to combat the isolation and stigma that many asexual individuals may face, and provide a sense of community and belonging. It's also important to recognize the importance of allyship in supporting asexual individuals. Allies can play a critical role in promoting understanding and acceptance of asexuality, challenging harmful myths and stereotypes, and advocating for policies and laws that protect the rights of asexual individuals.

By educating themselves about asexuality, listening to the experiences and perspectives of asexual individuals, and taking action to promote awareness and understanding, allies can help to create a more inclusive and equitable society for all individuals. Another important aspect of supporting asexual individuals is addressing the issue of asexual erasure, which occurs when asexual identities and experiences are ignored, invalidated, or erased from public discourse and mainstream media.

Asexual erasure can contribute to the marginalization and discrimination that asexual individuals face, and it's important to challenge and resist this erasure by actively promoting asexual visibility and representation.

This can include advocating for more accurate and inclusive representations of asexual individuals in media and popular culture, working to ensure that asexual identities are included in conversations about sexual and gender diversity, and promoting education and awareness about asexuality in schools, workplaces, and communities. It's also important to recognize and support the efforts of asexual activists and advocates who are working to promote visibility and acceptance of asexuality, and to amplify their voices and perspectives.

One additional way to support asexual individuals is to educate ourselves and others about the unique experiences and challenges that they may face. This can include learning about the various identities and labels within the asexual community, understanding the differences between asexuality and celibacy, and recognizing the impact of asexuality on mental health and well-being.

By educating ourselves and others about asexuality, we can challenge harmful myths and stereotypes, promote understanding and acceptance, and create a more supportive and inclusive environment for asexual individuals. It's also important to recognize that asexual individuals may face unique challenges when seeking medical and mental health care, as many healthcare providers may not be familiar with asexuality or may hold biases and stereotypes about asexual individuals.

As such, it's important to advocate for increased awareness and education about asexuality within the healthcare system, and to promote the development of resources and support networks for asexual individuals seeking medical and mental health care. Another important way to support asexual individuals is to advocate for policies and laws that protect their rights and ensure their full inclusion in society. This can include advocating for legal recognition of asexual identities, promoting policies that protect asexual individuals from discrimination in housing, employment, and public accommodations, and advocating for comprehensive sex education that includes information about asexuality and other diverse sexual orientations and gender identities.

By working to create a legal and policy environment that supports and affirms asexual identities and experiences, we can help to ensure that asexual individuals are able to fully participate in society and access the resources and opportunities that they need to thrive. One additional way to support asexual individuals is to challenge and resist harmful media representation and cultural narratives that perpetuate asexual erasure or negative stereotypes. This can include speaking out against media that presents asexuality as a pathology or a problem to be solved, and promoting media that includes positive and accurate representation of asexual individuals and relationships.

We can also work to create and support media and cultural narratives that center asexual experiences and perspectives. This can include supporting asexual creators and media that features asexual characters and storylines, as well as promoting diverse and intersectional representations of asexuality that reflect the full range of asexual experiences and identities.

By challenging harmful media representation and promoting positive and accurate representation of asexual individuals and relationships, we can help to shift cultural attitudes towards asexuality and create a more inclusive and accepting society. It's important to recognize that supporting asexual individuals is an ongoing and evolving process, and that there is no one-size-fits-all approach to allyship and advocacy. However, by taking proactive steps to educate ourselves and others, challenge harmful stereotypes and narratives, and advocate for policies and laws that protect asexual rights and inclusion, we can work towards a more just and equitable society that values and celebrates the diversity of human sexuality and relationships.

Another way to support asexual individuals is to prioritize self-care and mental health. Asexuality, like any other identity, can come with its own unique challenges and struggles, such as navigating relationships and feeling isolated or misunderstood. It's important for asexual individuals to prioritize their mental health and well-being, and seek out resources and support when needed. This can include seeking out therapy or counseling from a mental health professional who is knowledgeable and supportive of asexuality, connecting with online or in-person support groups and communities, and engaging in self-care practices that promote well-being, such as exercise, meditation, and creative expression.

For allies and advocates, it's important to prioritize self-care and boundary-setting as well, as supporting asexual individuals can be emotionally taxing and may require setting clear boundaries with others or taking breaks when needed.

By prioritizing mental health and self-care, both asexual individuals and their allies can better support and advocate for asexual rights and inclusion, and ensure that everyone involved is able to maintain their own well-being and resilience. Another important aspect of supporting asexual individuals is recognizing and addressing the intersections of asexuality with other identities and experiences, such as race, gender, and disability. Asexual individuals who also hold marginalized identities may face compounded discrimination and oppression, which can further impact their mental health and well-being.

As allies and advocates, it's important to educate ourselves about the intersections of asexuality with other identities and experiences, and work to address systemic barriers and injustices that may impact asexual individuals who also hold marginalized identities. This can include advocating for policies and laws that address systemic discrimination and promote equity and inclusion for all individuals, regardless of their identity or experiences. It can also include working to center the experiences and perspectives of asexual individuals who also hold marginalized identities in our advocacy and support efforts, and seeking out and amplifying their voices and leadership.

By recognizing and addressing the intersections of asexuality with other identities and experiences, we can work towards a more just and equitable society that values and celebrates the full diversity of human experiences and identities.

As allies and advocates, it's important to approach asexuality with openness and curiosity, and to be willing to listen and learn from asexual individuals themselves. This can include asking questions respectfully and without assumptions, and being open to the diverse range of experiences and perspectives that exist within the asexual community.

It's also important to recognize and address any biases or assumptions we may hold about asexuality, and to challenge any internalized or externalized beliefs that may limit our understanding or empathy towards asexual individuals.

By recognizing and embracing the diversity of experiences and identities within the asexual community, we can better support and advocate for asexual individuals and work towards a more inclusive and accepting society for all

SIX
Intersectionality

Intersectionality is a concept coined by scholar Kimberlé Crenshaw, which refers to the ways in which different forms of oppression (such as sexism, racism, homophobia, and ableism) intersect and overlap to create unique experiences of discrimination and marginalization for individuals who hold multiple marginalized identities. In the case of LGBTAI individuals, this means that their sexual orientation and gender identity intersect with other aspects of their identity such as race, class, and ability, to create complex experiences of discrimination and privilege.

For example, a Black transgender woman may experience discrimination not only because of her gender identity and sexual orientation but also because of her race. She may face discrimination and violence from both the LGBTQ+ community and the Black community, and she may also face barriers to employment, housing, and healthcare because of her race and gender identity.

Similarly, a low-income queer person with a disability may face unique challenges related to accessing healthcare, employment, and housing because of their intersecting identities. They may face discrimination in the healthcare system because of their sexual orientation, encounter physical barriers in the workplace because of their disability, and struggle to afford housing because of their economic status.

Understanding intersectionality is important because it helps us recognize that people's experiences of oppression are not singular or monolithic. Rather, people hold multiple marginalized identities that intersect and overlap, and these intersections shape their experiences of discrimination and privilege. By recognizing these intersections, we can work to create more inclusive and equitable communities for all individuals, including those who hold multiple marginalized identities.

To understand intersectionality, it's important to recognize that different forms of oppression do not exist in isolation. Instead, they intersect and interact with each other to create unique experiences of discrimination and marginalization. This means that individuals who hold multiple marginalized identities, such as being LGBTQ+ and a person of color or being disabled and transgender, may face a range of intersecting forms of discrimination and oppression.

For example, a queer woman of color may experience discrimination related to her gender, sexual orientation, and race. She may face gender-based violence and harassment, as well as racism and discrimination in her daily life. This can create a complex and challenging experience, as she may not be able to address these forms of oppression individually, and instead must navigate multiple forms of discrimination at the same time.

Intersectionality also helps us understand how power and privilege operate in society. Individuals who hold privileged identities, such as being white, male, or cisgender, may be less likely to experience the same kinds of intersecting forms of discrimination and marginalization as individuals who hold multiple marginalized identities. For example, a white gay man may experience homophobia but not racism, while a Black lesbian may experience racism and homophobia simultaneously.

By recognizing the ways in which different forms of oppression intersect and overlap, we can work to create more inclusive and equitable communities. This means understanding that individuals who hold multiple marginalized identities may face unique forms of discrimination and oppression, and working to address these intersecting forms of oppression in our policies, practices, and interactions. It also means recognizing our own privilege and working to use that privilege to create more equitable and inclusive spaces for everyone. It's important to note that intersectionality is not just a theoretical concept but also a framework for understanding and addressing social justice issues. Intersectional analysis helps us recognize the ways in which different forms of oppression intersect and interact, and how these intersections can create unique experiences of discrimination and marginalization. By using an intersectional lens, we can better understand the complexity of people's experiences and work towards more inclusive and equitable solutions.

For example, an intersectional approach to LGBTQ+ advocacy might recognize that the experiences of LGBTQ+ individuals differ based on other aspects of their identity, such as race, class, and ability. This means that LGBTQ+ advocacy efforts need to address these intersecting forms of oppression in order to create more inclusive and equitable outcomes for everyone in the community. It also means recognizing that not all LGBTQ+ individuals experience the same forms of discrimination and marginalization, and that our advocacy efforts need to be tailored to the specific needs of different communities.

Intersectionality also highlights the importance of centering the experiences and perspectives of those who hold multiple marginalized identities. For example, in LGBTQ+ advocacy, it's important to listen to and uplift the voices of queer people of color, transgender and gender non-conforming individuals, and those who experience intersecting forms of discrimination and marginalization. By centering these perspectives, we can ensure that our advocacy efforts are truly inclusive and equitable.

Intersectionality is a dynamic and evolving concept that has been applied to a wide range of social justice issues beyond LGBTQ+ advocacy, including feminism, anti-racism, disability rights, and environmental justice. By recognizing the interconnectedness of different forms of oppression, we can work towards creating more holistic solutions that address multiple issues at once.

Moreover, intersectionality also highlights the importance of recognizing and addressing systemic and institutionalized forms of oppression. It's not just about individual acts of discrimination, but also about the ways in which systemic discrimination and inequality are embedded in our institutions and structures. For example, the criminal justice system disproportionately targets and incarcerates people of color and LGBTQ+ individuals, perpetuating systemic oppression and inequality.

Intersectionality also highlights the importance of recognizing the diversity within marginalized communities. Not all LGBTQ+ individuals experience the same forms of discrimination and marginalization, and it's important to understand and address the specific needs and experiences of different communities within the broader LGBTQ+ community. This means recognizing and addressing the ways in which intersecting identities, such as race, class, and ability, shape people's experiences of discrimination and marginalization. Intersectionality also underscores the importance of allyship and solidarity between different marginalized communities. It's important to recognize that different communities may face different forms of oppression and discrimination, but there are also many shared experiences and struggles. For example, LGBTQ+ individuals and people of color may share experiences of discrimination and violence, and it's important for these communities to support each other and work together towards common goals.

Additionally, intersectionality can also help us recognize the ways in which privilege and power operate within and between different communities. It's important to acknowledge that some individuals hold privileged identities, such as being white, wealthy, or able-bodied, and that these forms of privilege can contribute to the marginalization of other communities. By recognizing and addressing privilege and power, we can work towards creating more equitable and just societies.

Intersectionality can also help us recognize the ways in which language and representation can shape our understanding of different communities and identities. For example, using gender-inclusive language and recognizing the diversity of gender identities can help create a more welcoming and inclusive environment for transgender and non-binary individuals within the LGBTQ+ community. Similarly, using language that recognizes and affirms different racial and cultural identities can help create a more inclusive and equitable environment for people of color within the LGBTQ+ community.

Furthermore, intersectionality can also help us understand the ways in which different forms of oppression intersect with and perpetuate each other. For example, transphobia and homophobia can intersect with ableism to create unique forms of discrimination and marginalization experienced by disabled LGBTQ+ individuals. Understanding these intersections can help us create more comprehensive and effective solutions that address the root causes of systemic oppression and inequality.

One important aspect of intersectionality is the recognition of the ways in which different forms of oppression and marginalization intersect with one another. For example, the experiences of a queer person of color are often different from those of a white queer person, as they may face not only homophobia and transphobia but also racism and xenophobia. Similarly, a disabled queer person may face unique forms of discrimination and marginalization due to ableism within both the queer community and broader society.

Furthermore, intersectionality emphasizes the importance of recognizing and addressing the ways in which different forms of oppression are institutionalized and systemic. For example, laws and policies that restrict access to healthcare or discriminate against LGBTQ+ individuals can perpetuate systemic oppression and inequality. Recognizing these systemic issues is crucial in working towards creating lasting change that benefits all members of our communities.

Intersectionality also underscores the importance of allyship and solidarity between different marginalized communities. Recognizing the ways in which different forms of oppression intersect can help us understand and support the struggles of other marginalized communities. For example, recognizing the ways in which racism and transphobia intersect can help create stronger allyship between the queer community and communities of color.

Another important aspect of intersectionality is recognizing the diversity of experiences within any given community. While LGBTQ+ individuals may share some common experiences related to their sexual orientation and gender identity, they also hold a wide range of other identities and experiences that shape their lives in unique ways. For example, a queer person may also be a parent, a person with a disability, or an immigrant, and each of these identities can impact their experiences and needs. Recognizing and honoring the diversity of experiences within the LGBTQ+ community is crucial in creating more inclusive and equitable solutions. This means centering the experiences and needs of those who are often overlooked or marginalized, such as LGBTQ+ youth, transgender and non-binary individuals, and LGBTQ+ individuals who hold multiple marginalized identities.

Furthermore, intersectionality highlights the importance of taking a holistic approach to social justice issues. Issues such as housing, healthcare, and employment discrimination can impact LGBTQ+ individuals in unique ways, and addressing these issues requires a comprehensive approach that considers the intersectionality of different forms of oppression. For example, addressing healthcare discrimination against LGBTQ+ individuals may require addressing issues related to both homophobia and transphobia as well as ableism.

One important application of intersectionality is in policy-making and advocacy work. An intersectional approach recognizes that social justice issues cannot be addressed in isolation, and that solutions must take into account the ways in which different forms of oppression intersect and compound one another. This means advocating for policies and programs that take into account the diversity of experiences within marginalized communities, and that address the root causes of systemic oppression.

For example, an intersectional approach to healthcare policy might involve advocating for policies that address not only healthcare discrimination against LGBTQ+ individuals, but also the ways in which racism, ableism, and economic inequality impact healthcare access and outcomes for marginalized communities. Similarly, an intersectional approach to employment policy might involve advocating for policies that address not only employment discrimination against LGBTQ+ individuals, but also the ways in which racism, sexism, and ableism impact employment opportunities and outcomes for marginalized communities.

Intersectionality can also inform the way we approach community organizing and activism. An intersectional approach recognizes that social justice issues are interconnected, and that organizing around a single issue or identity may not be sufficient to address the root causes of oppression. This means working towards building coalitions and alliances between different marginalized communities, and recognizing that the struggles of one community are intertwined with the struggles of others.

An important aspect of intersectionality is the recognition that individuals can hold both privileged and marginalized identities simultaneously. For example, a white cisgender gay man may experience marginalization due to his sexual orientation, but may also hold privilege due to his whiteness and cisgender identity. This means that intersectionality requires individuals to recognize and challenge their own privilege, and to actively work towards creating more equitable and inclusive systems that benefit all individuals, not just those who hold privileged identities.

Intersectionality also highlights the importance of centering the experiences and leadership of those who hold marginalized identities. This means recognizing the expertise and lived experiences of those who are most impacted by systemic oppression, and elevating their voices and leadership in advocacy work and decision-making processes. This approach is often referred to as "nothing about us without us," and recognizes that solutions to social justice issues must be informed and led by those who are most impacted.

Furthermore, an intersectional approach requires recognizing that different forms of oppression are not independent of one another, but are often interrelated and reinforcing. For example, homophobia and transphobia may intersect with racism, ableism, and classism to create unique forms of oppression and marginalization. This means that solutions to social justice issues must address the intersections between different forms of oppression, and must work towards dismantling systems of oppression in all their forms.

Another important aspect of intersectionality is the recognition that the experiences of LGBTQ+ individuals can vary depending on their geographic location and cultural context. For example, LGBTQ+ individuals living in more conservative or religiously influenced societies may face more overt discrimination and violence than those living in more progressive and accepting societies. This means that an intersectional approach to LGBTQ+ advocacy work must take into account the specific cultural and social contexts in which discrimination and marginalization occur, and must work towards creating solutions that are responsive to these unique contexts.

Intersectionality also highlights the importance of addressing the ways in which discrimination and marginalization can impact mental health and well-being. LGBTQ+ individuals may experience higher rates of mental health issues such as depression, anxiety, and substance abuse as a result of discrimination and marginalization. Additionally, the intersections of LGBTQ+ identity with other marginalized identities can further compound mental health issues. An intersectional approach to mental health care for LGBTQ+ individuals must take into account these unique experiences and work towards providing comprehensive and inclusive care that addresses the root causes of mental health issues.

An important consideration in an intersectional approach to LGBTQ+ advocacy is the recognition that individuals may not always identify solely within the LGBTQ+ community, and that their identities and experiences may be fluid and multifaceted. For example, an individual may identify as both LGBTQ+ and disabled, and may experience discrimination and marginalization based on both identities. An intersectional approach requires recognition of the complexity of individual identities and experiences, and the need for solutions that are responsive to these complexities.

Additionally, intersectionality emphasizes the importance of allyship and coalition building across different marginalized communities. This means recognizing the ways in which different forms of oppression are interrelated and interconnected, and working towards creating collaborative solutions that address these intersections. By building coalitions across different marginalized communities, we can amplify our voices and create more powerful movements for social justice.

Another key aspect of intersectionality is the importance of recognizing and addressing the ways in which LGBTQ+ individuals may be impacted by systemic inequities in areas such as education, employment, housing, and healthcare. For example, LGBTQ+ individuals may face discrimination in the workplace or may lack access to affordable healthcare. An intersectional approach requires addressing these systemic inequities and advocating for policies and practices that promote equity and inclusion for all individuals. Another important consideration in an intersectional approach to LGBTQ+ advocacy is the recognition that language and terminology can have a significant impact on the experiences of LGBTQ+ individuals. This means recognizing the importance of using language that is inclusive and affirming of all individuals, regardless of their gender identity, sexual orientation, race, ability, or other identities. For example, using gender-neutral language and avoiding gendered assumptions can help create more inclusive spaces and communities for non-binary and gender non-conforming individuals.

An intersectional approach to language also requires recognizing the ways in which language can be used to perpetuate discrimination and marginalization. For example, using slurs or derogatory language towards LGBTQ+ individuals can contribute to a culture of intolerance and hate. An intersectional approach requires actively challenging and addressing these harmful language practices, and promoting language that is affirming and inclusive of all individuals.

Additionally, an intersectional approach to LGBTQ+ advocacy work recognizes the importance of uplifting the voices and leadership of those who hold marginalized identities within the community. This means recognizing that LGBTQ+ individuals from historically marginalized communities, such as Black and Indigenous individuals, people of color, and people with disabilities, may face unique forms of discrimination and marginalization. An intersectional approach requires actively working to center these voices and experiences in advocacy work, and promoting inclusive leadership and decision-making practices. Another important aspect of an intersectional approach to LGBTQ+ advocacy is recognizing the importance of mental health and well-being for LGBTQ+ individuals. LGBTQ+ individuals may experience unique forms of stress and discrimination related to their sexual orientation, gender identity, and other marginalized identities, which can have a significant impact on their mental health and well-being.

An intersectional approach to mental health recognizes the importance of addressing the root causes of mental health disparities and promoting access to culturally responsive and affirming mental health services. This means recognizing the ways in which social determinants of health, such as discrimination and marginalization, can impact mental health outcomes, and working towards creating systems and policies that address these determinants.

Additionally, an intersectional approach to mental health requires recognizing the diversity of mental health needs and experiences within the LGBTQ+ community. For example, LGBTQ+ individuals from historically marginalized communities may experience unique forms of stress and trauma related to their identities, which may require tailored approaches to mental health care. An intersectional approach requires promoting access to mental health services that are responsive to the diverse needs and experiences of LGBTQ+ individuals. An important consideration in an intersectional approach to LGBTQ+ advocacy is recognizing the ways in which policy and legal frameworks can impact the experiences of LGBTQ+ individuals. An intersectional approach requires actively working towards creating policies and legal frameworks that are inclusive and affirming of all individuals, regardless of their sexual orientation, gender identity, race, ability, or other identities.

This means working towards the removal of discriminatory laws and policies, such as laws that criminalize same-sex activity or discriminate against transgender individuals in employment or housing. An intersectional approach also requires working towards the creation of policies and legal frameworks that promote equity and inclusion, such as laws that protect LGBTQ+ individuals from discrimination in all areas of life, including employment, housing, education, and healthcare.

Additionally, an intersectional approach requires recognizing the ways in which policy and legal frameworks intersect with other forms of oppression and discrimination. For example, policies that discriminate against LGBTQ+ individuals may also disproportionately impact individuals from historically marginalized communities, such as people of color, low-income individuals, and people with disabilities. An intersectional approach requires recognizing these intersections and working towards creating policies and legal frameworks that promote equity and inclusion for all individuals.

Another important aspect of an intersectional approach to LGBTQ+ advocacy is recognizing the importance of education and awareness-raising efforts. Education and awareness-raising efforts are essential for challenging misconceptions and stereotypes about LGBTQ+ individuals and promoting understanding and acceptance.

An intersectional approach to education and awareness-raising efforts requires recognizing the diversity of experiences within the LGBTQ+ community and the ways in which different forms of oppression and discrimination intersect. This means acknowledging the ways in which race, class, ability, and other identities intersect with sexual orientation and gender identity, and working towards promoting understanding and acceptance across all intersections of identity. Additionally, an intersectional approach to education and awareness-raising efforts requires recognizing the importance of centering the voices and experiences of LGBTQ+ individuals from historically marginalized communities. This means promoting the leadership and visibility of LGBTQ+ individuals from these communities in educational and awareness-raising efforts, and working towards creating spaces and platforms for these individuals to share their experiences and perspectives. Another important consideration in an intersectional approach to LGBTQ+ advocacy is recognizing the importance of mental health and well-being. LGBTQ+ individuals experience higher rates of mental health issues, including depression, anxiety, and suicidal ideation, compared to their cisgender and heterosexual peers. These mental health issues are often linked to experiences of discrimination, violence, and social isolation.

An intersectional approach to mental health and well-being requires recognizing the ways in which different forms of oppression and discrimination intersect to impact the mental health of LGBTQ+ individuals. This means recognizing that experiences of discrimination and violence may be compounded by other forms of marginalization, such as racism, ableism, and poverty, which can further impact mental health and well-being.

Additionally, an intersectional approach to mental health and well-being requires recognizing the importance of culturally responsive and affirming mental health services. This means ensuring that mental health services are inclusive of the diversity of experiences and identities within the LGBTQ+ community and that mental health providers are trained to provide culturally responsive and affirming care. Another important aspect of an intersectional approach to LGBTQ+ advocacy is recognizing the importance of legal protections and policies that promote equity and inclusion for LGBTQ+ individuals. Legal protections are essential for ensuring that LGBTQ+ individuals have equal access to employment, housing, healthcare, and other basic rights and services.

An intersectional approach to legal protections requires recognizing the ways in which different forms of oppression and discrimination intersect to impact the legal rights and protections of LGBTQ+ individuals. This means recognizing that LGBTQ+ individuals from historically marginalized communities may face additional barriers to accessing legal protections and may require targeted policies and programs to address these barriers.

Additionally, an intersectional approach to legal protections requires recognizing the importance of policies and programs that address the specific needs and experiences of LGBTQ+ individuals. This includes policies and programs that promote inclusion and diversity in the workplace, provide access to affordable healthcare, and address issues of violence and discrimination against LGBTQ+ individuals. Another important consideration in an intersectional approach to LGBTQ+ advocacy is the need to address the impact of environmental factors on the health and well-being of LGBTQ+ individuals. Environmental factors, such as pollution and climate change, can have a disproportionate impact on the health and well-being of marginalized communities, including LGBTQ+ individuals.

An intersectional approach to environmental justice requires recognizing the ways in which different forms of oppression and discrimination intersect to impact the environmental health and well-being of LGBTQ+ individuals. For example, LGBTQ+ individuals from historically marginalized communities may be more likely to live in areas with high levels of pollution or environmental hazards, which can lead to higher rates of health problems.

Additionally, an intersectional approach to environmental justice requires recognizing the importance of policies and programs that promote environmental justice and address the specific needs and experiences of LGBTQ+ individuals. This includes policies and programs that promote access to clean air and water, reduce exposure to environmental hazards, and address the impact of climate change on the health and well-being of LGBTQ+ individuals. Another important aspect of intersectionality in LGBTQ+ advocacy is the recognition of the impact of language and cultural competency. Language and cultural competency are essential in ensuring that LGBTQ+ individuals from diverse backgrounds feel seen, heard, and respected in all areas of their lives, including healthcare, education, and social services.

An intersectional approach to language and cultural competency requires recognizing the ways in which different forms of oppression and discrimination intersect to impact the language and cultural needs of LGBTQ+ individuals. This means recognizing that LGBTQ+ individuals from historically marginalized communities may require targeted outreach and support to address language and cultural barriers.

Additionally, an intersectional approach to language and cultural competency requires recognizing the importance of policies and programs that promote cultural competency and address the specific needs and experiences of LGBTQ+ individuals. This includes policies and programs that provide training and support for healthcare providers and educators to better understand and address the unique needs of LGBTQ+ individuals from diverse backgrounds. One important area where intersectionality is essential in LGBTQ+ advocacy is in the criminal justice system. LGBTQ+ individuals, particularly those who are transgender, non-binary, or people of color, are often subjected to discrimination, harassment, and violence within the criminal justice system.

An intersectional approach to criminal justice reform requires recognizing the ways in which different forms of oppression and discrimination intersect to impact the experiences of LGBTQ+ individuals within the criminal justice system. This means recognizing that LGBTQ+ individuals from historically marginalized communities may face additional barriers to accessing justice, and may be more likely to experience discrimination and violence at the hands of law enforcement and within the criminal justice system.

Additionally, an intersectional approach to criminal justice reform requires recognizing the importance of policies and programs that address the specific needs and experiences of LGBTQ+ individuals within the criminal justice system. This includes policies and programs that provide training and support for law enforcement and criminal justice professionals to better understand and address the unique needs of LGBTQ+ individuals, as well as policies and programs that work to end the criminalization of LGBTQ+ identities and experiences. Another important area where intersectionality is crucial in LGBTQ+ advocacy is in the workplace. LGBTQ+ individuals face significant barriers to employment, including discrimination, harassment, and unequal treatment in the workplace.

An intersectional approach to workplace advocacy requires recognizing the ways in which different forms of oppression and discrimination intersect to impact the experiences of LGBTQ+ individuals in the workplace. This means recognizing that LGBTQ+ individuals from historically marginalized communities may face additional barriers to employment, including discrimination based on their sexual orientation or gender identity, as well as discrimination based on other aspects of their identity, such as race, ethnicity, or disability. Additionally, an intersectional approach to workplace advocacy requires recognizing the importance of policies and programs that address the specific needs and experiences of LGBTQ+ individuals in the workplace. This includes policies and programs that provide protections against discrimination, harassment, and unequal treatment, as well as policies and programs that promote workplace diversity and inclusion.

Intersectionality is a concept that recognizes the ways in which different forms of oppression and discrimination intersect to impact individuals' experiences. In the context of LGBTQ+ advocacy, intersectionality is essential to understanding the experiences of LGBTQ+ individuals from diverse backgrounds and promoting policies and programs that address their specific needs.

An intersectional approach to LGBTQ+ advocacy requires recognizing the ways in which different aspects of an individual's identity, such as race, class, and ability, intersect with their sexual orientation and gender identity to shape their experiences. This includes recognizing the ways in which LGBTQ+ individuals from historically marginalized communities may face additional barriers to accessing healthcare, education, employment, and justice, and may be more vulnerable to discrimination and violence.

Intersectionality is also essential in promoting policies and programs that address the specific needs and experiences of LGBTQ+ individuals in various contexts, including healthcare, education, criminal justice, and the workplace. This requires recognizing the importance of community-led advocacy and organizing efforts to advance LGBTQ+ rights and promote the well-being of all individuals within the LGBTQ+ community.

<u>SEVEN</u>
The Coming Out Process

The process of coming out as lesbian, LGBTAI can be a difficult and complex journey for individuals. It involves revealing one's sexual orientation or gender identity to family, friends, and society, which can bring about a range of emotions and reactions from those around them.

One of the primary challenges that individuals face during the coming out process is fear of rejection and discrimination from loved ones and society. This can create feelings of isolation and anxiety, leading to a delay or avoidance of coming out. Additionally, some individuals may struggle with accepting their own sexual orientation or gender identity, which can make it difficult to reveal their true selves to others.

As a friend, family member, or ally, it's important to offer support and understanding during this process. Here are some tips on how to support someone who is coming out:

1. **Listen Without Judgment:** When someone comes out to you, it's essential to listen to them without interrupting or judging them. Let them share their feelings and experiences with you, and validate their emotions.

2. **Educate Yourself:** Take the time to educate yourself about different sexual orientations and gender identities, and learn about the challenges that individuals face during the coming out process. This will help you to understand and empathize with their journey.

3. **Use Inclusive Language:** Using inclusive language, such as using someone's correct pronouns or not assuming someone's sexual orientation, can make a big difference in creating a safe and supportive environment.

4. **Offer Your Support:** Let the individual know that you support them and that you're there for them. Offer to accompany them to LGBTIA events or to be a sounding board for their thoughts and feelings.

5. **Respect Their Privacy:** It's important to respect the individual's privacy and allow them to come out to others on their own terms. Don't pressure them to come out to others before they're ready.

In addition to the challenges mentioned earlier, coming out can also be difficult due to the societal stigma and discrimination that still exists towards the LGBTAI community. Discrimination can manifest in various forms, including job loss, housing discrimination, and even physical violence. These factors can create a sense of fear and uncertainty, making the decision to come out even more challenging. It's important to understand that coming out is a personal decision, and it should be done at the individual's own pace. Some individuals may feel comfortable coming out to certain people before others, and that's okay. It's important to respect the individual's decision and not push them to come out before they're ready.

As a society, it's crucial to create safe and accepting spaces for the LGBTAI community. This can involve advocating for equal rights and protections, creating inclusive policies and practices, and challenging harmful stereotypes and biases. It's also important to recognize and celebrate the diversity within the LGBTAI community, including different cultural and ethnic backgrounds, religions, and gender identities.

If you are an individual who is struggling with coming out, know that there are resources and support available to you. You can reach out to local LGBTAI organizations, counseling services, or support groups to find individuals who can relate to your experiences and provide guidance and support.

It's also important to understand that coming out is not a one-time event. It's an ongoing process that individuals may navigate throughout their lives. Even after coming out to family and friends, individuals may continue to face challenges and discrimination in other areas of their lives, such as in the workplace or in accessing healthcare.

As allies, we can also work towards creating safe and inclusive environments in these areas. This can involve advocating for policies and practices that protect the rights of the LGBTAI community, challenging harmful stereotypes and biases, and providing education and training to others.

It's important to recognize that the experiences of individuals in the LGBTAI community are diverse and unique. Some individuals may experience multiple forms of marginalization, such as individuals who identify as both transgender and a person of color. It's important to approach each individual's experience with empathy and understanding, and to recognize and celebrate the diversity within the community. It's also important to acknowledge that the coming out process can be especially difficult for individuals who belong to certain cultural or religious groups that may be less accepting of diverse sexual orientations and gender identities. These individuals may face additional challenges, such as the risk of rejection from their community or family, and the possibility of losing their cultural or religious identity. Allies need to understand and respect the cultural and religious background of individuals in the LGBTAI community, and to work towards creating a safe and supportive environment that honors and celebrates diversity.

Furthermore, it's important to recognize that individuals in the LGBTAI community may have different experiences and needs throughout the coming out process. For example, some individuals may be more comfortable with public displays of affection, while others may not be. It's important to respect and accommodate each individual's needs and preferences, and to communicate openly and honestly with them about your own needs and boundaries.

Ultimately, the coming out process is a deeply personal and ongoing journey for individuals in the LGBTAI community. As allies, it's important to approach each individual's experience with empathy and understanding, and to provide support and advocacy towards creating a more equitable and inclusive society. By working together, we can create a world where all individuals are celebrated and accepted for who they are. In addition, it's important to recognize that coming out is not a linear process. Individuals may experience different stages of acceptance and disclosure throughout their lives, and may face setbacks or challenges along the way. As allies, it's important to provide ongoing support and validation throughout this journey, and to be patient and understanding as individuals navigate their own unique path.

It's also important to recognize that the language we use to discuss the LGBTAI community can have a significant impact on individuals' experiences. Using inclusive and affirming language can help create a safe and welcoming environment for individuals in the community. This can involve using gender-neutral pronouns and avoiding assumptions about individuals' sexual orientation or gender identity.

As allies, it's important to educate ourselves on the experiences and needs of individuals in the LGBTAI community, and to challenge our own biases and stereotypes. This can involve seeking out resources and education, engaging in meaningful conversations with individuals in the community, and being open to feedback and growth. It's also important to recognize that coming out can be a difficult and vulnerable experience for individuals in the LGBTAI community. As allies, it's important to create a safe and supportive environment that respects each individual's privacy and autonomy. This can involve respecting an individual's decision to come out or not, and providing them with resources and support regardless of their choice. It's important to recognize that coming out is a deeply personal decision, and individuals should never feel pressured to disclose their sexual orientation or gender identity before they are ready.

Furthermore, as allies, it's important to recognize and challenge the systemic discrimination and marginalization faced by the LGBTAI community. This can involve advocating for policies and practices that protect the rights of the community, such as anti-discrimination laws and inclusive healthcare policies. It's also important to support and uplift the voices of individuals in the LGBTAI community, especially those who may be more marginalized or underrepresented. This can involve amplifying their stories and experiences, and actively working towards creating space for them to be heard and valued. It's important to recognize that the coming out process is not just a one-time event, but rather an ongoing process of self-discovery and self-expression. Even after an individual has come out, they may continue to face challenges and discrimination in their personal and professional lives.

As allies, it's important to be mindful of these ongoing challenges and to provide ongoing support and validation. This can involve actively advocating for the rights of the LGBTAI community, challenging discriminatory practices and beliefs, and being a visible and vocal ally. It's also important to recognize that coming out can be a difficult and emotional experience for the family and friends of individuals in the LGBTAI community. As allies, it's important to provide support and validation to those who may be struggling to understand and accept their loved one's sexual orientation or gender identity. This can involve actively listening to their concerns and fears, providing resources and education, and modeling inclusive and affirming behavior. It's important to recognize that the journey of acceptance and understanding is unique for each individual, and to respect each person's own process and timeline.

One important aspect of being an ally in the coming out process is to create a safe and welcoming environment for individuals in the LGBTAI community. This can involve educating oneself on the experiences and needs of the community, as well as actively challenging discriminatory practices and beliefs.

As allies, it's important to recognize the intersectional experiences of individuals in the LGBTAI community, and to work towards creating a more inclusive and equitable society for all. This can involve advocating for the rights and needs of individuals who may face additional marginalization, such as those who are BIPOC, disabled, or low-income.

Furthermore, it's important to recognize the power of language in shaping our perceptions and attitudes towards the LGBTAI community. As allies, we can work towards using inclusive and affirming language that respects each individual's gender identity and sexual orientation.

This can involve using gender-neutral pronouns, avoiding assumptions about individuals' sexual orientation or gender identity, and being open to feedback and growth. By creating a language of inclusivity and respect, we can work towards creating a more welcoming and accepting environment for individuals in the LGBTAI community. It's important to recognize that the coming out process can be a transformative and empowering experience for individuals in the LGBTAI community. By embracing and affirming their true selves, individuals can find a sense of belonging and community that may have been missing before.

As allies, it's important to celebrate and uplift the experiences and achievements of individuals in the LGBTAI community. This can involve celebrating Pride month and other important milestones, as well as actively supporting and promoting the work of organizations that serve the community.

Furthermore, it's important to recognize the role of mental health in the coming out process. For many individuals, the journey of coming out can be accompanied by feelings of isolation, anxiety, and depression. As allies, we can work towards creating a more supportive and inclusive environment that prioritizes mental health and wellbeing.

This can involve connecting individuals with resources and support, such as therapy or peer support groups, as well as modeling self-care and compassion. By recognizing the unique challenges and needs of individuals in the LGBTAI community, we can work towards creating a more inclusive and affirming society for all. Another important aspect of being an ally in the coming out process is to support individuals in their pursuit of self-expression and authenticity. This can involve actively challenging gender norms and stereotypes, as well as embracing and celebrating the diverse ways in which individuals express their gender identity and sexual orientation.

As allies, it's important to recognize that the journey of coming out is not just about disclosing one's sexual orientation or gender identity, but also about exploring and affirming one's own sense of self. By actively validating and affirming the identities and experiences of individuals in the LGBTAI community, we can work towards creating a more inclusive and affirming society for all.

Furthermore, it's important to recognize that the journey of coming out is not just about the individual, but also about the broader societal and cultural contexts in which they exist. By working towards creating more inclusive and affirming policies and practices, we can create a world where all individuals are able to live authentically and without fear of discrimination. This can involve advocating for policies that protect the rights of individuals in the LGBTAI community, such as anti-discrimination laws and marriage equality, as well as supporting and promoting the work of organizations that serve the community.

In addition to supporting individuals in the LGBTAI community during their coming out process, it's also important to acknowledge the ongoing challenges and discrimination that they may face even after coming out.

As allies, it's important to remain vigilant against discrimination and actively work towards creating a more inclusive and equitable society for all. This can involve advocating for policies and practices that protect the rights of individuals in the LGBTAI community, as well as challenging discriminatory beliefs and practices when they arise. It's also important to recognize that the journey of coming out is not a one-time event, but an ongoing process that can involve new challenges and obstacles along the way. As allies, we can provide ongoing support and validation, as well as model self-care and compassion in our own lives.

This can involve being open to feedback and growth, practicing active listening and empathy, and educating ourselves on the experiences and needs of the LGBTAI community. By creating a culture of inclusivity and respect, we can work towards creating a world where all individuals are able to live authentically and without fear of discrimination. Another important aspect of supporting individuals in the LGBTAI community during their coming out process is to recognize and address intersectional issues that may arise.

For example, individuals who identify as both LGBTQ+ and a person of color may face unique challenges and discrimination that require a specific approach to support. As allies, it's important to acknowledge and address these intersectional issues, and work towards creating a more inclusive and equitable society for all individuals, regardless of their race, ethnicity, sexual orientation, or gender identity.

Additionally, it's important to recognize that not all individuals in the LGBTAI community may have the same experiences or perspectives. While some individuals may feel empowered and validated by the process of coming out, others may feel pressure or fear of rejection from their family, friends, or society.

As allies, it's important to be respectful and understanding of each individual's unique experiences and needs, and to avoid making assumptions about their journey. Providing a safe and supportive space for individuals to share their experiences can be a crucial aspect of being an effective ally in the coming out process. It's important to recognize that the coming out process is not a linear or one-time event, but an ongoing journey that involves navigating personal and societal challenges. As allies, it's important to provide ongoing support and validation, even after an individual has come out.

This can involve checking in with individuals to see how they are doing, listening to their concerns and experiences, and offering resources and support when needed. It's also important to respect each individual's autonomy and allow them to define their own journey and identity, rather than imposing our own expectations or assumptions onto them.

Additionally, it's important to recognize that the coming out process can have a significant impact on an individual's mental health and well-being. As allies, we can encourage individuals to seek support from mental health professionals, and advocate for policies and practices that promote mental health and well-being within the LGBTAI community. One important way that allies can support individuals in the LGBTAI community during their coming out process is by advocating for policies and practices that promote equality and inclusion. This can involve supporting LGBTQ+ organizations, volunteering for LGBTQ+ events and initiatives, and advocating for LGBTQ+ rights at the local, national, and international levels. Additionally, allies can work to challenge discrimination and promote inclusivity within their own personal and professional networks. This can involve speaking out against homophobic or transphobic language and behavior, actively seeking out diverse perspectives and voices, and creating safe and inclusive spaces for individuals in the LGBTAI community. It's also important for allies to educate themselves on issues affecting the LGBTAI community, including the history and context of discrimination, intersectional issues, and the impact of discrimination on mental health and well-being. By being informed and knowledgeable, allies can be better equipped to provide support and advocacy for individuals in the LGBTAI community.

Another important way that allies can support individuals in the LGBTAI community during their coming out process is by recognizing and addressing the unique challenges faced by individuals with intersecting marginalized identities. For example, individuals who identify as both LGBTQ+ and people of color, individuals with disabilities, or individuals who are immigrants or refugees may face additional challenges and barriers when coming out.

As allies, we can work to recognize and address these intersecting issues by actively seeking out and amplifying the voices and perspectives of individuals with intersecting identities, advocating for policies and practices that promote equity and inclusion for all individuals, and working to create safe and inclusive spaces that prioritize the needs and experiences of individuals with intersecting marginalized identities. It's also important for allies to recognize that the coming out process can look different for different individuals, and that not all individuals may choose to come out in the same way or at the same time. It's important to respect each individual's decision and to avoid making assumptions or judgments about their identity or journey.

Furthermore, allies can work to create a culture of acceptance and affirmation within their personal and professional networks, by celebrating diversity and promoting understanding and empathy. This can involve challenging harmful stereotypes and assumptions, actively listening to the experiences and perspectives of individuals in the LGBTAI community, and creating spaces where individuals feel safe and supported to express their identities.

Additionally, allies can encourage individuals in the LGBTAI community to prioritize their own self-care and mental health, by seeking out supportive resources and communities, practicing self-care and self-compassion, and accessing mental health support when needed. Allies can also work to destigmatize seeking mental health support and to promote the importance of mental health care as an essential aspect of overall health and well-being.

In summary, the coming out process can be challenging for individuals in the LGBTAI community, and allies can play a crucial role in supporting them. Allies can offer support and validation, advocate for policies and practices that promote equity and inclusion, recognize and address intersecting issues, create a culture of acceptance and affirmation, and prioritize self-care and mental health. It's important for allies to listen to and respect each individual's journey and decision, create safe and inclusive spaces, challenge harmful stereotypes and assumptions, and promote understanding and empathy. By being intentional and committed allies, we can help to create a world where all individuals are able to live authentically and without fear of discrimination or stigma.

EIGHT
Discrimination And Violence

Discrimination and violence against LGBTAI individuals are unfortunately still prevalent in many societies today. Discrimination can manifest in various forms, including hate speech, harassment, and exclusion from opportunities or institutions. Additionally, violence towards LGBTAI individuals, including physical assault, sexual violence, and hate crimes, can have devastating consequences.

Hate crimes are particularly concerning, as they are often motivated by bias or prejudice towards an individual's sexual orientation or gender identity. These crimes can range from verbal abuse to physical assault and even murder. In addition to hate crimes, LGBTAI individuals are also at higher risk of experiencing bullying, particularly during adolescence.

Employment discrimination is another form of discrimination that LGBTAI individuals may face. This can include being denied job opportunities, being treated unfairly in the workplace, or being subject to harassment or bullying by colleagues or superiors. Such discrimination can lead to economic disadvantages and can even affect an individual's mental and physical health.

It is crucial to combat discrimination and promote equality for all individuals, regardless of their sexual orientation or gender identity. One way to do this is to raise awareness about the impact of discrimination and violence on LGBTAI individuals. Educating the public on the issue can help reduce prejudice and promote tolerance and acceptance.

Additionally, governments and institutions can pass laws and policies that protect LGBTAI individuals from discrimination in the workplace, housing, and other areas of life. This can include anti-discrimination legislation, hate crime laws, and policies that promote diversity and inclusion. Individuals can also help combat discrimination by being allies to the LGBTAI community. This can involve speaking out against hate speech and discriminatory behavior, promoting acceptance and understanding, and supporting LGBTAI individuals in their personal and professional lives.

In summary, discrimination and violence against LGBTAI individuals are still widespread, and it is essential to combat these issues through education, legislation, and support from allies. By promoting acceptance and understanding, we can help create a more inclusive and equitable society for all individuals.

In addition to raising awareness, passing laws, and promoting allyship, there are other ways to combat discrimination and promote equality for LGBTAI individuals. One important way is to provide resources and support for those who have experienced discrimination or violence. This can include access to mental health services, legal aid, and community organizations that offer support and resources. Another way to combat discrimination is to promote representation and visibility for LGBTAI individuals. This can involve promoting positive portrayals of LGBTAI individuals in media and entertainment, as well as in politics and other areas of public life. This can help reduce stereotypes and promote understanding and acceptance.

Education is also crucial in combating discrimination. This can involve teaching young people about the history and experiences of the LGBTAI community, as well as promoting diversity and inclusion in schools and other educational institutions.

Another crucial step in combatting discrimination and promoting equality for LGBTAI individuals is to promote self-acceptance and resilience within the community. Discrimination and violence can have significant impacts on the mental health and well-being of LGBTAI individuals, and it is important to provide resources and support to help individuals cope with these challenges. This can include promoting self-care and mental health resources, such as counseling services and support groups. It can also involve creating safe spaces for LGBTAI individuals, where they can connect with others who have similar experiences and feel accepted and supported.

Advocacy and activism are also essential in combatting discrimination and promoting equality. This can involve speaking out against discriminatory laws and policies, organizing protests and rallies, and advocating for the rights of LGBTAI individuals. By using their voices and working together, LGBTAI individuals and their allies can create meaningful change and push for greater acceptance and equality. Another crucial aspect of combatting discrimination and violence against LGBTAI individuals is to promote cultural competency and sensitivity among service providers, including healthcare providers, law enforcement officials, and educators. These professionals can play a vital role in supporting LGBTAI individuals and promoting equality, but they must also be aware of the unique challenges faced by this community.

For example, healthcare providers should be trained to provide culturally sensitive care to LGBTAI patients, including addressing their unique health needs and concerns. Law enforcement officials should be trained to identify and respond to hate crimes and discrimination against LGBTAI individuals, and educators should be trained to promote diversity and inclusion in their classrooms and to address instances of bullying and discrimination.

Promoting cultural competency and sensitivity can also involve creating policies and guidelines that promote equality and inclusivity in various sectors. For example, schools can develop anti-bullying policies that specifically address discrimination against LGBTAI students, and employers can adopt non-discrimination policies that protect employees from discrimination based on sexual orientation or gender identity. Another important strategy in combatting discrimination and promoting equality for LGBTAI individuals is to encourage community engagement and activism. This can involve creating opportunities for LGBTAI individuals to connect with one another, to organize and advocate for their rights, and to contribute to their communities in meaningful ways.

One way to encourage community engagement is to create safe spaces and community centers where LGBTAI individuals can gather and connect with one another. These spaces can provide a sense of community and belonging, as well as access to resources and support. Another way to encourage community engagement is to create opportunities for LGBTAI individuals to get involved in activism and advocacy efforts. This can involve organizing rallies and protests, lobbying lawmakers for policy changes, and contributing to campaigns that promote equality and inclusivity.

In addition to these strategies, it is also important to recognize the role of intersectionality in promoting equality and combatting discrimination. LGBTAI individuals who also belong to other marginalized communities, such as people of color or those with disabilities, may experience unique forms of discrimination and violence. It is essential to recognize and address these intersectionalities and to work towards creating a more inclusive and equitable society for all individuals. Also, education and awareness-raising are also crucial in combatting discrimination and promoting equality for LGBTAI individuals. This can involve creating educational programs that promote understanding and acceptance, as well as increasing visibility of LGBTAI individuals in the media and in popular culture.

Educational programs can take many forms, including workshops, seminars, and training sessions for educators, healthcare providers, and law enforcement officials. These programs can provide information about the unique challenges faced by LGBTAI individuals, as well as strategies for promoting acceptance and inclusivity.

Increasing visibility of LGBTAI individuals in the media and in popular culture can also have a significant impact on attitudes towards this community. This can involve featuring LGBTAI individuals in television shows, movies, and advertisements, as well as promoting LGBTAI representation in politics and other positions of power.

It is also important to recognize the role of social media and online communities in promoting acceptance and combating discrimination. Social media platforms can provide a space for LGBTAI individuals to connect with one another, share their stories, and advocate for their rights. These platforms can also be used to promote educational resources and to challenge discriminatory attitudes and behaviors. Another important strategy in combatting discrimination and promoting equality for LGBTAI individuals is to advocate for legal protections and policies that support the rights of this community. This can involve working with lawmakers to pass legislation that prohibits discrimination based on sexual orientation and gender identity, as well as promoting policies that support the well-being of LGBTAI individuals.

One way to advocate for legal protections is to support organizations that are working to promote equality and inclusivity for LGBTAI individuals. These organizations may work on a local, national, or international level, and may focus on a range of issues, from promoting anti-discrimination laws to providing support and resources for LGBTAI individuals.

Another way to advocate for legal protections is to lobby lawmakers and policymakers for policy changes that support the rights of LGBTAI individuals. This can involve attending rallies and protests, writing letters and emails to elected officials, and meeting with lawmakers to discuss issues of importance to the LGBTAI community.

In addition to advocating for legal protections, it is also important to promote policies that support the well-being of LGBTAI individuals. This can involve promoting access to healthcare, including mental healthcare, and supporting programs that provide resources and support for LGBTAI individuals who are experiencing discrimination or violence. Another important strategy to combat discrimination and promote equality for LGBTAI individuals is to support intersectional approaches that recognize and address the unique challenges faced by individuals who are members of multiple marginalized communities. For example, a person who identifies as both Black and transgender may face compounded discrimination and marginalization that is different from someone who only identifies as transgender or only as Black. It is important to recognize and address these unique challenges through intersectional approaches that take into account the multiple identities and experiences of individuals. This can involve promoting policies and programs that are specifically designed to address the needs of individuals who are members of multiple marginalized communities.

In addition to supporting intersectional approaches, it is important to promote cultural competency and sensitivity in healthcare, education, and other institutions. Cultural competency involves understanding and respecting the cultural differences and unique experiences of individuals from diverse backgrounds, including LGBTAI individuals. This can involve providing training and education to healthcare providers, educators, and other professionals to ensure that they are able to provide culturally competent care and support.

Another important aspect of combatting discrimination and promoting equality for LGBTAI individuals is promoting representation and visibility in media, politics, and other spheres of influence. This can involve supporting LGBTAI individuals who are running for political office, advocating for greater representation of LGBTAI individuals in media and entertainment, and promoting the work and achievements of LGBTAI individuals in a range of fields.

Representation and visibility can help to challenge stereotypes and promote greater understanding and acceptance of LGBTAI individuals in society. It can also provide role models for individuals who may be struggling with their own sexual orientation or gender identity, and help them to feel less isolated and marginalized.

In addition to promoting representation and visibility, it is important to provide education and resources to help individuals and communities understand and address the unique challenges faced by LGBTAI individuals. This can involve providing training and education to educators, healthcare providers, and other professionals, as well as providing resources and support for families and friends of LGBTAI individuals. One important aspect to consider in combatting discrimination and promoting equality for LGBTAI individuals is addressing the intersection of discrimination and mental health. Discrimination can have a significant impact on the mental health of LGBTAI individuals, contributing to higher rates of depression, anxiety, and suicide.

Therefore, it is important to provide mental health resources and support for LGBTAI individuals who may be experiencing discrimination or other forms of stress related to their sexual orientation or gender identity. This can involve providing access to therapy and counseling, as well as connecting individuals with peer support groups and other resources that can provide a sense of community and belonging. It is also important to address the underlying social and cultural factors that contribute to discrimination and marginalization of LGBTAI individuals. This can involve challenging stereotypes and promoting greater understanding and acceptance of diverse sexual orientations and gender identities.

In addition to addressing discrimination, it is also important to support and promote the positive aspects of LGBTAI identities and experiences. This can involve celebrating diversity, promoting positive representations of LGBTAI individuals in media and entertainment, and supporting cultural events and organizations that celebrate LGBTAI cultures and communities. Another important aspect to consider in combatting discrimination and promoting equality for LGBTAI individuals is addressing the intersection of religion and sexual orientation or gender identity. Many individuals who identify as LGBTAI also hold religious beliefs, and may face discrimination or rejection from religious communities that do not accept their sexual orientation or gender identity.

Therefore, it is important to promote greater understanding and acceptance of diverse religious and spiritual beliefs within the LGBTAI community, and to support individuals who may be experiencing conflict between their religious beliefs and their sexual orientation or gender identity. This can involve connecting individuals with affirming religious communities and resources, as well as promoting dialogue and understanding between different religious and spiritual communities. It is also important to address the impact of religious-based discrimination on the mental health and well-being of LGBTAI individuals. This can involve providing access to mental health resources and support, as well as promoting positive representations of LGBTAI individuals within religious communities and promoting greater acceptance and understanding of diverse sexual orientations and gender identities within religious communities.

In addition to addressing religious-based discrimination, it is important to continue advocating for legal protections and policies that support the rights and well-being of LGBTAI individuals. This can involve working to challenge discriminatory laws and practices, and advocating for greater legal recognition and protections for individuals who identify as LGBTAI.

Another important strategy in combatting discrimination and promoting equality for LGBTAI individuals is education and awareness-building. Education can play a crucial role in helping individuals and communities understand the experiences of LGBTAI individuals, and in promoting greater acceptance and understanding of diverse sexual orientations and gender identities. This can involve providing education and training for educators, healthcare providers, employers, and other professionals on issues related to LGBTAI individuals, as well as promoting greater awareness and understanding of LGBTAI experiences within the broader community. It can also involve promoting the inclusion of LGBTAI perspectives and experiences within school curricula, media and entertainment, and other cultural institutions.

In addition to education, it is important to continue supporting and promoting the voices and experiences of LGBTAI individuals themselves. This can involve promoting greater visibility and representation of LGBTAI individuals in media and entertainment, supporting LGBTAI-led organizations and advocacy efforts, and encouraging greater participation and leadership from LGBTAI individuals within all sectors of society. It is also important to recognize and address the unique challenges faced by individuals who belong to multiple marginalized groups, such as LGBTAI individuals who also face racism, ableism, or other forms of discrimination. This can involve addressing the intersection of multiple forms of discrimination in policy and practice, and promoting greater understanding and support for individuals who may face multiple forms of discrimination.

Another key aspect of promoting equality for LGBTAI individuals is providing access to resources and support services. Discrimination and violence can have a significant impact on the mental health and well-being of LGBTAI individuals, and it is important to provide resources and support to help individuals cope with these experiences. This can involve providing access to mental health resources, including therapy and counseling services, as well as support groups and community-based resources. It can also involve providing legal support to individuals who have experienced discrimination or violence, and connecting individuals with resources related to healthcare, housing, and employment.

In addition to providing resources and support services, it is important to promote greater access to healthcare services for LGBTAI individuals. This can involve working to eliminate discriminatory practices within the healthcare system, promoting greater cultural competency among healthcare providers, and addressing disparities in healthcare access and outcomes for LGBTAI individuals. Another important aspect to consider is promoting greater visibility and acceptance of LGBTAI individuals within the workplace. This can involve advocating for workplace policies that promote greater inclusion and support for LGBTAI employees, as well as supporting LGBTAI-led organizations and initiatives within the workplace.

Another important strategy for combatting discrimination and promoting equality for LGBTAI individuals is political advocacy and policy change. This can involve advocating for policies and legislation that promote greater protection and support for LGBTAI individuals, as well as holding political leaders accountable for upholding these policies and addressing issues related to discrimination and violence.

Some key policy areas to focus on include anti-discrimination laws, hate crime legislation, marriage equality, and transgender rights. It is also important to advocate for policies that promote greater inclusion and support for LGBTAI individuals in all areas of society, including healthcare, education, housing, and employment.

In addition to political advocacy, it is important to promote greater visibility and representation of LGBTAI individuals in all levels of government and political leadership. This can involve supporting LGBTAI individuals who are running for political office, and advocating for greater representation of LGBTAI perspectives and experiences within political decision-making.

Another important strategy for promoting equality for LGBTAI individuals is through education and awareness-raising efforts. Educating individuals and communities about the experiences of LGBTAI individuals and the impact of discrimination and violence can help to foster greater understanding, empathy, and support. This can involve promoting education and awareness about LGBTAI issues within schools and universities, as well as within workplaces, community organizations, and other settings. It can also involve supporting and promoting media and cultural representations that accurately reflect the diversity and complexity of LGBTAI experiences.

In addition to education and awareness-raising efforts, it is important to support and uplift the voices and experiences of LGBTAI individuals themselves. This can involve promoting LGBTAI-led organizations and initiatives, as well as providing opportunities for LGBTAI individuals to share their experiences and perspectives through storytelling, art, and other creative outlets.

One important aspect of promoting equality for LGBTAI individuals is addressing intersecting forms of oppression and discrimination that can impact their experiences. This can include recognizing and addressing the ways in which racism, ableism, classism, and other forms of oppression intersect with homophobia, transphobia, and other forms of discrimination.

For example, LGBTAI individuals who also experience racism may face additional barriers and challenges related to discrimination in housing, employment, healthcare, and other areas of life. Similarly, LGBTAI individuals who also experience ableism may face additional challenges related to accessing healthcare, education, and employment, among other areas.

Recognizing and addressing these intersecting forms of oppression is important for promoting greater understanding and support for LGBTAI individuals, and for promoting a more inclusive and equitable society for all individuals. This can involve supporting and promoting initiatives and organizations that focus on intersectional approaches to promoting equality, as well as recognizing and addressing intersectional discrimination in policy and advocacy efforts. Another important aspect of promoting equality for LGBTAI individuals is addressing the unique challenges faced by specific subgroups within the broader community. For example, transgender individuals often face significant discrimination and violence, and may face additional barriers related to accessing healthcare, employment, and other essential services.

Similarly, bisexual individuals may experience invisibility and erasure, both within the broader LGBTAI community and in society at large. Bisexual individuals may face additional challenges related to accessing supportive resources and services, and may also face discrimination from both the heterosexual and LGBTAI communities.

Recognizing and addressing the unique challenges faced by specific subgroups within the LGBTAI community is important for promoting greater understanding and support for all members of the community. This can involve supporting and promoting initiatives and organizations that focus on the specific needs of these subgroups, as well as advocating for policy changes and public awareness campaigns that address these challenges.

In addition to addressing these challenges, it is also important to celebrate the diversity and resilience of the LGBTAI community. The LGBTAI community is made up of individuals from a wide range of backgrounds, cultures, and identities, and has a rich history of activism and resilience in the face of discrimination and oppression.

By promoting greater understanding and support for the LGBTAI community as a whole, while also recognizing and addressing the unique challenges faced by specific subgroups within the community, we can work towards creating a more inclusive and equitable society for all individuals, regardless of their sexual orientation or gender identity.

Finally, it is important to recognize the role that allies can play in promoting equality and supporting LGBTAI individuals. Allies are individuals who do not identify as LGBTAI themselves, but who support and advocate for the rights and well-being of LGBTAI individuals.

By actively supporting and advocating for LGBTAI individuals, allies can help to create more inclusive and supportive environments in schools, workplaces, and other settings. This can involve speaking out against discrimination and violence, promoting policies and practices that support LGBTAI individuals, and actively working to create more inclusive and equitable communities.

One important way that allies can support LGBTAI individuals is by educating themselves about LGBTAI issues and experiences, and by listening to and learning from LGBTAI individuals themselves. Allies can also use their own privilege and influence to advocate for LGBTAI individuals and to promote greater understanding and support within their own communities.

<u>NINE</u>
Mental Health

Mental health is a vital aspect of overall wellbeing, yet it often goes overlooked and neglected. For members of the LGBTAI community, mental health challenges are especially prevalent due to the unique stressors and discrimination they face. This can result in an increased risk of depression, anxiety, and suicidality.

Depression and anxiety are two of the most common mental health challenges that LGBTAI individuals experience. The stress of coming out, discrimination, and stigma can lead to feelings of hopelessness, sadness, and anxiety. Additionally, the fear of rejection from family, friends, and society can be a significant source of stress and can lead to ongoing anxiety.

Suicidality is another significant challenge faced by members of the LGBTAI community. LGBTAI individuals are significantly more likely to attempt suicide than their heterosexual counterparts. This increased risk is a result of the discrimination, bullying, and stigma that they face.

To promote mental health and well-being in the LGBTAI community, it is essential to provide resources and support. One way to do this is through the use of mental health services. Counseling and therapy can be a valuable tool in helping LGBTAI individuals cope with the unique challenges they face. Many organizations and therapists specialize in serving the LGBTAI community and can offer a safe and supportive environment for individuals seeking help. Another way to promote mental health is through community involvement. Joining a local LGBTQIA+ group or organization can provide a sense of belonging and social support. These groups can also provide education and resources for mental health services and support. Additionally, it is crucial to educate friends, family, and society about the unique challenges faced by the LGBTAI community. By raising awareness and understanding, we can help reduce stigma and discrimination and promote acceptance and support.

Mental health challenges are prevalent among members of the LGBTAI community, but with the right resources and support, individuals can find help and support to overcome these challenges. It is essential to promote awareness and understanding, provide mental health services and support, and promote community involvement to help promote mental health and well-being in the LGBTAI community.

To better understand the mental health challenges faced by members of the LGBTAI community, it is essential to recognize the unique stressors they experience. Discrimination, stigma, and marginalization are all significant stressors that can contribute to poor mental health outcomes.

For example, discrimination and stigma can lead to internalized homophobia or transphobia, which can negatively impact mental health. Members of the LGBTAI community may feel shame or self-loathing for their sexual orientation or gender identity, which can lead to depression, anxiety, and other mental health challenges.

Bullying and harassment are also common experiences for many LGBTAI individuals, particularly for youth. Bullying can lead to social isolation, which can contribute to depression and anxiety. It can also result in trauma, which can have long-term effects on mental health.

In addition to these stressors, members of the LGBTAI community may also face additional challenges such as family rejection, employment discrimination, and lack of legal protections. These stressors can have a significant impact on mental health and can contribute to depression, anxiety, and suicidality.

To promote mental health in the LGBTAI community, it is essential to provide resources and support that address these unique stressors. Mental health services that specialize in serving the LGBTAI community can provide a safe and supportive environment for individuals seeking help. These services can offer counseling and therapy, support groups, and education on mental health issues affecting the LGBTAI community.

Community involvement can also play an important role in promoting mental health. Joining a local LGBTQIA+ group or organization can provide a sense of belonging and social support. These groups can also provide education and resources for mental health services and support. Additionally, involvement in advocacy efforts can help reduce stigma and discrimination and promote acceptance and support.

It is important to educate friends, family, and society about the unique challenges faced by the LGBTAI community. By raising awareness and understanding, we can help reduce stigma and discrimination and promote acceptance and support. This can include providing education on mental health issues affecting the LGBTAI community and advocating for policies and practices that promote mental health and well-being. It is also important to note that the mental health challenges faced by members of the LGBTAI community can vary depending on a variety of factors, such as age, race, ethnicity, and socioeconomic status. For example, LGBTQIA+ youth may face additional challenges such as lack of support from parents or caregivers, bullying in schools, and difficulties accessing mental health services.

Transgender individuals, in particular, face significant challenges in accessing appropriate mental health care. Transgender individuals may experience gender dysphoria, which can cause significant distress and require specialized care. However, many mental health professionals may not have the necessary training or expertise to provide appropriate care to transgender individuals. It is important to address these disparities and ensure that mental health services are accessible and inclusive for all members of the LGBTAI community. This can include providing training and education for mental health professionals on the unique mental health challenges faced by the LGBTAI community and how to provide culturally competent care.

In addition to professional mental health services, there are also a variety of self-care strategies that can help promote mental health and well-being. These strategies can include engaging in regular physical activity, practicing mindfulness and meditation, and connecting with supportive friends and family members. It is important to seek help when needed. Many individuals may feel ashamed or embarrassed to seek help for mental health challenges, but it is important to remember that seeking help is a sign of strength. There are many resources available, including crisis hotlines and online support groups that can provide immediate support and connect individuals with mental health services. It is also important to recognize the intersectionality of identities within the LGBTAI community and how these intersections can impact mental health. For example, members of the LGBTAI community who also identify as people of color, immigrants, or individuals with disabilities may face additional challenges that can impact mental health.

Intersectional identities can also impact access to mental health services. For example, individuals who are uninsured or underinsured may have difficulty accessing mental health services, which can have a negative impact on mental health outcomes.

Addressing these disparities requires a systemic approach that addresses social determinants of health and promotes equitable access to mental health services. This can include advocating for policies and practices that promote equitable access to mental health care, increasing funding for mental health services in underserved communities, and promoting culturally competent care.

One of the most effective ways to promote mental health in the LGBTAI community is through community-based interventions. These interventions are designed to provide support and resources to individuals who may be experiencing mental health challenges, as well as to promote community engagement and social connectedness.

Community-based interventions can take many different forms, including peer support groups, community education and outreach programs, and online support networks. These interventions provide a safe and supportive environment for individuals to connect with others who share similar experiences and to access information and resources related to mental health.

Research has shown that community-based interventions can be particularly effective for promoting mental health and reducing mental health disparities in the LGBTAI community. These interventions can provide a sense of social support and connectedness, which can help reduce feelings of isolation and promote resilience in the face of mental health challenges. Another important aspect of promoting mental health in the LGBTAI community is reducing stigma and discrimination. Stigma and discrimination can contribute to feelings of shame and isolation, which can have a negative impact on mental health outcomes.

Reducing stigma and discrimination requires a multi-faceted approach that includes educating individuals about the experiences and challenges faced by the LGBTAI community, promoting diversity and inclusivity in all aspects of society, and advocating for policies and practices that promote equity and social justice. It is also important to recognize the role of families and support systems in promoting mental health in the LGBTAI community. Many individuals in the LGBTAI community may experience rejection or lack of support from their families, which can have a significant impact on mental health outcomes.

Family-based interventions, such as family therapy or parent support groups, can be effective in promoting acceptance and support for LGBTAI individuals within their families. These interventions can help families better understand the experiences and challenges faced by their loved ones and provide them with the tools and resources needed to provide support and promote mental health and well-being. It is also important to recognize that promoting mental health in the LGBTAI community requires a commitment to social justice and equity. Discrimination and marginalization can have a profound impact on mental health outcomes, and addressing these disparities requires a comprehensive approach that includes advocacy, policy change, and social action.

This includes advocating for policies that promote equity and social justice, such as anti-discrimination laws and policies that promote access to mental health services for all individuals, regardless of their sexual orientation or gender identity. It also involves challenging harmful societal attitudes and beliefs that contribute to stigma and discrimination, and promoting diversity and inclusivity in all aspects of society. It is also important to address the unique mental health challenges faced by transgender and gender non-conforming individuals within the LGBTAI community. Transgender and gender non-conforming individuals may experience higher rates of depression, anxiety, and suicidality compared to cisgender individuals, and may also face barriers to accessing gender-affirming healthcare.

Promoting mental health in the transgender and gender non-conforming community requires a comprehensive approach that includes addressing barriers to healthcare access, reducing stigma and discrimination, and providing support and resources for individuals who may be experiencing mental health challenges.

One way to address barriers to healthcare access is through advocacy for policies that promote gender-affirming healthcare, including insurance coverage for gender-affirming treatments and procedures. It is also important to promote culturally competent care and to educate healthcare providers on the unique needs and experiences of transgender and gender non-conforming individuals.

Reducing stigma and discrimination is also critical for promoting mental health in the transgender and gender non-conforming community. This includes challenging harmful societal attitudes and beliefs about gender identity and promoting inclusive policies and practices in all aspects of society. It is important to also address the impact of intersectionality on mental health outcomes within the LGBTAI community. Intersectionality refers to the ways in which multiple aspects of identity, such as race, ethnicity, socioeconomic status, and disability, intersect to create unique experiences of oppression and discrimination.

LGBTAI individuals who also belong to marginalized groups may experience compounded stigma and discrimination, which can have a significant impact on mental health outcomes. For example, a Black transgender individual may face both racism and transphobia, which can lead to increased levels of stress and anxiety.

Promoting mental health in the LGBTAI community therefore requires an intersectional approach that acknowledges and addresses the unique experiences and challenges faced by individuals who belong to multiple marginalized groups. This can include promoting inclusive policies and practices that address issues of racism, ableism, and other forms of discrimination.

It is important to ensure that mental health services and resources are accessible and culturally competent for individuals from diverse backgrounds. This can involve hiring mental health professionals who reflect the diversity of the LGBTAI community and providing training on cultural humility and sensitivity. It is also important to recognize the impact of historical and ongoing trauma on mental health outcomes within the LGBTAI community. Many LGBTAI individuals have experienced trauma, such as bullying, harassment, and violence, due to their sexual orientation, gender identity, or other aspects of their identity.

This trauma can have lasting effects on mental health and well-being, including increased rates of depression, anxiety, and post-traumatic stress disorder (PTSD). It is important to provide trauma-informed care and support to individuals who have experienced trauma, and to work towards preventing future trauma through education, advocacy, and policy change.

Another important aspect of promoting mental health in the LGBTAI community is promoting self-care and resilience. Self-care can involve a range of activities, such as exercise, mindfulness, and social support, that help individuals to manage stress and maintain a positive outlook on life. Resilience, on the other hand, refers to the ability to bounce back from adversity and to adapt to change.

Promoting self-care and resilience can help individuals to cope with the challenges and stressors that they may face in their lives, and can contribute to overall mental health and well-being. It is important to provide resources and education on self-care and resilience to individuals in the LGBTAI community, and to promote a culture of self-care and resilience within the community as a whole. Another important aspect of promoting mental health in the LGBTAI community is addressing the impact of social isolation and loneliness. LGBTAI individuals may face unique challenges when it comes to building and maintaining social connections, such as stigma, discrimination, and lack of acceptance from family and friends.

Social isolation and loneliness can have a significant impact on mental health outcomes, including increased rates of depression, anxiety, and suicidality. It is important to promote social connectedness and community building within the LGBTAI community as a means of promoting mental health and well-being. This can involve creating safe and welcoming spaces for LGBTAI individuals to connect and build community, such as community centers, support groups, and social events. It can also involve promoting education and awareness around the importance of social connectedness and providing resources and support for individuals who may be experiencing social isolation and loneliness.

Another important aspect of promoting mental health in the LGBTAI community is promoting allyship and support from non-LGBTAI individuals and organizations. Allies can play an important role in reducing stigma and discrimination and promoting acceptance and inclusion within the broader community. This can involve advocating for policies and practices that promote equality and inclusion, speaking out against discrimination and harassment, and providing support and resources for LGBTAI individuals. It can also involve promoting education and awareness around issues related to sexual orientation and gender identity and providing opportunities for individuals to learn and engage in allyship. One additional aspect of promoting mental health in the LGBTAI community is addressing the impact of minority stress. Minority stress refers to the chronic stress that individuals from stigmatized groups experience as a result of their marginalized status.

LGBTAI individuals may experience minority stress due to a range of factors, including discrimination, prejudice, and social rejection. This chronic stress can have a significant impact on mental health outcomes, including increased rates of depression, anxiety, and substance abuse.

It is important to address the impact of minority stress and promote resilience within the LGBTAI community. This can involve promoting education and awareness around minority stress and its impact on mental health, providing resources and support for individuals who may be experiencing minority stress, and promoting resilience-building activities, such as mindfulness and cognitive-behavioral therapy. Another important aspect of promoting mental health in the LGBTAI community is addressing the impact of healthcare disparities. LGBTAI individuals may face unique challenges when it comes to accessing healthcare, such as discrimination, lack of acceptance, and inadequate healthcare coverage. These healthcare disparities can have a significant impact on mental health outcomes, including decreased rates of mental health treatment and increased rates of negative health outcomes. It is important to work towards reducing healthcare disparities and promoting equitable access to mental health care for all individuals within the LGBTAI community. This can involve advocating for policies and practices that promote equitable healthcare access, promoting education and awareness around healthcare disparities, and providing resources and support for individuals who may be experiencing challenges accessing mental health care.

Another important aspect of promoting mental health in the LGBTAI community is addressing the impact of intersectionality. Intersectionality refers to the ways in which individuals may experience multiple forms of marginalization and oppression based on their various identities and social locations.

LGBTAI individuals may experience intersectional forms of discrimination and marginalization based on factors such as race, ethnicity, religion, disability, and socioeconomic status. These forms of intersectionality can have a significant impact on mental health outcomes, including increased rates of depression, anxiety, and suicidal ideation. It is important to address the impact of intersectionality and promote inclusive and intersectional approaches to mental health promotion and support. This can involve promoting education and awareness around intersectionality and its impact on mental health, providing resources and support for individuals who may be experiencing intersectional forms of discrimination and marginalization, and promoting inclusive and intersectional approaches to mental health care and support.

Another important aspect of promoting mental health in the LGBTAI community is addressing the impact of trauma. LGBTAI individuals may experience a range of traumas, including hate crimes, intimate partner violence, and sexual assault. These traumas can have a significant impact on mental health outcomes, including increased rates of post-traumatic stress disorder, depression, and anxiety. It is important to address the impact of trauma and provide trauma-informed care and support for individuals who may be experiencing trauma-related mental health challenges. This can involve promoting education and awareness around trauma and its impact on mental health, providing trauma-informed care and support for individuals who may be experiencing trauma-related mental health challenges, and promoting community-based approaches to healing and recovery from trauma.

Another important aspect of promoting mental health in the LGBTAI community is addressing the impact of internalized homophobia and transphobia. Internalized homophobia and transphobia refer to the internalization of negative attitudes and beliefs towards oneself as a result of living in a society that stigmatizes and marginalizes individuals based on their sexual orientation or gender identity.

LGBTAI individuals may experience internalized homophobia and transphobia, which can lead to increased rates of depression, anxiety, and self-harm. It is important to address the impact of internalized homophobia and transphobia and provide support and resources for individuals who may be struggling with these challenges. This can involve promoting education and awareness around internalized homophobia and transphobia, providing individual and group counseling and support services, and promoting self-acceptance and self-love through self-care practices and self-compassion exercises. Another important aspect of promoting mental health in the LGBTAI community is addressing the impact of social isolation and loneliness. LGBTAI individuals may experience social isolation and loneliness as a result of stigma, discrimination, and rejection from family and peers.

Social isolation and loneliness can have a significant impact on mental health outcomes, including increased rates of depression, anxiety, and substance abuse. It is important to address the impact of social isolation and loneliness and provide resources and support for individuals who may be experiencing these challenges. This can involve promoting social connection and community building, providing resources and support for individuals who may be experiencing social isolation and loneliness, and promoting inclusive and supportive environments in schools, workplaces, and community organizations.

An important aspect of promoting mental health in the LGBTAI community is addressing the impact of discrimination and stigma. Discrimination and stigma based on sexual orientation and gender identity can have a significant impact on mental health outcomes, including increased rates of depression, anxiety, and suicidality. It is important to address the impact of discrimination and stigma and promote inclusive and supportive environments in schools, workplaces, and community organizations. This can involve promoting education and awareness around discrimination and stigma, providing training and resources for individuals and organizations to become more inclusive and supportive, and advocating for policies and laws that protect the rights and well-being of LGBTAI individuals.

Another important aspect of promoting mental health in the LGBTAI community is addressing the impact of access to mental health care. LGBTAI individuals may experience barriers to accessing mental health care, including lack of insurance coverage, discrimination and stigma within the healthcare system, and limited availability of culturally competent care. It is important to address the barriers to accessing mental health care and promote accessible and culturally competent mental health care for LGBTAI individuals. This can involve advocating for policies and laws that promote access to mental health care, providing resources and support for individuals who may be experiencing barriers to accessing mental health care, and promoting the development and training of mental health professionals who are culturally competent in working with LGBTAI individuals. Another important aspect of promoting mental health in the LGBTAI community is addressing the impact of trauma. LGBTAI individuals may experience trauma related to discrimination, violence, and rejection based on their sexual orientation or gender identity. Trauma can have a significant impact on mental health outcomes, including increased rates of post-traumatic stress disorder (PTSD), depression, and anxiety.

It is important to address the impact of trauma and provide support and resources for individuals who may be experiencing trauma-related mental health challenges. This can involve promoting education and awareness around trauma, providing trauma-informed care and support services, and promoting self-care and coping strategies for individuals who may be experiencing trauma-related mental health challenges. Another important aspect of promoting mental health in the LGBTAI community is addressing the impact of substance abuse. LGBTAI individuals may experience higher rates of substance abuse compared to the general population, which can have a significant impact on mental health outcomes. It is important to address the impact of substance abuse and provide support and resources for individuals who may be experiencing substance abuse-related mental health challenges. This can involve promoting education and awareness around substance abuse, providing substance abuse treatment and support services, and promoting harm reduction strategies for individuals who may be experiencing substance abuse-related mental health challenges.

Another important aspect of promoting mental health in the LGBTAI community is addressing the impact of family and social support. LGBTAI individuals may experience rejection or lack of support from their families and social networks, which can have a significant impact on mental health outcomes, including increased rates of depression, anxiety, and suicidality. It is important to address the impact of family and social support and provide resources and support for individuals who may be experiencing challenges related to these issues. This can involve promoting education and awareness around family and social support, providing support services for individuals who may be experiencing rejection or lack of support, and advocating for policies and laws that protect the rights and well-being of LGBTAI individuals within families and social networks. Another important aspect of promoting mental health in the LGBTAI community is addressing the impact of intersectionality. LGBTAI individuals may experience multiple forms of marginalization and oppression, including racism, ableism, and classism, which can have a significant impact on mental health outcomes.

It is important to address the impact of intersectionality and provide support and resources for individuals who may be experiencing mental health challenges related to multiple forms of marginalization and oppression. This can involve promoting education and awareness around intersectionality, providing culturally competent care and support services, and advocating for policies and laws that address systemic barriers and promote equity and justice for all individuals. Another important aspect of promoting mental health in the LGBTAI community is addressing the impact of healthcare discrimination. LGBTAI individuals may experience discrimination and stigma within healthcare settings, which can result in negative mental health outcomes such as avoidance of healthcare services, increased stress, and poor self-esteem. It is important to address the impact of healthcare discrimination and provide support and resources for individuals who may be experiencing challenges related to these issues. This can involve promoting education and awareness around healthcare discrimination, providing culturally competent care and support services, and advocating for policies and laws that protect the rights and well-being of LGBTAI individuals within healthcare settings.

Another important aspect of promoting mental health in the LGBTAI community is addressing the impact of housing discrimination. LGBTAI individuals may experience discrimination and stigma in accessing safe and affordable housing, which can have a significant impact on mental health outcomes. It is important to address the impact of housing discrimination and provide support and resources for individuals who may be experiencing challenges related to these issues. This can involve promoting education and awareness around housing discrimination, providing support services for individuals who may be experiencing housing insecurity, and advocating for policies and laws that address systemic barriers and promote equity and justice for all individuals. Another important aspect of promoting mental health in the LGBTAI community is addressing the impact of workplace discrimination. LGBTAI individuals may experience discrimination and stigma in the workplace, which can result in negative mental health outcomes such as increased stress, anxiety, and depression.

It is important to address the impact of workplace discrimination and provide support and resources for individuals who may be experiencing challenges related to these issues. This can involve promoting education and awareness around workplace discrimination, providing support services for individuals who may be experiencing discrimination or harassment in the workplace, and advocating for policies and laws that protect the rights and well-being of LGBTAI individuals in the workplace. Another important aspect of promoting mental health in the LGBTAI community is addressing the impact of violence and hate crimes. LGBTAI individuals may experience violence and hate crimes, which can result in trauma and negative mental health outcomes such as PTSD, depression, and anxiety. It is important to address the impact of violence and hate crimes and provide support and resources for individuals who may be experiencing challenges related to these issues. This can involve promoting education and awareness around violence and hate crimes, providing support services for individuals who have experienced violence or hate crimes, and advocating for policies and laws that address systemic barriers and promote safety and justice for all individuals.

In addition to addressing discrimination and violence, it is also important to focus on positive coping mechanisms and strategies for promoting mental health and well-being in the LGBTAI community. This can include promoting self-care practices, such as mindfulness, exercise, and healthy eating, as well as connecting with supportive community resources and engaging in advocacy and activism work.

Community-based organizations, such as LGBTQ centers and support groups, can be valuable resources for individuals seeking support and connection. These organizations often offer a range of services, including mental health counseling, peer support, and social events, that can help to promote mental health and well-being.

It is also important to recognize the unique challenges and strengths of different subgroups within the LGBTAI community. For example, individuals who are transgender or gender nonconforming may face additional challenges related to accessing healthcare, navigating legal barriers, and experiencing discrimination and violence. It is important to recognize and address these challenges, while also celebrating the resilience and strength of these individuals and their communities.

One key factor in promoting mental health and well-being in the LGBTAI community is building supportive and inclusive social networks. Research has shown that social support is a key protective factor for mental health, and that LGBTAI individuals who feel connected to supportive communities have better mental health outcomes.

Creating supportive social networks can involve connecting with others who share similar experiences and identities, as well as building relationships with allies and advocates who are committed to promoting equality and justice for all individuals. This can involve participating in community-based events and organizations, volunteering for advocacy and support work, and engaging in online and offline social networks that promote positivity and inclusivity. It is also important to recognize that mental health challenges are a normal part of the human experience, and that seeking help is a sign of strength, not weakness. LGBTAI individuals may face unique challenges related to accessing mental health care, including barriers related to insurance coverage, cultural competency, and stigma. It is important to advocate for accessible and culturally competent mental health care services that meet the unique needs of the LGBTAI community, and to work towards reducing the stigma associated with seeking mental health care.

In addition to seeking professional support, individuals can also engage in self-care practices that promote mental health and well-being. This can involve developing a regular exercise routine, practicing mindfulness or meditation, engaging in creative expression or hobbies, and connecting with supportive friends and family members. By prioritizing self-care and well-being, individuals can build resilience and improve their mental health outcomes.

Another important aspect of promoting mental health in the LGBTAI community is recognizing and addressing the impact of discrimination and prejudice on mental health outcomes. Discrimination and prejudice can take many forms, including microaggressions, harassment, and violence, and can have a significant negative impact on mental health and well-being. It is important to acknowledge the experiences of individuals who have faced discrimination and prejudice, and to provide support and resources to help them cope with these experiences. This can involve providing access to mental health care, connecting individuals with supportive social networks, and advocating for policies and laws that protect the rights and well-being of LGBTAI individuals.

At the same time, it is important to address the root causes of discrimination and prejudice, and to work towards creating a more just and equitable society for all individuals. This can involve challenging stereotypes and misinformation about the LGBTAI community, promoting education and awareness about the diversity and complexity of human identity, and advocating for policies and laws that protect the rights and well-being of all individuals, regardless of their sexual orientation, gender identity, or other aspects of their identity.

Ultimately, promoting mental health and well-being in the LGBTAI community requires a sustained commitment to education, advocacy, and community building. By working together to address the challenges facing the LGBTAI community, we can create a more inclusive and supportive society that values and celebrates the diversity of human experience. Another important factor in promoting mental health in the LGBTAI community is addressing the unique challenges faced by individuals who belong to multiple marginalized groups. For example, individuals who identify as both LGBTAI and people of color may face intersectional discrimination, which can compound the negative effects on their mental health.

To address this issue, it is important to recognize and celebrate the diversity and complexity of human identity, and to create inclusive communities that value and respect all individuals, regardless of their race, ethnicity, sexual orientation, gender identity, or other aspects of their identity. This can involve engaging in conversations and activities that promote understanding and allyship, building bridges between communities, and advocating for policies and laws that protect the rights and well-being of all individuals.

It is also important to recognize the role of trauma in mental health outcomes for LGBTAI individuals. Trauma can result from a wide range of experiences, including violence, abuse, neglect, and discrimination, and can have long-lasting effects on mental health and well-being. It is important to provide access to trauma-informed care and support services, and to create safe spaces for individuals to share their experiences and seek healing.

To further promote mental health in the LGBTAI community, it is important to prioritize access to mental health care and resources. This includes addressing the barriers that many LGBTAI individuals face in accessing mental health care, such as stigma, discrimination, and lack of insurance or financial resources.

One way to improve access to mental health care is by increasing the availability and affordability of mental health services, including therapy, medication, and support groups. This can involve advocating for policies and laws that require insurance providers to cover mental health care, increasing funding for mental health services, and expanding access to teletherapy and online support resources. Another way to promote mental health is by increasing awareness and education about mental health issues within the LGBTAI community. This can involve providing information and resources about common mental health conditions, such as depression, anxiety, and PTSD, as well as strategies for coping with mental health challenges and building resilience. It is also important to promote self-care and self-compassion within the LGBTAI community. This can involve encouraging individuals to prioritize their own well-being, engage in healthy coping strategies, and seek out support when needed. It can also involve promoting a culture of acceptance and understanding, where individuals feel safe and supported in expressing their emotions and seeking help.

Ultimately, promoting mental health in the LGBTAI community requires a multifaceted approach that addresses the social, economic, and political factors that shape mental health outcomes, as well as the individual experiences and challenges faced by members of the community. By working together to build more inclusive and supportive communities, we can create a world where all individuals feel valued and empowered to pursue their best possible mental health and well-being. It is also important to acknowledge and address the impact of historical and ongoing trauma on mental health in the LGBTAI community. Many members of the community have experienced trauma as a result of historical and current discrimination, violence, and marginalization. This can include trauma related to experiences of homophobia, transphobia, biphobia, racism, sexism, ableism, and other forms of oppression.

In order to promote healing and resilience in the face of this trauma, it is important to create safe spaces and supportive communities where individuals can share their experiences and receive validation and support. This can involve creating opportunities for dialogue and healing, such as support groups, therapy, and peer-to-peer mentoring programs. It is also important to recognize and validate the diversity of experiences within the LGBTAI community, and to avoid assumptions about the experiences and needs of individuals based on their identities. This can involve creating spaces that are welcoming and inclusive of diverse gender identities, sexual orientations, races, ethnicities, abilities, and other aspects of identity.

The LGBTAI community faces unique mental health challenges, including depression, anxiety, and suicidality, which can be exacerbated by experiences of discrimination and marginalization. To promote mental health and well-being in this community, it is important to prioritize access to mental health care and resources, increase awareness and education about mental health issues, promote self-care and self-compassion, acknowledge and address the impact of historical and ongoing trauma, create safe and inclusive spaces, and engage in ongoing advocacy and activism to promote social justice and equity. A multifaceted and intersectional approach is necessary to promote mental health and well-being for all members of the LGBTAI community. Another important factor in promoting mental health in the LGBTAI community is addressing the unique challenges faced by individuals who belong to multiple marginalized groups. For example, individuals who identify as both LGBTAI and people of color may face intersectional discrimination, which can compound the negative effects on their mental health.

To address this issue, it is important to recognize and celebrate the diversity and complexity of human identity, and to create inclusive communities that value and respect all individuals, regardless of their race, ethnicity, sexual orientation, gender identity, or other aspects of their identity. This can involve engaging in conversations and activities that promote understanding and allyship, building bridges between communities, and advocating for policies and laws that protect the rights and well-being of all individuals. It is also important to recognize the role of trauma in mental health outcomes for LGBTAI individuals. Trauma can result from a wide range of experiences, including violence, abuse, neglect, and discrimination, and can have long-lasting effects on mental health and well-being. It is important to provide access to trauma-informed care and support services, and to create safe spaces for individuals to share their experiences and seek healing.

One way to improve access to mental health care is by increasing the availability and affordability of mental health services, including therapy, medication, and support groups. This can involve advocating for policies and laws that require insurance providers to cover mental health care, increasing funding for mental health services, and expanding access to teletherapy and online support resources.

Another way to promote mental health is by increasing awareness and education about mental health issues within the LGBTAI community. This can involve providing information and resources about common mental health conditions, such as depression, anxiety, and PTSD, as well as strategies for coping with mental health challenges and building resilience.

It is also important to promote self-care and self-compassion within the LGBTAI community. This can involve encouraging individuals to prioritize their own well-being, engage in healthy coping strategies, and seek out support when needed. It can also involve promoting a culture of acceptance and understanding, where individuals feel safe and supported in expressing their emotions and seeking help.

Ultimately, promoting mental health in the LGBTAI community requires a multifaceted approach that addresses the social, economic, and political factors that shape mental health outcomes, as well as the individual experiences and challenges faced by members of the community. By working together to build more inclusive and supportive communities, we can create a world where all individuals feel valued and empowered to pursue their best possible mental health and well-being.

It is also important to acknowledge and address the impact of historical and ongoing trauma on mental health in the LGBTAI community. Many members of the community have experienced trauma as a result of historical and current discrimination, violence, and marginalization. This can include trauma related to experiences of homophobia, transphobia, biphobia, racism, sexism, ableism, and other forms of oppression.

In order to promote healing and resilience in the face of this trauma, it is important to create safe spaces and supportive communities where individuals can share their experiences and receive validation and support. This can involve creating opportunities for dialogue and healing, such as support groups, therapy, and peer-to-peer mentoring programs.

It is also important to recognize and validate the diversity of experiences within the LGBTAI community, and to avoid assumptions about the experiences and needs of individuals based on their identities.

This can involve creating spaces that are welcoming and inclusive of diverse gender identities, sexual orientations, races, ethnicities, abilities, and other aspects of identity.

The LGBTAI community faces unique mental health challenges, including depression, anxiety, and suicidality, which can be exacerbated by experiences of discrimination and marginalization. To promote mental health and well-being in this community, it is important to prioritize access to mental health care and resources, increase awareness and education about mental health issues, promote self-care and self-compassion, acknowledge and address the impact of historical and ongoing trauma, create safe and inclusive spaces, and engage in ongoing advocacy and activism to promote social justice and equity. A multifaceted and intersectional approach is necessary to promote mental health and well-being for all members of the LGBTAI community.

<u>TEN</u>
Allies

Allies play a crucial role in supporting LGBTAI individuals in creating a more inclusive and accepting society. Being an ally means actively advocating for and supporting the rights of the LGBTAI community, even if you are not a member of that community yourself.

Understanding allies means acknowledging that LGBTAI individuals face significant challenges and discrimination, often rooted in homophobia, transphobia, and other forms of prejudice. As an ally, it is essential to educate yourself about these issues and to listen to the experiences of the people you are trying to support.

One key aspect of allyship is recognizing the unique challenges faced by different groups within the LGBTAI community. For example, transgender individuals may face different forms of discrimination than gay or bisexual individuals. Understanding these differences and being mindful of them can help you be a more effective ally. Another important aspect of allyship is speaking out against discrimination and prejudice when you see it. This can mean challenging homophobic or transphobic language, supporting LGBTAI-inclusive policies and legislation, or simply being a supportive and accepting friend or family member.

The importance of allyship cannot be overstated. By standing up for the rights of LGBTAI individuals, allies can help create a more inclusive and accepting society for everyone. Allies can also help provide a sense of community and support for LGBTAI individuals who may feel isolated or marginalized.

If you want to become a better ally, there are many resources available to help you educate yourself and become more informed. These might include books, articles, podcasts, or organizations dedicated to LGBTAI rights and advocacy. You can also reach out to LGBTAI individuals and ask them how you can best support them.

Ultimately, being an ally is about recognizing the humanity and dignity of all people, regardless of their sexual orientation, gender identity, or other characteristics. By working together, allies and LGBTAI individuals can create a more just and equitable society for all.

In addition to speaking out against discrimination, there are many other ways that allies can support the LGBTAI community. For example, allies can:

1. **Educate Themselves:** This involves learning about the experiences and challenges faced by LGBTAI individuals. This might involve reading books or articles, attending workshops or training sessions, or seeking out conversations with LGBTAI individuals.

2. **Speak Up:** Allies can use their voices and their platforms to raise awareness about LGBTAI issues and advocate for change. This might involve writing letters to lawmakers, speaking out on social media, or participating in protests or rallies.

3. **Be A Supportive Friend Or Family Member:** Allies can offer a listening ear, a shoulder to cry on, or just a friendly face to LGBTAI individuals who may be struggling with discrimination or other challenges.

4. **Use Inclusive Language:** Allies can make a conscious effort to use gender-neutral language and avoid making assumptions about someone's sexual orientation or gender identity.

5. **Donate To LGBTAI Organizations:** There are many organizations dedicated to advocating for the rights of LGBTAI individuals. Allies can support these organizations by donating money or volunteering their time.

Another important aspect of allyship is recognizing the intersectionality of LGBTAI identities. People who identify as LGBTAI also have other intersecting identities, such as race, ethnicity, religion, ability, and socioeconomic status, that can shape their experiences and the forms of discrimination they face. Being an effective ally means recognizing these intersections and taking them into account when advocating for LGBTAI rights and supporting the community. It is also important for allies to recognize that they will make mistakes and may not always get it right. It is important to approach allyship with humility, a willingness to listen, and a commitment to learning from feedback. Allies should be open to feedback and criticism, and use it to grow and improve their allyship skills.

As an ally, it is important to recognize that your role is to support and amplify the voices of LGBTAI individuals, not to speak on their behalf. This means being mindful of your own privilege and using it to create space for LGBTAI individuals to share their experiences and perspectives. Allies should also recognize that LGBTAI individuals have a wide range of experiences and viewpoints, and should not make assumptions about what they need or want.

Another key aspect of allyship is recognizing the importance of self-care. Supporting the LGBTAI community can be emotionally challenging and draining, and allies should take the time to care for themselves and seek support when needed. This might involve taking a break from activism, seeking out a supportive community, or engaging in self-care practices like meditation, exercise, or therapy.

In addition to supporting the LGBTAI community, allies can also work to create change within their own communities and spheres of influence. This might involve advocating for LGBTAI-inclusive policies and practices in the workplace, schools, or other organizations, or challenging discriminatory practices when they arise.

Ultimately, allyship is about recognizing that we are all connected and that we all have a responsibility to create a more just and equitable world for everyone. By working together, allies and LGBTAI individuals can build a society that is truly inclusive and accepting of all people, regardless of their sexual orientation, gender identity, or other characteristics.

Allyship is a continual journey that requires ongoing education and reflection. It is important to recognize that allyship is not a one-time action or a fixed identity, but a continuous process of learning, growth, and action. Allies should be open to feedback, willing to make mistakes, and committed to constantly improving their allyship skills. It is also important for allies to recognize that their work is not done until everyone in the LGBTAI community is free from discrimination and oppression. This means continuing to advocate for change, even when it is uncomfortable or difficult, and pushing for more inclusive policies and practices in all areas of society.

One important way that allies can continue to support the LGBTAI community is by using their privilege to advocate for change at the systemic level. This might involve lobbying lawmakers to pass laws that protect the rights of LGBTAI individuals, or pushing for changes in school curricula to include more inclusive content.

Allies can also work to create safe and inclusive spaces for LGBTAI individuals in their own communities. This might involve organizing events, creating supportive networks, or pushing for more inclusive policies and practices in local organizations. Another important aspect of allyship is recognizing and addressing internalized biases and prejudices. Allies should be aware of their own biases and work to challenge them, both within themselves and in others. This might involve speaking up when someone makes a discriminatory comment, or challenging stereotypes and assumptions about LGBTAI individuals.

One key aspect of allyship that is often overlooked is the importance of financial support. LGBTAI individuals often face economic challenges due to discrimination in the workplace and in society as a whole. Allies can help by donating to LGBTAI organizations, supporting LGBTAI-owned businesses, and advocating for economic policies that benefit marginalized communities.

Additionally, allies should recognize that allyship is not a one-size-fits-all approach. The experiences and needs of LGBTAI individuals can vary widely depending on factors such as race, gender, socioeconomic status, and location. Effective allyship requires taking these differences into account and being mindful of the unique challenges faced by different members of the community.

An important aspect of allyship is recognizing the role of intersectionality. LGBTAI individuals often face discrimination not just based on their sexual orientation or gender identity, but also due to their race, ethnicity, religion, or other characteristics. Allies should be aware of these intersecting identities and work to address the multiple forms of discrimination that LGBTAI individuals may face. Another important aspect of allyship is creating spaces for LGBTAI individuals to share their experiences and perspectives. Allies can help amplify the voices of LGBTAI individuals by sharing their stories on social media, providing opportunities for them to speak at events, and creating platforms for their voices to be heard.

It is also important for allies to recognize the importance of self-care for LGBTAI individuals. Members of the community often face significant stress and discrimination, which can take a toll on their mental and physical health. Allies can support LGBTAI individuals by promoting self-care practices, providing resources for mental health support, and creating safe and supportive spaces where individuals can come together for support and connection.

One way that allies can deepen their understanding of the experiences of LGBTAI individuals is by engaging in dialogue with members of the community. This requires a willingness to listen, learn, and reflect on one's own beliefs and biases. Allies can participate in community events, attend workshops and trainings, and seek out opportunities to learn from the experiences of LGBTAI individuals.

Another important aspect of allyship is recognizing the impact of allyship on the ally themselves. By becoming an ally, individuals can experience personal growth and development, as well as a sense of purpose and connection to a larger community. This can be particularly powerful for individuals who have been impacted by discrimination and prejudice in their own lives. It is also important for allies to recognize the impact of their actions on the broader community. By taking a stand against discrimination and prejudice, allies can create ripple effects that extend beyond their immediate sphere of influence. This can lead to broader societal change and a more accepting and equitable society for everyone.

One important aspect of allyship is taking action to create change. Allies can use their positions of privilege and power to advocate for policies and practices that promote equity and inclusion for LGBTAI individuals. This can involve advocating for anti-discrimination laws, supporting LGBTAI candidates and causes, and promoting education and awareness of LGBTAI issues.

Another key aspect of allyship is recognizing the impact of language and terminology on the experiences of LGBTAI individuals. Allies should be mindful of the language they use and strive to use inclusive and respectful language that reflects the diversity of the community. This can include using gender-neutral pronouns, avoiding stereotypes and assumptions, and being open to learning about new terminology and identities.

In addition, allies can use their social and professional networks to create opportunities for LGBTAI individuals to connect, network, and support one another. This can involve hosting events and gatherings, providing mentorship and guidance, and creating safe and inclusive spaces where individuals can be themselves without fear of judgment or discrimination. It is also important for allies to recognize that allyship is not a one-size-fits-all approach, as the LGBTAI community is not a monolith. Each individual's experiences and identities are unique, and it is important for allies to approach allyship with an intersectional lens that recognizes the ways in which different forms of oppression intersect and compound.

For example, a trans person of color may face different forms of discrimination and marginalization than a white cisgender gay man. Allies should be mindful of these differences and work to create inclusive and equitable spaces that recognize and honor the diversity of the community.

Another important aspect of allyship is recognizing that mistakes will inevitably be made along the way. No one is perfect, and allies may unintentionally say or do things that are hurtful or offensive. In these situations, it is important for allies to take responsibility for their actions, apologize sincerely, and strive to do better in the future.

One important way that allies can demonstrate their commitment to the LGBTAI community is by using their platforms and positions of influence to speak out against discrimination and prejudice. This can involve using social media, public speaking engagements, and other forms of advocacy to raise awareness of LGBTAI issues and promote greater understanding and acceptance.

Allies can also support LGBTAI individuals in their personal and professional lives by being vocal allies in their workplaces, schools, and communities. This can involve advocating for workplace policies that support LGBTAI employees, speaking out against homophobic and transphobic language and behavior, and supporting LGBTAI individuals in their personal lives.

Another important aspect of allyship is supporting the mental health and well-being of LGBTAI individuals. This can involve advocating for increased access to mental health services, supporting LGBTAI organizations that provide mental health resources, and being a supportive and understanding friend or family member. It is also important for allies to recognize and challenge their own biases and assumptions about LGBTAI individuals. This can involve educating themselves about LGBTAI issues, listening to and learning from the experiences of LGBTAI individuals, and challenging stereotypes and assumptions.

Allies can also use their privilege and power to create opportunities for LGBTAI individuals, particularly those from marginalized communities who may face additional barriers to success. This can involve advocating for policies and initiatives that promote equity and inclusion, mentoring and sponsoring LGBTAI individuals in their personal and professional lives, and creating opportunities for LGBTAI individuals to share their perspectives and experiences.

In addition, allies can help to create safe and supportive environments for LGBTAI individuals by taking an active role in promoting inclusion and diversity. This can involve speaking out against discrimination and prejudice, creating opportunities for LGBTAI individuals to connect and build community, and challenging exclusionary policies and practices. It is also important for allies to recognize that allyship is an ongoing process and requires ongoing education and growth. This means staying up-to-date on current issues and challenges facing the LGBTAI community, and being open to feedback and critique from LGBTAI individuals.

Allies should also be willing to take action even when it may be uncomfortable or challenging. This can involve challenging friends, family, and colleagues when they engage in homophobic or transphobic behavior, advocating for policy changes even in the face of opposition, and standing up for the rights and dignity of LGBTAI individuals even in the face of harassment or threats.

Moreover, allies should recognize the intersectionality of identities and experiences within the LGBTAI community. This means acknowledging and addressing the unique challenges and discrimination faced by LGBTAI individuals who are also people of color, people with disabilities, immigrants, or members of other marginalized communities.

Ultimately, effective allyship requires a willingness to listen, learn, and take action in support of the LGBTAI community. By prioritizing the voices and leadership of LGBTAI individuals, challenging biases and assumptions, promoting equity and inclusion, and staying engaged in the ongoing struggle for LGBTAI rights and acceptance, allies can play a critical role in creating a more just and equitable world for all.

One important aspect of allyship is recognizing that LGBTAI individuals have diverse experiences and perspectives, and there is no one "right" way to be LGBTAI. Allies should be mindful of this diversity and avoid making assumptions or generalizations about LGBTAI individuals based on their identity. Another important aspect of allyship is recognizing that allyship is not a one-way street. While allies can provide support and advocacy for LGBTAI individuals, they can also learn from and be enriched by the experiences and perspectives of the LGBTAI community.

Moreover, allyship can have a powerful ripple effect, inspiring others to take action and creating a more inclusive and accepting society for all. By modeling allyship and promoting inclusion and equity in their personal and professional lives, allies can help to create a culture of acceptance and respect that benefits everyone. It is important to note that allyship is not a fixed or static identity, but rather a continuous and evolving process. As the LGBTAI community and societal attitudes towards them continue to evolve, allyship must also evolve to remain effective and relevant.

This means that allies must be willing to adapt and change their approach based on the needs and experiences of the LGBTAI community. They must be open to feedback and critique, and willing to learn and grow from their mistakes.

Furthermore, effective allyship requires a deep commitment to social justice and human rights, not just for LGBTAI individuals, but for all marginalized communities. Allies must recognize the interconnectedness of all forms of oppression and work to challenge systemic discrimination and inequality in all its forms.

Ultimately, allyship is about more than just supporting the LGBTAI community; it is about creating a more just and equitable world for all. By standing up for the rights and dignity of LGBTAI individuals, challenging biases and assumptions, promoting inclusion and equity, and working to dismantle systems of oppression and inequality, allies can help to create a world that is more accepting, more just, and more equitable for everyone.

Another important aspect of allyship is recognizing and challenging the ways in which systemic discrimination and marginalization impact the lives of LGBTAI individuals. This includes advocating for policy changes and social reforms that address the unique challenges faced by LGBTAI individuals in areas such as employment, healthcare, housing, and education. It also means actively working to create inclusive and welcoming spaces for LGBTAI individuals in all aspects of society, including in schools, workplaces, and religious institutions. Allies can play a crucial role in creating these spaces by challenging homophobic and transphobic language and behavior, promoting understanding and acceptance, and actively seeking out and amplifying the voices and perspectives of LGBTAI individuals.

Moreover, allies can help to create positive social change by using their privilege and influence to advocate for the LGBTAI community. This can involve using their social media platforms to raise awareness about important issues, writing letters to elected officials, or volunteering with local advocacy organizations.

Allyship is a critical component of creating a more just and equitable society for LGBTAI individuals. Effective allyship requires ongoing learning, challenging biases and assumptions, promoting inclusion and equity, and prioritizing the voices and leadership of LGBTAI individuals. Allies must be willing to adapt and change their approach based on the needs and experiences of the LGBTAI community, and recognize the interconnectedness of all forms of oppression. They must advocate for policy changes, create inclusive spaces, use their privilege and influence to advocate for the LGBTAI community, and be present and engaged in their lives. Ultimately, allyship is about creating a more just and equitable world for all.

<u>ELEVEN</u>
LGBTAI Relationships

LGBTAI individuals, like everyone else, seek love, companionship, and fulfilling relationships. However, they may face unique challenges in pursuing these relationships due to societal biases and discrimination. In this section, we will explore the various types of relationships that LGBTAI individuals may have, the challenges they may face, and the benefits of these relationships.

Same-Sex Relationships

Same-sex relationships refer to romantic and sexual relationships between individuals of the same gender. While same-sex relationships are increasingly accepted and legal in many parts of the world, they can still face discrimination and stigma in some places. However, there are many benefits to being in a same-sex relationship, including a deeper understanding of each other's experiences and shared perspectives. Same-sex relationships also offer the opportunity to redefine traditional gender roles and expectations.

Non-Monogamous Relationships

Non-monogamous relationships refer to relationships in which partners have multiple romantic and/or sexual partners. While non-monogamy is not exclusive to LGBTAI individuals, it has been historically stigmatized in mainstream society. However, non-monogamous relationships can offer many benefits, such as greater emotional and sexual freedom, increased communication skills, and the ability to explore different types of intimacy.

Challenges

LGBTAI relationships can face unique challenges, including:

1. **Discrimination And Stigma:** LGBTAI individuals may face discrimination and stigma from society, which can affect their relationships and mental health.

2. **Legal Barriers:** In some parts of the world, same-sex relationships may not be recognized or protected by law, making it difficult for couples to access legal rights and protections.
3. **Family Rejection:** LGBTAI individuals may face rejection or disapproval from their families, which can put a strain on their relationships.
4. **Limited Access To Support:** LGBTAI individuals may have limited access to support and resources that are specifically designed for their needs.

Benefits

LGBTAI relationships can also offer unique benefits, including:

-   **Greater Understanding And Empathy:** Same-sex relationships can offer a deeper understanding of each other's experiences and perspectives.
-   **Redefining Gender Roles:** Same-sex relationships offer the opportunity to redefine traditional gender roles and expectations.
-   **Emotional And Sexual Freedom:** Non-monogamous relationships can offer greater emotional and sexual freedom and the opportunity to explore different types of intimacy.
-   **Stronger Communication Skills:** Non-monogamous relationships require strong communication skills to navigate the complexities of multiple partners, which can lead to stronger communication skills overall.

LGBTAI relationships are an important aspect of LGBTQIA+ culture and history. They have been an essential part of the LGBTQIA+ community, providing individuals with a sense of belonging, acceptance, and support. LGBTAI relationships are diverse and include a wide range of orientations, identities, and expressions. Some individuals identify as gay, lesbian, bisexual, or queer, while others may identify as gender non-conforming or non-binary.

Same-sex relationships, in particular, have been the focus of significant social and legal battles for LGBTQIA+ rights. These relationships have been historically stigmatized and discriminated against, leading to a lack of legal recognition and protection. However, in recent years, there have been significant strides in legalizing same-sex marriage and providing greater protections for LGBTQIA+ individuals in many parts of the world.

Non-monogamous relationships are also an important part of LGBTAI relationships. While non-monogamy may not be for everyone, it can offer unique benefits to those who choose to engage in it. These benefits can include increased emotional and sexual freedom, the ability to explore different types of intimacy, and stronger communication skills. Non-monogamous relationships require a high level of communication, honesty, and trust, which can lead to stronger overall relationship skills.

One of the significant challenges that LGBTAI individuals may face is the discrimination and stigma that they experience from society. This discrimination can lead to internalized homophobia or transphobia, which can cause a lack of self-acceptance and self-love. It can also lead to issues in relationships, such as insecurity, distrust, and a lack of support. It is important for LGBTAI individuals to find supportive communities and allies who can provide them with acceptance and understanding.

Another challenge that LGBTAI individuals may face is family rejection. Many LGBTAI individuals experience rejection or disapproval from their families when they come out, which can cause a strain on their relationships. It is essential for families to support and accept their LGBTQIA+ children and loved ones, as this can greatly improve their mental health and overall well-being.

One of the unique aspects of LGBTAI relationships is the way they challenge traditional gender roles and expectations. In same-sex relationships, there are no prescribed roles for "masculine" and "feminine" behaviors or responsibilities, allowing individuals to define their own gender expression and roles within the relationship. This can lead to a greater sense of freedom and authenticity in relationships.

Non-monogamous relationships also challenge traditional relationship structures and expectations. While monogamy is still the norm in many cultures, non-monogamous relationships can offer an alternative for those who desire more than one romantic or sexual partner. This can lead to a greater sense of emotional and sexual freedom, but it can also require more communication, trust, and boundaries than traditional monogamous relationships.

Despite the challenges and unique aspects of LGBTAI relationships, research has shown that these relationships can be just as healthy and fulfilling as heterosexual relationships. In fact, some studies have shown that same-sex couples may have stronger relationship satisfaction and communication skills than heterosexual couples. This is likely due to the unique challenges that LGBTAI couples face, such as discrimination and stigma, which can foster a stronger sense of support and communication within the relationship. It is also important to note that LGBTAI relationships are not immune to the same issues and conflicts that can arise in any relationship. Relationships require work, communication, and compromise, regardless of sexual orientation or gender identity. It is important for individuals in LGBTAI relationships to prioritize open and honest communication, set clear boundaries and expectations, and work towards resolving conflicts in a healthy and constructive way.

In addition, LGBTAI individuals may face unique challenges when seeking out relationship support and resources. Traditional relationship counseling or therapy may not always be equipped to address the specific issues that LGBTAI individuals may face, such as discrimination or family rejection. It is important for individuals to seek out therapists or counselors who are knowledgeable and supportive of LGBTAI issues, or to seek out specialized support groups or resources.

Furthermore, LGBTAI relationships can also face additional legal challenges and barriers. In many parts of the world, same-sex couples may still face discrimination in accessing legal protections and benefits, such as adoption or healthcare benefits. It is important to continue advocating for legal recognition and protections for LGBTAI individuals and relationships.

Ultimately, LGBTAI relationships are an important aspect of LGBTQIA+ culture and history, providing individuals with a sense of belonging, acceptance, and support. While they may face unique challenges and require additional support and resources, they can also offer unique benefits and opportunities for growth and exploration. By recognizing and supporting LGBTAI relationships, we can work towards creating a more inclusive and accepting society for all individuals, regardless of sexual orientation or gender identity. Another important aspect to consider when discussing LGBTAI relationships is the intersectionality of identities. Individuals in LGBTAI relationships may also identify with other marginalized identities, such as race, ethnicity, religion, or ability. These intersections can compound discrimination and oppression, and may impact the dynamics and experiences within the relationship.

For example, a same-sex couple who are also people of color may face discrimination and racism in addition to homophobia or transphobia. This can impact the way they navigate their relationship and the outside world, and may require additional support and resources to address these intersecting issues.

It is also important to recognize the diversity within the LGBTAI community and the range of relationships and identities that exist. Not all individuals in the community may identify with the labels of "LGBT" or "AI," and some may identify with multiple labels or identities. It is essential to support and respect the unique experiences and identities of all individuals within the community. It is also important to acknowledge the historical and cultural context of LGBTAI relationships. For many years, same-sex relationships were criminalized and stigmatized, leading to significant discrimination and oppression. Even today, many parts of the world still criminalize same-sex relationships or fail to recognize them legally.

As a result, LGBTAI individuals and couples have had to create their own communities and support networks, often in the face of significant obstacles. These communities have played an important role in providing support, resources, and advocacy for LGBTAI relationships and rights.

Furthermore, the fight for LGBTAI rights and recognition has been closely tied to other social justice movements, such as the civil rights movement and the feminist movement. LGBTAI individuals have often joined forces with other marginalized groups to fight for equality and justice for all.

It is important to note the role that media and representation play in shaping societal attitudes towards LGBTAI relationships. Positive representation of LGBTAI relationships in media can help to increase acceptance and understanding, while negative or stereotypical portrayals can reinforce harmful attitudes and discrimination. It is also worth noting that LGBTAI relationships can offer unique benefits and opportunities for personal growth and self-discovery. For many individuals, coming out and exploring their sexual orientation or gender identity within a relationship can be a transformative experience.

In same-sex relationships, individuals may have the opportunity to challenge traditional gender roles and expectations, and to create a relationship dynamic that is based on equality and mutual respect. Non-monogamous relationships can also provide opportunities for exploration and self-discovery, as individuals navigate their own boundaries and desires within the relationship.

Additionally, LGBTAI relationships may provide a sense of community and belonging that may be difficult to find in other areas of life. Many individuals may feel isolated or rejected by family or friends due to their sexual orientation or gender identity, and finding a partner or community who shares similar experiences can be a source of comfort and support.

It is important to recognize that while LGBTAI relationships may offer unique benefits, they are not inherently better or worse than any other type of relationship. It is up to each individual to decide what type of relationship works best for them, based on their own values, beliefs, and desires. Another important aspect of understanding LGBTAI relationships is recognizing the role of allies. Allies are individuals who do not necessarily identify as LGBTAI themselves, but who actively support and advocate for the rights and acceptance of the community.

Allies play a crucial role in creating a more accepting and inclusive society for LGBTAI individuals and relationships. They can help to challenge harmful stereotypes and discrimination, and create safe and welcoming spaces for LGBTAI individuals to express themselves and form relationships.

There are many ways for individuals to become allies for the LGBTAI community. This can include educating oneself on the experiences and issues faced by the community, using inclusive language, standing up against discrimination and hate speech, and supporting LGBTAI individuals and organizations in a variety of ways.

It is important to recognize that being an ally is an ongoing process of learning, growth, and action. It is not enough to simply express support for the community without taking concrete steps to create change. It is also important to recognize that LGBTAI relationships are not monolithic, and that there is a great deal of diversity within the community. Individuals within the LGBTAI community may have different experiences, identities, and relationship preferences.

For example, some individuals may identify as bisexual, meaning that they are attracted to both genders. Others may identify as pansexual, meaning that they are attracted to individuals regardless of gender identity. Transgender individuals may also have unique experiences within relationships, as they navigate the intersection of their gender identity and sexual orientation.

Additionally, there is a growing recognition of the diversity within non-monogamous relationships within the LGBTAI community. Some individuals may practice polyamory, meaning that they have multiple romantic and/or sexual relationships with the consent of all involved. Others may practice open relationships, meaning that they have the freedom to pursue outside relationships while still maintaining a primary relationship.

Understanding and respecting the diversity within the LGBTAI community is crucial for creating a more inclusive and accepting society. It involves recognizing that individuals have different experiences and identities, and that there is no one "right" way to express one's gender or sexuality within a relationship.

Another important aspect of understanding LGBTAI relationships is recognizing the impact of discrimination and stigma on individuals within the community. LGBTAI individuals may face discrimination and marginalization in a variety of settings, including at work, in healthcare, and in their personal relationships.

This discrimination can have significant impacts on the mental health and well-being of individuals within the community. LGBTAI individuals are at a higher risk of experiencing mental health issues such as depression, anxiety, and suicidal ideation, as well as physical health issues such as substance abuse and HIV/AIDS.

In relationships, LGBTAI individuals may face unique challenges related to discrimination and stigma. For example, they may face discrimination from family members or friends who do not accept their sexual orientation or gender identity, or may face challenges in finding healthcare providers who are knowledgeable and accepting of their needs.

Additionally, LGBTAI individuals may experience microaggressions or other forms of discrimination within their relationships. For example, they may be subjected to questions or comments about their sexual orientation or gender identity, or may face pressure to conform to traditional gender roles within their relationship.

Recognizing and addressing discrimination and stigma within LGBTAI relationships is crucial for creating safe and supportive environments for individuals within the community. This involves advocating for policies and practices that promote equality and acceptance, as well as providing education and resources to support individuals in navigating discrimination and stigma. Another important aspect of understanding LGBTAI relationships is recognizing the intersectionality of identities within the community. Individuals within the LGBTAI community may also identify with other marginalized identities, such as race, ethnicity, religion, disability, and socio-economic status.

These intersecting identities can have complex and overlapping impacts on individuals within the LGBTAI community. For example, LGBTAI individuals who are also members of racial or ethnic minority groups may face unique challenges related to both their sexual orientation or gender identity and their race or ethnicity.

Additionally, LGBTAI individuals who are also members of other marginalized groups may face compounded discrimination and marginalization. This can have significant impacts on their mental health and well-being, as well as their ability to form and maintain healthy relationships.

Understanding and respecting the intersectionality of identities within the LGBTAI community is crucial for creating a more inclusive and accepting society. It involves recognizing that individuals may face unique and complex challenges based on their various identities, and that there is no one-size-fits-all approach to addressing these challenges.

Another important aspect of understanding LGBTAI relationships is recognizing the importance of communication and consent. Communication is crucial in any relationship, but it can be especially important for individuals within the LGBTAI community, who may be navigating complex issues related to their sexual orientation, gender identity, and relationships.

Individuals within the LGBTAI community may need to communicate about issues such as sexual preferences, boundaries, and expectations within their relationships. This can involve having difficult conversations about topics such as monogamy, open relationships, and sexual health.

Consent is also a crucial aspect of any relationship, and it is particularly important within the LGBTAI community, where individuals may face unique challenges related to sexual consent. For example, individuals within the community may be more likely to experience sexual assault or coercion, or may face challenges in asserting their sexual boundaries and preferences.

Recognizing the importance of communication and consent within LGBTAI relationships involves creating safe and supportive environments for individuals to express their needs and preferences. It involves respecting individuals' boundaries and consent, and working to create a culture of enthusiastic consent within relationships. Another important aspect of understanding LGBTAI relationships is recognizing the diversity within the community. LGBTAI individuals come from diverse backgrounds and may have a wide range of experiences related to their sexual orientation, gender identity, and relationships.

This diversity can be seen in the different types of relationships that LGBTAI individuals may have. While some individuals may identify as monogamous and may be seeking long-term, committed relationships, others may be interested in exploring non-monogamous relationships or may prefer casual dating.

Furthermore, LGBTAI relationships may take on different forms, depending on cultural or religious beliefs, personal preferences, or the needs of the individuals involved. For example, some individuals within the community may choose to form non-romantic, platonic relationships that are based on emotional intimacy and support.

Recognizing and respecting the diversity within the LGBTAI community involves avoiding assumptions about individuals' sexual orientation, gender identity, or relationship preferences based on stereotypes or generalizations. It involves creating space for individuals to express their unique experiences and needs, and working to create inclusive and accepting environments that honor the diversity within the community.

An important aspect of understanding LGBTAI relationships is recognizing the impact of societal attitudes and discrimination on individuals within the community. LGBTAI individuals may face a wide range of challenges related to discrimination, stigma, and social exclusion. This can include experiencing bullying, harassment, or violence due to their sexual orientation or gender identity, facing employment or housing discrimination, or feeling excluded from social or religious communities due to their identity. These challenges can have significant impacts on individuals' mental health and well-being, as well as their ability to form and maintain healthy relationships. For example, individuals who have experienced discrimination or stigma may be more likely to struggle with issues such as anxiety, depression, or trauma, which can impact their ability to form and maintain healthy relationships.

Recognizing the impact of societal attitudes and discrimination on individuals within the LGBTAI community involves working to create more inclusive and accepting environments for individuals within the community. This may involve advocating for policies that protect the rights of LGBTAI individuals, educating others about the harmful impacts of discrimination and stigma, and creating safe and supportive spaces for individuals within the community.

This community can take many different forms, including support groups, online forums, or social organizations. It can involve connecting with others who share similar experiences or identities, or building relationships with individuals who are allies and advocates for the LGBTAI community.

Support and community can also be important for individuals who are navigating issues related to their sexual orientation or gender identity. This may involve seeking out resources or support from other individuals who have gone through similar experiences, or connecting with individuals who can offer guidance or advice.

Recognizing the importance of community and support within the LGBTAI community involves creating safe and supportive environments where individuals can connect with others who share similar experiences or identities. It involves advocating for policies and resources that support the mental health and well-being of individuals within the community, and working to create a culture of acceptance and support for all individuals, regardless of their sexual orientation or gender identity.

Understanding LGBTAI relationships involves recognizing the diversity within the community, which includes a range of relationship types, cultural and religious beliefs, and personal preferences. It is important to avoid making assumptions based on stereotypes and to create inclusive and accepting environments that honor the unique needs and preferences of individuals within the community. Additionally, it is important to recognize the impact of societal attitudes and discrimination on individuals within the community, and to work towards creating more inclusive and supportive environments. Finally, recognizing the importance of community and support within the LGBTAI community is crucial for promoting the mental health and well-being of individuals and creating a more inclusive and accepting society.

TWELVE
LGBTAI Parenting

LGBTAI parenting refers to the experience of individuals who identify as lesbian, gay, bisexual, transgender, asexual, intersex, or other non-heterosexual orientations or gender identities, who are also parents. Becoming a parent is an important life decision, and for LGBTAI individuals, the path to parenthood may look different from that of heterosexual individuals.

There are various ways in which LGBTAI individuals can become parents, including adoption, surrogacy, and fostering. Adoption is a legal process that allows individuals to become the legal parents of a child who is not biologically related to them. Adoption laws vary by jurisdiction, but same-sex couples and individuals are generally allowed to adopt. Surrogacy involves a woman carrying a pregnancy for another person or couple, and can be done through traditional surrogacy (where the surrogate uses her own eggs) or gestational surrogacy (where the surrogate carries an embryo created with the intended parents' or donors' eggs and sperm). Fostering involves providing temporary care for a child who is in the custody of a state or other agency, with the goal of eventually reunifying the child with their birth family or finding a permanent home through adoption.

While becoming a parent can be a fulfilling experience, LGBTAI parents may face unique challenges. For example, they may experience discrimination or stigma from healthcare providers, social workers, or others involved in the adoption or surrogacy process. They may also face legal barriers, such as restrictions on adoption or surrogacy based on sexual orientation or gender identity. Additionally, LGBTAI parents may need to navigate questions about their family structure from their children's schools, healthcare providers, or other institutions.

Fortunately, there are resources available for LGBTAI parents. Organizations like the Family Equality Council and the Human Rights Campaign provide advocacy and support for LGBTAI families. Legal resources, such as Lambda Legal and the National Center for Lesbian Rights, can assist with navigating legal barriers. Additionally, support groups and online communities, such as the Gay Fathers Association and the Mombian blog, can provide social and emotional support for LGBTAI parents.

In addition to the challenges discussed above, LGBTAI parents may also face challenges related to their children's development and wellbeing. For example, some research has suggested that children raised by same-sex parents may experience more discrimination and stigma from their peers, which can impact their mental health and wellbeing. LGBTAI parents may also face challenges related to their children's access to healthcare, especially in cases where the healthcare provider is not supportive of their family structure.

Despite these challenges, research has consistently shown that children raised by same-sex parents fare just as well as children raised by heterosexual parents. A meta-analysis of 79 studies found that children raised by same-sex parents had similar outcomes in terms of cognitive development, emotional wellbeing, and gender identity development as children raised by heterosexual parents.

It is important to note that LGBTAI parenting is not a new phenomenon, and has been a part of human history and culture for centuries. However, societal attitudes and legal frameworks have not always been supportive of LGBTAI families. In recent years, there have been significant advances in legal recognition of same-sex relationships and parenting, including the legalization of same-sex marriage in many countries, and the adoption of laws allowing for adoption and surrogacy by same-sex couples.

One area of concern for LGBTAI parents is the impact of their sexual orientation or gender identity on their children's development. Some studies have suggested that children raised by LGBTAI parents may be more likely to experience bullying or harassment from their peers, which can impact their mental health and wellbeing. However, it is important to note that these negative outcomes are often a result of societal stigma and discrimination, rather than the parenting skills or abilities of LGBTAI parents themselves.

LGBTAI parents may also face challenges related to their legal rights and protections. While same-sex marriage has been legalized in many countries, there are still places where LGBTAI parents may not have the same legal recognition or protections as heterosexual parents. This can impact issues related to custody, adoption, and access to healthcare for themselves and their children.

In addition to legal challenges, LGBTAI parents may also face challenges related to social support and acceptance. While attitudes towards LGBTAI parenting have become more positive in recent years, there are still some who hold negative attitudes or beliefs about non-heterosexual or non-cisgender individuals as parents. This can impact LGBTAI parents' ability to access resources and support, and may contribute to feelings of isolation or exclusion.

Despite these challenges, LGBTAI parents have demonstrated resilience and creativity in building families that are loving, supportive, and healthy. Many LGBTAI parents have formed networks and communities of support with other LGBTAI parents, which can provide social and emotional support as well as practical advice and resources. Additionally, there are many advocacy organizations that provide legal and social support for LGBTAI families, including the Human Rights Campaign, Lambda Legal, and the National Center for Lesbian Rights.

Another important aspect of understanding LGBTAI parenting is recognizing the diversity of experiences within the community. LGBTAI individuals may become parents through a variety of pathways, including adoption, foster care, surrogacy, and donor insemination. Each of these pathways has its own unique challenges and considerations, and it is important to recognize that not all LGBTAI individuals may have equal access to these options due to legal or financial barriers.

Adoption is one common pathway for LGBTAI individuals to become parents. While same-sex couples are legally allowed to adopt in many countries, there are still some places where adoption by same-sex couples is not recognized or supported. Additionally, some adoption agencies or social workers may hold negative attitudes towards LGBTAI individuals as parents, which can impact the adoption process.

Foster care is another pathway for LGBTAI individuals to become parents. However, LGBTAI individuals may face challenges related to finding a supportive agency or foster parent network. Additionally, children in foster care may have experienced trauma or abuse, which can require additional support and resources for their caregivers.

Surrogacy and donor insemination are other pathways for LGBTAI individuals to become parents. However, these options may be financially inaccessible for many due to the high cost of assisted reproductive technologies. Additionally, laws around surrogacy and donor insemination vary widely by country and may not always be supportive of LGBTAI individuals as parents.

In addition to these pathways, some LGBTAI individuals may also become parents through co-parenting arrangements or through blended families. Co-parenting arrangements involve two or more individuals coming together to raise a child together, without necessarily being in a romantic relationship. Blended families involve the merging of two families through remarriage or partnership, which can involve navigating complex relationships and dynamics.

Another important aspect of understanding LGBTAI parenting is recognizing the importance of affirming and supportive environments for children raised by LGBTAI parents. Research has shown that children who are raised in environments that affirm their parents' sexual orientation or gender identity are more likely to experience positive outcomes, such as higher self-esteem and better mental health.

Affirming environments can include a range of factors, such as positive messages about LGBTAI individuals in the media and education systems, policies and laws that support LGBTAI families, and support from family members and peers. It is important for schools, healthcare providers, and other institutions to create welcoming and inclusive environments for children raised by LGBTAI parents, and to provide education and resources for parents and caregivers.

LGBTAI parenting also intersects with issues related to intersectionality, such as race, ethnicity, religion, and socioeconomic status. LGBTAI individuals who belong to marginalized communities may face additional barriers and challenges in accessing resources and support for parenting. It is important to recognize and address these intersections in order to create a more equitable and inclusive society for all families. Another important consideration when discussing LGBTAI parenting is the unique challenges that may arise within the family unit itself. For example, same-sex couples may face additional stress and pressure due to societal stigma and discrimination. They may also have to navigate complex legal and financial issues related to parenting, such as adoption or custody arrangements.

LGBTAI parents may also face challenges related to their children's development and identity formation. Children of LGBTAI parents may be more likely to experience bullying or discrimination from their peers or within their communities, which can impact their mental health and wellbeing. Additionally, children may struggle with their own identity formation, particularly if they are questioning their sexual orientation or gender identity. It is important for LGBTAI parents to provide a supportive and affirming environment for their children, and to be aware of the unique challenges that their children may face. Parents may need to provide additional support, such as counseling or therapy, for their children as they navigate their identities and relationships.

One important issue related to LGBTAI parenting is the legal recognition and protection of LGBTAI families. In many parts of the world, LGBTAI individuals and families face legal barriers and discrimination that can impact their ability to form and maintain families. For example, same-sex marriage may not be legally recognized, making it difficult for same-sex couples to access legal protections and benefits related to marriage.

Lack of legal recognition and protection can also impact LGBTAI parents' ability to adopt, foster, or have custody of their children. In some countries, LGBTAI individuals may be prohibited from adopting or fostering children, or may face barriers in accessing these processes. Additionally, in cases of divorce or separation, LGBTAI parents may face challenges related to custody and visitation rights. It is important for laws and policies to recognize and protect LGBTAI families, and to provide them with the same legal rights and protections as heterosexual families. This includes legal recognition of same-sex marriage, adoption and fostering rights, and equal custody and visitation rights.

Another important aspect to consider when discussing LGBTAI parenting is the impact of societal attitudes and biases on LGBTAI families. Unfortunately, LGBTAI individuals and families continue to face discrimination and stigma in many parts of the world, which can impact their mental health and wellbeing.

LGBTAI parents may face discrimination and bias from teachers, healthcare providers, and other professionals who may hold negative attitudes towards LGBTAI families. Children of LGBTAI parents may also experience bullying or discrimination from their peers, which can have a significant impact on their mental health and wellbeing.

To support LGBTAI families, it is important to work towards creating more inclusive and accepting communities. This includes providing education and resources to help combat stereotypes and biases, as well as advocating for policies and practices that promote inclusivity and respect for diversity.

Additionally, LGBTAI families may benefit from support groups or other resources that provide a safe and supportive environment for parents and children to connect with others who share similar experiences. Such resources can help to reduce isolation and provide a sense of community and support. It is also important to recognize the resilience and strength of LGBTAI families, who may face unique challenges but also have unique strengths and coping mechanisms. LGBTAI families often display strong bonds and resilience in the face of discrimination and adversity, and can provide important role models for other families and children.

Another important consideration when discussing LGBTAI parenting is the potential impact on the children raised in LGBTAI families. Research has consistently shown that children raised by LGBTAI parents are just as likely to thrive as those raised by heterosexual parents, and that they do not experience negative outcomes related to their parents' sexual orientation or gender identity.

Children raised by LGBTAI parents may have unique experiences and perspectives on issues related to diversity and inclusivity, and may have the opportunity to develop a greater understanding and appreciation for differences among people.

However, it is important to recognize that children of LGBTAI parents may face additional challenges related to their parents' sexual orientation or gender identity, such as facing discrimination or bullying from peers or others in their community. It is important to provide resources and support to help children of LGBTAI parents navigate these challenges and promote their mental health and wellbeing.

It is also important to recognize that LGBTAI families are diverse and may have unique needs and experiences related to their family structure, cultural background, or other factors. For example, families with transgender or non-binary parents may have unique experiences related to gender identity, and may face additional challenges related to accessing healthcare or legal recognition.

To fully understand and support LGBTAI parenting, it is important to recognize and celebrate the diversity of LGBTAI families, and to provide resources and support that meet their unique needs. This includes providing education and training to professionals who work with LGBTAI families, such as healthcare providers and educators, as well as advocating for policies and practices that promote inclusivity and respect for diversity. Another important aspect to consider when discussing LGBTAI parenting is the legal and policy landscape surrounding LGBTAI families. In many parts of the world, LGBTAI individuals and families face legal barriers and discrimination when it comes to accessing healthcare, legal recognition of their family structure, and other important rights and services.

For example, in some countries, LGBTAI individuals may face legal barriers when it comes to adopting or fostering children, or may not have access to reproductive healthcare services such as surrogacy or fertility treatments. Similarly, legal recognition of same-sex relationships and families can vary widely around the world, with some countries offering marriage equality and others offering no legal recognition at all.

To support LGBTAI families, it is important to advocate for policies and practices that promote equality and respect for diversity. This includes working towards legal recognition of same-sex relationships and families, as well as promoting inclusive healthcare policies and practices that meet the unique needs of LGBTAI families. It is also important to support advocacy efforts that aim to challenge discriminatory laws and policies, and to promote the rights and wellbeing of LGBTAI families and their children. This can include supporting local and national advocacy organizations, as well as engaging in political and social activism to promote change.

Another important topic to consider when discussing LGBTAI parenting is the role of allies in supporting and advocating for LGBTAI families. Allies are individuals who do not identify as LGBTAI themselves, but who support and advocate for the rights and wellbeing of LGBTAI individuals and families.

Allies can play a crucial role in promoting inclusivity and respect for diversity in their communities, workplaces, and social networks. This can include actively challenging discrimination and bias when they witness it, educating others about LGBTAI issues and experiences, and advocating for policies and practices that promote equality and respect for diversity.

For example, allies can support LGBTAI families by advocating for policies that promote legal recognition of same-sex relationships and families, as well as policies that support access to healthcare and other important services. Allies can also play a role in promoting inclusive environments in schools and workplaces, by challenging discriminatory attitudes and behaviors and advocating for policies and practices that promote respect and inclusivity.

To support LGBTAI families and their children, it is important for allies to actively engage in advocacy efforts and to educate themselves and others about LGBTAI issues and experiences. This can include attending workshops or training sessions on LGBTAI issues, reading books and articles written by LGBTAI individuals, and seeking out opportunities to engage in social and political activism to promote equality and respect for diversity.

Another important aspect to consider when discussing LGBTAI parenting is the impact of stigma and discrimination on the wellbeing of LGBTAI families and their children. LGBTAI individuals and families are often subject to stigma, discrimination, and prejudice due to their sexual orientation, gender identity, or family structure. This can have a negative impact on their mental health and wellbeing, as well as their ability to access important resources and services.

For example, LGBTAI parents may face discrimination and bias when trying to access healthcare services for themselves or their children. They may also face discrimination and barriers when trying to enroll their children in schools or extracurricular activities, or when seeking legal recognition of their family structure.

To support the wellbeing of LGBTAI families and their children, it is important to challenge stigma and discrimination when it occurs, and to provide support and resources to help LGBTAI families cope with these challenges. This can include providing access to counseling and mental health services, as well as connecting families with supportive social networks and advocacy organizations. It is also important to promote inclusive policies and practices in schools, healthcare settings, and other important institutions, to ensure that LGBTAI families are treated with respect and dignity. This can include promoting inclusive language and policies that acknowledge the diversity of families, as well as providing training and education for service providers to help them better understand and support LGBTAI families and their children.

Another important topic to consider when discussing LGBTAI parenting is the need for legal protections and recognition of LGBTAI families. Legal recognition of same-sex relationships and families can provide important protections for LGBTAI families and their children, including access to healthcare benefits, inheritance rights, and legal recognition of parent-child relationships.

In many countries, LGBTAI families may face legal barriers to adoption, surrogacy, or other forms of family formation. This can create additional challenges for LGBTAI families who may face discrimination or bias in the legal system, or who may not have access to the same legal protections as heterosexual families.

To support the legal recognition and protection of LGBTAI families, it is important to advocate for inclusive laws and policies that acknowledge the diversity of families and protect the rights and wellbeing of all individuals and families, regardless of sexual orientation or gender identity. This can include advocating for same-sex marriage or civil union laws, as well as laws that protect LGBTAI parents and their children from discrimination in employment, housing, and other areas. It is also important to work with legal and policy experts to develop inclusive policies and practices that reflect the needs and experiences of LGBTAI families. This can include providing training and education for legal professionals and policymakers to help them better understand and support LGBTAI families, as well as advocating for changes to laws and policies that create barriers or discrimination for LGBTAI families.

Another important aspect to consider when discussing LGBTAI parenting is the role of allies and community support. Allies are individuals who support and advocate for LGBTAI individuals and families, and can play an important role in promoting inclusion and equality.

Supportive communities can provide important resources and support for LGBTAI families, including access to social networks, resources, and advocacy organizations. For LGBTAI parents, community support can help to counteract the negative effects of stigma and discrimination, and provide a sense of belonging and acceptance.

To support LGBTAI families and promote community support and allyship, it is important to raise awareness and educate others about the experiences and needs of LGBTAI families. This can include providing resources and training for allies, as well as creating safe spaces for LGBTAI families to connect and share experiences.

It is also important to challenge harmful stereotypes and biases about LGBTAI families, and to promote positive representations of diverse families in media and popular culture. This can help to counteract the negative effects of stigma and discrimination, and promote acceptance and inclusion of all families. Another important consideration when discussing LGBTAI parenting is the potential impact on the children of LGBTAI parents. Some studies have shown that children of same-sex parents do not experience negative developmental outcomes compared to children of heterosexual parents. In fact, research suggests that the quality of the parent-child relationship and family functioning is more important for children's well-being than the sexual orientation of the parents.

However, LGBTAI parents may face additional challenges in parenting, including navigating social stigma and discrimination, and addressing questions or concerns from their children about their family structure. It is important for LGBTAI parents to have access to support and resources to help them navigate these challenges, including counseling, peer support groups, and educational materials. It is also important for LGBTAI parents to create a supportive and inclusive environment for their children, and to educate their children about diversity and acceptance. This can help to promote positive self-esteem and a sense of belonging for children of LGBTAI families, and can help to counteract the negative effects of social stigma and discrimination. Another important aspect of LGBTAI parenting is the legal and political landscape surrounding the rights of LGBTAI parents and their families. LGBTAI individuals and couples may face legal barriers in accessing parenting rights and protections, such as the right to adopt or obtain custody of a child, or to make medical decisions for their child.

In recent years, there have been legal and political advancements in recognizing and protecting the rights of LGBTAI parents and their families. For example, many countries now allow same-sex couples to adopt children, and there have been legal battles to recognize the parental rights of same-sex parents who have not given birth to their children.

However, there is still much work to be done to ensure that LGBTAI parents and their families have equal rights and protections under the law. LGBTAI individuals and families may face discrimination and barriers to accessing healthcare, education, and other important resources, and it is important for advocates and allies to continue to push for change and progress in this area.

In addition to legal protections, it is also important for LGBTAI parents to have access to healthcare and social services that are inclusive and supportive of their needs and experiences. This can include access to LGBTQ+ affirming mental health services, as well as support groups and resources for LGBTAI parents and their families.

Another aspect to consider when discussing LGBTAI parenting is the intersectionality of identities within the community. LGBTAI individuals come from diverse racial, ethnic, cultural, and religious backgrounds, and may also identify as disabled or neurodivergent. These intersecting identities can create unique challenges and experiences for LGBTAI parents and their families.

For example, LGBTAI parents who are also people of color may face discrimination and bias from both the LGBTAI community and from society at large. They may also face additional barriers in accessing healthcare and social services due to systemic racism and discrimination.

Similarly, LGBTAI parents who are also disabled or neurodivergent may face unique challenges in parenting, such as navigating inaccessible environments or needing accommodations to parent effectively. They may also experience ableism or discrimination from others in the LGBTAI community or from society at large.

It is important for LGBTAI parents to have access to resources and support that are inclusive of their intersecting identities and experiences. This can include support groups and resources that focus specifically on the needs of LGBTAI parents who are people of color, disabled, or neurodivergent. Another important aspect to consider when discussing LGBTAI parenting is the role of allyship and support from family, friends, and the broader community. LGBTAI parents and their families may face discrimination, stigma, and harassment from individuals who do not accept or understand their identities and experiences. It is important for allies to educate themselves on the unique challenges and experiences faced by LGBTAI parents and their families and to actively support and advocate for their rights and well-being. This can include supporting LGBTAI parents in accessing resources and services, standing up against discrimination and stigma, and creating inclusive and welcoming environments for LGBTAI families.

In addition, LGBTAI parents can also benefit from connecting with other LGBTAI parents and families who have similar experiences. This can provide a sense of community and support, as well as opportunities to share resources and advice on parenting and navigating the challenges that come with it.

One additional aspect to consider when discussing LGBTAI parenting is the impact of societal and cultural norms on the experiences of LGBTAI parents and their families. LGBTAI families may face pressure to conform to traditional gender roles and family structures, which can create additional stress and anxiety for parents and children.

For example, same-sex parents may face questions or criticisms about which parent takes on more traditional maternal or paternal roles, or assumptions that one parent must be the biological parent while the other parent is a non-biological parent or caregiver. These assumptions and pressures can lead to feelings of inadequacy, confusion, or frustration for LGBTAI parents and may also impact the well-being of their children. It is important for society to recognize and respect the diversity of family structures and parenting styles that exist within the LGBTAI community. This includes challenging stereotypes and assumptions about gender roles and family structures, and creating policies and social norms that support the needs and experiences of LGBTAI parents and their families.

Another important consideration when discussing LGBTAI parenting is the impact of legal and policy barriers on LGBTAI individuals' ability to become parents and raise children. Legal barriers may include discriminatory laws that restrict or prohibit LGBTAI individuals from adopting, fostering, or pursuing surrogacy or fertility treatments.

For example, some states or countries may have laws that prohibit same-sex couples from adopting or fostering children, or that restrict access to fertility treatments for individuals or couples who do not meet certain criteria (such as being married to someone of the opposite sex). These legal barriers can make it more difficult or impossible for LGBTAI individuals to become parents, or can create additional financial or emotional burdens in the process.

It is important for legal systems to recognize and protect the rights of LGBTAI individuals to become parents and raise children, without discrimination or barriers. This includes advocating for policies that support equal access to adoption, foster care, surrogacy, and fertility treatments for all individuals, regardless of sexual orientation or gender identity.

In addition, it is important for LGBTAI parents and their families to understand their legal rights and protections, and to seek out legal resources and support if necessary. This can include working with attorneys who specialize in family law and LGBTAI rights, as well as connecting with advocacy organizations that work to protect the rights of LGBTAI parents and their families.

Another important aspect to consider when discussing LGBTAI parenting is the impact of social support on the well-being of LGBTAI parents and their families. Research has consistently shown that social support can have a positive impact on mental health, stress levels, and overall well-being, and this is particularly true for LGBTAI individuals who may face additional stressors related to their sexual orientation or gender identity.

Social support can come from a variety of sources, including friends, family members, support groups, and healthcare providers. For LGBTAI parents and their families, social support can be especially important in helping them navigate the challenges and complexities of parenting, and in providing a sense of community and belonging.

There are many resources available for LGBTAI parents and their families to access social support, including online communities and support groups, local community organizations, and national advocacy groups. These resources can provide a safe and supportive space for LGBTAI parents and their families to connect with others who share similar experiences and challenges, and to receive guidance and support from those who have been through similar situations.

In addition to seeking out social support, it is also important for LGBTAI parents and their families to prioritize self-care and to take steps to manage stress and maintain their mental and physical health. This can include engaging in regular exercise, getting enough sleep, eating a healthy diet, and engaging in activities that bring joy and relaxation.

Another important aspect to consider when discussing LGBTAI parenting is the impact of discrimination and stigma on the mental health and well-being of LGBTAI parents and their families. Discrimination and stigma can take many forms, including verbal harassment, physical violence, social exclusion, and legal barriers. For LGBTAI parents and their families, discrimination and stigma can create significant stress and anxiety, and can have a negative impact on mental health and well-being.

Research has shown that LGBTAI parents and their families may be at increased risk for discrimination and stigma, particularly in settings such as schools, healthcare facilities, and community organizations. This can make it difficult for LGBTAI parents to access support and resources, and can create additional stress and anxiety for them and their families. It is important for healthcare providers, educators, and other professionals who work with families to be aware of the unique challenges and needs of LGBTAI parents and their families, and to provide inclusive and supportive care. This can include taking steps to create a safe and welcoming environment, using inclusive language and terminology, and providing access to resources and support services.

In addition to seeking out supportive professionals and organizations, LGBTAI parents and their families can also take steps to advocate for their rights and to raise awareness about the challenges and needs of LGBTAI families. This can include getting involved in advocacy organizations, speaking out about discrimination and stigma, and working to change policies and laws that create barriers for LGBTAI parents and their families.

LGBTAI individuals can become parents through adoption, surrogacy, fostering, or biological means. However, LGBTAI parents may face unique challenges, such as discrimination and stigma, legal barriers, and social isolation. Seeking out social support and prioritizing self-care can help LGBTAI parents and their families navigate these challenges and maintain their mental and physical health. Healthcare providers, educators, and other professionals can help by providing inclusive and supportive care and creating a safe and welcoming environment. Advocating for their rights and raising awareness about the unique challenges and needs of LGBTAI families can also help create a more inclusive and supportive environment.

THIRTEEN
LGBTAI Faith

The relationship between LGBTAI individuals and religion has been complex and fraught with tension for many years. While some religious institutions have provided a supportive and welcoming space for members of the LGBTAI community, others have historically been unwelcoming and even actively hostile towards LGBTAI individuals.

For many LGBTAI individuals, religion is an important part of their lives, providing them with a sense of community, purpose, and meaning. However, when religious teachings and doctrines promote intolerance and discrimination towards LGBTAI individuals, it can cause significant emotional and psychological harm.

Many religious institutions have traditionally viewed homosexuality, bisexuality, and transgender identity as sinful or immoral, and have used religious texts to justify discrimination against LGBTAI individuals. This has led many LGBTAI individuals to feel alienated from their faith communities, and to experience shame, guilt, and rejection as a result.

However, in recent years, there has been a growing movement towards greater acceptance and inclusivity within many faith communities. Many religious leaders have spoken out in support of LGBTAI rights, and some churches, synagogues, and mosques have actively worked to create more welcoming spaces for LGBTAI individuals.

There are several ways in which faith communities can become more accepting and inclusive of LGBTAI individuals. One important step is for religious leaders to speak out against discrimination and to promote a message of love and acceptance towards all members of their communities. It is also important for faith communities to actively work to create safe and inclusive spaces for LGBTAI individuals, and to provide support and resources to those who may be struggling with their sexual or gender identity.

In addition, it is important for faith communities to educate themselves about the experiences and struggles of LGBTAI individuals, and to actively work to combat stereotypes and misinformation about the community. This can involve partnering with local LGBTAI organizations to learn more about the issues facing the community, and to find ways to support and advocate for LGBTAI rights.

Ultimately, it is important for faith communities to recognize that LGBTAI individuals are a valued and important part of their communities, and to work towards creating a more inclusive and welcoming environment for all members. By promoting acceptance, understanding, and love, faith communities can play an important role in helping LGBTAI individuals feel valued, supported, and empowered.

Another important step towards creating more inclusive faith communities is for religious institutions to examine their own teachings and beliefs about sexuality and gender identity. Many religious texts and doctrines have been interpreted in ways that promote intolerance and discrimination towards LGBTAI individuals. However, there are also many religious scholars and leaders who have worked to reinterpret these texts in a more accepting and inclusive light.

For example, some scholars have argued that biblical passages that are often cited as condemning homosexuality may have been mistranslated or taken out of context, and that the Bible actually promotes love and acceptance towards all individuals, regardless of their sexual orientation or gender identity. Similarly, many religious leaders have worked to promote a message of inclusivity and acceptance within their own traditions, often drawing on the core principles of compassion, justice, and equality.

In addition to changing attitudes and beliefs within faith communities, there are also practical steps that religious institutions can take to create more welcoming and inclusive spaces for LGBTAI individuals. This can include things like offering gender-neutral restrooms, providing sensitivity training for clergy and staff members, and creating support groups or programming specifically for LGBTAI individuals.

Some religious institutions have also taken a more active role in advocating for LGBTAI rights outside of their own communities. For example, many faith-based organizations have spoken out in support of marriage equality and other legal protections for LGBTAI individuals. Some have even worked to mobilize their congregations to take action on these issues, such as organizing rallies, letter-writing campaigns, and other forms of advocacy. It is important to note that while there has been progress towards greater acceptance and inclusion of LGBTAI individuals within some faith communities, there is still a long way to go. Discrimination and intolerance towards LGBTAI individuals continues to exist within many religious institutions, and many individuals still feel unwelcome and unsupported in their faith communities.

In addition, it is important to recognize that not all LGBTAI individuals are interested in finding acceptance within religious institutions. Some individuals may choose to distance themselves from religious traditions altogether due to the harm and trauma they have experienced within these communities. It is also important to acknowledge that LGBTAI individuals are not a monolithic group, and that there is diversity within the community in terms of religious beliefs and practices. Some individuals may be deeply committed to their faith traditions, while others may reject religion altogether. It is important for faith communities to recognize this diversity and to work to create spaces that are welcoming to all individuals, regardless of their beliefs or practices.

Ultimately, creating more inclusive faith communities for LGBTAI individuals requires a commitment to ongoing learning, growth, and dialogue. It requires a willingness to examine and challenge one's own assumptions and beliefs, and to be open to new perspectives and experiences. By working towards greater understanding and inclusivity, faith communities have the potential to promote healing, justice, and equality for all individuals, regardless of their sexual orientation or gender identity.

One of the most important ways to create more inclusive faith communities for LGBTAI individuals is through education and awareness-building. This can involve offering workshops, training sessions, or other educational opportunities for clergy, staff members, and congregants to learn about issues related to sexual orientation, gender identity, and the experiences of LGBTAI individuals.

It is also important for religious institutions to create spaces for open dialogue and conversation, where individuals can share their stories and experiences and work together to build greater understanding and acceptance. This can involve creating support groups or affinity groups for LGBTAI individuals within the community, as well as offering opportunities for interfaith dialogue and collaboration with other faith communities.

Another important step towards creating more inclusive faith communities for LGBTAI individuals is to actively work to combat discrimination and stigma within the broader society. This can involve advocating for policies and legislation that promote equality and justice for LGBTAI individuals, as well as speaking out against discrimination and intolerance wherever it occurs.

Ultimately, creating more inclusive faith communities for LGBTAI individuals requires a deep commitment to compassion, understanding, and justice. It requires a willingness to listen to the voices and experiences of those who have been marginalized and to work towards building a more just and equitable world for all individuals, regardless of their sexual orientation or gender identity.

While the journey towards greater acceptance and inclusion of LGBTAI individuals within faith communities is a long and ongoing one, it is a journey that is essential for building a more just and compassionate world. By working together to build greater understanding, compassion, and justice, we can create faith communities that are truly welcoming and inclusive for all individuals, regardless of their sexual orientation or gender identity.

It is important to recognize that creating more inclusive faith communities for LGBTAI individuals is not just a matter of tolerance, but of celebrating and affirming the diversity of all individuals. This means actively working to dismantle the systems of oppression that have historically marginalized and excluded LGBTAI individuals from religious institutions, and creating spaces where individuals can fully express and celebrate their identities.

One way that faith communities can work to celebrate and affirm the diversity of all individuals is through the use of inclusive language and imagery in their religious practices and rituals. This can involve using gender-neutral language in prayers and liturgies, creating sacred spaces that are inclusive of all gender identities, and incorporating symbols and imagery that celebrate the diversity of all individuals. It is also important for faith communities to actively work to address the unique challenges and experiences faced by LGBTAI individuals within their communities. This can involve offering pastoral care and counseling services that are specifically tailored to the needs of LGBTAI individuals, as well as providing resources and support for families and loved ones of LGBTAI individuals.

Another important aspect of creating more inclusive faith communities for LGBTAI individuals is the recognition of the intersectionality of identities. LGBTAI individuals may also face other forms of marginalization and oppression, such as racism, ableism, or socioeconomic inequality, and it is important for faith communities to actively work to address these intersecting forms of oppression. This can involve offering resources and support for individuals who may face multiple forms of marginalization, such as individuals who are both LGBTAI and people of color or individuals who are both LGBTAI and disabled. It can also involve actively working to address the ways in which systems of oppression intersect and compound, such as the impact of poverty on access to healthcare and support for LGBTAI individuals.

Creating more inclusive faith communities for LGBTAI individuals is not always an easy or straightforward process, but it is an essential one for building a more just and compassionate world. By actively working to address discrimination and exclusion within religious institutions, and by celebrating and affirming the diversity of all individuals, we can create spaces that are truly welcoming and inclusive for all individuals, regardless of their sexual orientation or gender identity.

One key aspect of creating more inclusive faith communities for LGBTAI individuals is to prioritize the voices and experiences of those who have been marginalized within the community. This may involve actively seeking out the perspectives of LGBTAI individuals and creating spaces where they can share their stories and experiences.

In addition, it is important for faith communities to actively work to address the harm that has been caused to LGBTAI individuals by religious institutions in the past. This may involve acknowledging the ways in which religious institutions have historically excluded and oppressed LGBTAI individuals, and taking steps to repair the harm that has been caused.

One way to repair the harm caused by religious institutions is through the practice of reparative justice, which involves acknowledging the harm that has been caused, taking responsibility for that harm, and taking action to repair the harm. This may involve offering formal apologies, creating spaces for dialogue and healing, and making reparations for the harm that has been caused.

Ultimately, creating more inclusive faith communities for LGBTAI individuals is about building communities that are truly welcoming and affirming for all individuals, regardless of their sexual orientation or gender identity. It requires a deep commitment to compassion, understanding, and justice, and a willingness to actively work towards greater inclusivity and equity for all members of the community. By working together towards greater inclusivity and justice, we can create faith communities that are truly transformative and healing for all individuals.

Another important aspect of creating more inclusive faith communities for LGBTAI individuals is to engage in advocacy work that supports LGBTAI rights and equality more broadly. This may involve working to change discriminatory laws and policies that impact LGBTAI individuals, supporting organizations and movements that are advocating for LGBTAI rights, and engaging in community organizing and activism that centers the needs and experiences of LGBTAI individuals.

In addition, faith communities can play an important role in educating their members and the broader community about the experiences and needs of LGBTAI individuals. This may involve hosting educational workshops, panels, and events that provide information and resources about LGBTAI issues, and creating resources and materials that can be shared with members of the community.

Faith communities can also work to create partnerships with other organizations and movements that are advocating for LGBTAI rights and equality. This may involve partnering with LGBTAI organizations, social justice organizations, and other faith communities that are working towards greater inclusivity and equity for all individuals.

Ultimately, creating more inclusive faith communities for LGBTAI individuals requires a deep commitment to justice, equity, and compassion. It requires a willingness to listen to the voices and experiences of those who have been marginalized, to actively work to address systems of oppression and discrimination, and to build communities that are truly welcoming and affirming for all individuals, regardless of their sexual orientation or gender identity. By working together towards greater inclusivity and justice, we can create faith communities that are truly transformative and healing for all individuals. Another important aspect of creating more inclusive faith communities for LGBTAI individuals is to provide resources and support for those who are struggling with their sexual orientation or gender identity. This may involve creating spaces where individuals can receive counseling and support from trained professionals, as well as creating support groups and communities for LGBTAI individuals within the faith community.

It is also important for faith communities to provide support and resources for the families and loved ones of LGBTAI individuals. This may involve offering education and resources to help families better understand and support their LGBTAI loved ones, as well as creating spaces for families to connect and share their experiences.

In addition, faith communities can work to create more inclusive religious texts and teachings that reflect the experiences and needs of LGBTAI individuals. This may involve reinterpreting religious texts and traditions in more inclusive ways, or creating new liturgical materials that reflect the diversity of sexual orientations and gender identities.

Ultimately, creating more inclusive faith communities for LGBTAI individuals requires a willingness to listen to the voices and experiences of those who have been marginalized, to actively work to address systems of oppression and discrimination, and to build communities that are truly welcoming and affirming for all individuals, regardless of their sexual orientation or gender identity. By working together towards greater inclusivity and justice, we can create faith communities that are transformative and healing for all individuals.

Another important aspect of creating more inclusive faith communities for LGBTAI individuals is to address the intersectional experiences of those who face multiple forms of oppression. For example, LGBTAI individuals who also belong to racial, ethnic, or religious minority groups may face unique challenges that are not experienced by other LGBTAI individuals. It is important for faith communities to recognize and address these intersectional experiences, and to create spaces and resources that are responsive to the needs of those who are most marginalized. This may involve partnering with other social justice organizations and movements that are working to address issues of racism, xenophobia, ableism, and other forms of oppression.

Ultimately, creating more inclusive faith communities for LGBTAI individuals is a complex and ongoing process that requires a deep commitment to compassion, justice, and understanding. It requires a willingness to listen to the voices and experiences of those who have been marginalized, and to actively work to address systems of oppression and discrimination. By working together towards greater inclusivity and justice, we can create faith communities that are truly transformative and healing for all individuals.

One important step towards creating more inclusive faith communities for LGBTAI individuals is to address the historical role that religion has played in oppressing and marginalizing these communities. Many LGBTAI individuals have experienced discrimination and rejection from religious communities, and this has often been justified using religious teachings and beliefs.

As a result, it is important for faith communities to acknowledge and address this history of harm, and to work to create spaces that are welcoming and affirming for all individuals, regardless of their sexual orientation or gender identity. This may involve engaging in self-reflection and education about the ways in which religious teachings and traditions have been used to justify discrimination and exclusion, and actively working to reinterpret these teachings in more inclusive ways. It is also important for faith communities to work towards greater accountability and transparency in their relationships with LGBTAI individuals. This may involve creating clear policies and procedures that address issues such as discrimination, harassment, and exclusion, as well as creating mechanisms for reporting and addressing these issues when they occur.

Another important aspect of creating more inclusive faith communities for LGBTAI individuals is to ensure that leadership and decision-making roles within the community are open to all individuals, regardless of their sexual orientation or gender identity. This may involve actively recruiting and supporting LGBTAI individuals to serve in leadership roles within the faith community, and ensuring that they have access to the resources and support they need to be successful. It is also important for faith communities to recognize and celebrate the diversity of sexual orientations and gender identities within their communities. This may involve creating spaces and programming that specifically address the needs and experiences of LGBTAI individuals, as well as actively working to incorporate LGBTAI perspectives and experiences into broader community programming and teaching.

In addition, faith communities can work to create partnerships with other organizations and movements that are working towards greater inclusivity and justice for LGBTAI individuals. This may involve partnering with local advocacy organizations, participating in pride events and other LGBTAI-centered programming, and actively working to build relationships across different communities and identities.

Ultimately, creating more inclusive faith communities for LGBTAI individuals requires a deep commitment to compassion, justice, and understanding. It requires a willingness to listen to the voices and experiences of those who have been marginalized, and to actively work to address systems of oppression and discrimination. By working together towards greater inclusivity and justice, we can create faith communities that are truly transformative and healing for all individuals. Another important way to create more inclusive faith communities for LGBTAI individuals is to offer resources and support for individuals who may be struggling with issues related to their sexual orientation or gender identity. This may involve offering counseling or therapy services, as well as creating support groups and peer-to-peer networks for LGBTAI individuals within the faith community.

It is also important for faith communities to address the unique challenges that LGBTAI individuals may face when it comes to finding and building romantic relationships. This may involve offering programming and support for individuals who are single or dating, as well as creating resources and support for individuals who are in committed relationships or marriages. Another important way to create more inclusive faith communities for LGBTAI individuals is to recognize and address the unique challenges that may be faced by families and parents of LGBTAI individuals. This may involve creating spaces and programming that specifically address the needs and experiences of LGBTAI parents and families, as well as actively working to incorporate LGBTAI perspectives and experiences into broader community programming and teaching.

Ultimately, creating more inclusive faith communities for LGBTAI individuals requires a deep commitment to compassion, justice, and understanding. It requires a willingness to listen to the voices and experiences of those who have been marginalized, and to actively work to address systems of oppression and discrimination. By working together towards greater inclusivity and justice, we can create faith communities that are truly transformative and healing for all individuals.

In addition to offering resources and support, it is important for faith communities to actively engage in advocacy work on behalf of LGBTAI individuals. This may involve working to change discriminatory laws and policies, advocating for greater protections and rights for LGBTAI individuals, and supporting broader movements for social justice and equality.

Faith communities can also play an important role in creating safe and supportive spaces for LGBTAI individuals outside of traditional religious settings. This may involve creating or supporting LGBTAI-centered community organizations, such as social and support groups, as well as providing space and resources for LGBTAI-affirming events and programming.

Furthermore, creating more inclusive faith communities for LGBTAI individuals requires ongoing communication and collaboration between faith leaders, community members, and LGBTAI individuals themselves. It is important to continually solicit feedback from the LGBTAI community and to actively work to address concerns and issues as they arise.

Ultimately, creating more inclusive faith communities for LGBTAI individuals requires a deep commitment to compassion, justice, and understanding. It requires a willingness to listen to the voices and experiences of those who have been marginalized, and to actively work to address systems of oppression and discrimination. By working together towards greater inclusivity and justice, we can create faith communities that are truly transformative and healing for all individuals.

Faith communities can also work to build bridges and cultivate understanding between the LGBTAI community and the broader religious community. This may involve organizing dialogue and education events, inviting LGBTAI individuals to speak at religious services or events, and actively working to build relationships across different communities and identities.

Ultimately, creating more inclusive faith communities for LGBTAI individuals requires a deep commitment to compassion, justice, and understanding. It requires a willingness to listen to the voices and experiences of those who have been marginalized, and to actively work to address systems of oppression and discrimination. By working together towards greater inclusivity and justice, we can create faith communities that are truly transformative and healing for all individuals.

One important aspect of creating more inclusive faith communities for LGBTAI individuals is the role of education. It is important for faith communities to provide accurate and affirming education on LGBTAI issues, including the experiences of LGBTAI individuals, the history of discrimination and oppression faced by the LGBTAI community, and the role that faith communities can play in supporting and advocating for LGBTAI individuals.

Education can take many forms, including sermons, classes, workshops, and other programming. It is important for faith leaders and educators to approach this work with humility and a willingness to learn from the experiences and perspectives of LGBTAI individuals themselves.

In addition to education, faith communities can also take action to promote visibility and representation of LGBTAI individuals within their communities. This may involve creating spaces for LGBTAI individuals to share their stories and experiences, as well as actively working to include LGBTAI perspectives and experiences in community programming, leadership, and decision-making.

Ultimately, creating more inclusive faith communities for LGBTAI individuals requires a deep commitment to compassion, justice, and understanding. It requires a willingness to listen to the voices and experiences of those who have been marginalized, and to actively work to address systems of oppression and discrimination. By working together towards greater inclusivity and justice, we can create faith communities that are truly transformative and healing for all individuals.

Another important aspect of creating more inclusive faith communities for LGBTAI individuals is the role of allyship. Allies are individuals who may not identify as LGBTAI themselves, but who actively support and advocate for the LGBTAI community.

Allies can play a crucial role in creating more inclusive faith communities by using their privilege and platform to amplify the voices and experiences of LGBTAI individuals, advocating for greater inclusion and acceptance within their faith communities, and actively working to challenge discrimination and oppression wherever it arises.

To be an effective ally, it is important to listen to and learn from the experiences and perspectives of LGBTAI individuals, to recognize and challenge one's own biases and assumptions, and to take concrete actions to support and advocate for the LGBTAI community.

Ultimately, creating more inclusive faith communities for LGBTAI individuals requires a deep commitment to compassion, justice, and understanding from all members of the community. It requires a willingness to listen to the voices and experiences of those who have been marginalized, and to actively work to address systems of oppression and discrimination. By working together towards greater inclusivity and justice, we can create faith communities that are truly transformative and healing for all individuals.

Another important way that faith communities can become more inclusive for LGBTAI individuals is by examining their policies and practices to ensure that they are not contributing to discrimination or exclusion.

For example, faith communities can examine their policies around marriage and family to ensure that they are not excluding same-sex couples or non-traditional families. They can also examine their policies around gender and gender expression to ensure that they are not reinforcing harmful gender stereotypes or excluding individuals who do not conform to traditional gender norms.

In addition, faith communities can examine their practices around language and communication to ensure that they are inclusive and affirming of all individuals, regardless of their sexual orientation, gender identity, or other identities.

Creating more inclusive policies and practices requires a willingness to listen to and learn from the experiences and perspectives of LGBTAI individuals, as well as a commitment to ongoing self-reflection and examination. It also requires a willingness to actively work towards change and to address any areas of discrimination or exclusion that may exist within the community.

Ultimately, creating more inclusive faith communities for LGBTAI individuals requires a deep commitment to compassion, justice, and understanding from all members of the community. It requires a willingness to listen to the voices and experiences of those who have been marginalized, and to actively work to address systems of oppression and discrimination. By working together towards greater inclusivity and justice, we can create faith communities that are truly transformative and healing for all individuals.

Creating more inclusive faith communities requires a deep commitment to empathy, compassion, and understanding, and a willingness to engage in ongoing self-reflection and examination. By working together towards greater inclusivity and justice, we can create faith communities that are truly transformative and healing for all individuals.

The relationship between LGBTAI individuals and religion can be complex, with some faith communities providing support and acceptance, while others contribute to discrimination and exclusion. Creating more inclusive faith communities requires a deep commitment to empathy, compassion, and understanding, as well as ongoing efforts to challenge discrimination and oppression. This can involve examining policies and practices to ensure they are inclusive, working towards greater allyship and advocacy, and engaging in ongoing conversations around issues of sexual orientation, gender identity, and other marginalized identities. Ultimately, creating more inclusive faith communities requires a willingness to listen to and learn from the experiences and perspectives of LGBTAI individuals, and a commitment to ongoing self-reflection and examination.

FOURTEEN
LGBTAI In The Workplace

Understanding LGBTAI individuals in the workplace is an important aspect of creating an inclusive and supportive work environment. While many workplaces have made progress in promoting diversity and inclusion, there are still challenges that LGBTAI individuals may face in the workplace.

One of the biggest challenges that LGBTAI individuals may face is discrimination and harassment. Discrimination can come in many forms, such as being passed over for a promotion, being treated unfairly compared to coworkers, or being subject to negative stereotypes and assumptions. Harassment can also take many forms, including verbal abuse, physical violence, and unwanted sexual advances.

In order to promote inclusivity and support LGBTAI employees, it is important for workplaces to have policies and procedures in place that explicitly prohibit discrimination and harassment based on sexual orientation, gender identity, and other related factors. These policies should be communicated clearly to all employees, and training should be provided to ensure that everyone is aware of the expectations and requirements.

It is also important for workplaces to create a culture of inclusivity and support. This can be done by promoting awareness and understanding of the challenges faced by LGBTAI individuals, providing resources and support for employees who may be struggling, and celebrating the contributions and accomplishments of LGBTAI employees. Creating a safe and welcoming environment for all employees can help to foster a sense of community and belonging, which can ultimately benefit the workplace as a whole.

In addition, workplaces can also consider offering benefits and resources that are specifically designed to support LGBTAI employees. This can include access to mental health services, support groups, and other resources that can help individuals navigate the unique challenges that they may face.

To further promote inclusivity and support for LGBTAI employees, workplaces can take additional steps to create a more welcoming environment. This can include initiatives such as forming employee resource groups or diversity committees that are dedicated to promoting diversity, equity, and inclusion in the workplace. These groups can help to raise awareness of the unique challenges faced by LGBTAI individuals, and can work with management to develop policies and programs that address these challenges.

Another way that workplaces can support LGBTAI employees is by offering training and education programs. These programs can help employees to better understand issues related to sexual orientation and gender identity, and can provide them with tools and strategies for promoting inclusivity and respect in the workplace. Training can also help to build empathy and understanding among employees, which can lead to a more supportive and collaborative work environment.

In addition to the steps mentioned earlier, workplaces can also implement policies and practices that promote gender-neutral language and facilities. For example, bathrooms and changing facilities can be made gender-neutral, or separate facilities can be provided for employees who prefer a more private setting. This can help to create a more inclusive environment for transgender and non-binary employees, who may face challenges when using gendered facilities.

Workplaces can also ensure that their health insurance policies cover transition-related healthcare, such as hormone therapy and gender confirmation surgery, to support transgender employees in their journey. This can include offering mental health support to employees who may be experiencing gender dysphoria or other related challenges.

Another way that workplaces can support LGBTAI employees is by creating mentorship or sponsorship programs. These programs can connect LGBTAI employees with experienced mentors or sponsors who can provide guidance and support, and can help them to navigate the unique challenges that they may face in their careers. This can be particularly beneficial for employees who may not have access to role models or mentors who share their experiences and perspectives.

Workplaces can also engage in outreach and recruitment efforts that specifically target LGBTAI job seekers. This can include partnering with LGBTQ+ advocacy organizations, attending career fairs and events that cater to the LGBTQ+ community, and using inclusive language in job postings and recruiting materials. By actively seeking out and recruiting LGBTAI talent, workplaces can create a more diverse and inclusive workforce that reflects the communities that they serve.

To further support LGBTAI employees, workplaces can also consider offering benefits and policies that address the unique needs and challenges that these individuals may face. This can include offering flexible work arrangements, such as telecommuting or flexible schedules, to accommodate the needs of employees who may be caring for a same-sex partner, raising children, or dealing with health-related issues.

Workplaces can also provide resources and support for employees who may be dealing with discrimination or harassment outside of the workplace. This can include offering legal assistance, connecting employees with community resources, and providing emotional support and counseling.

Additionally, workplaces can make a commitment to being transparent and open about their diversity, equity, and inclusion efforts. This can involve sharing data and metrics on the diversity of their workforce, their hiring and promotion practices, and their employee engagement and satisfaction rates. By being transparent about their efforts to create an inclusive workplace, organizations can build trust and credibility with employees, customers, and the broader community.

Another way that workplaces can support LGBTAI employees is by promoting allyship and advocacy among all employees. This can involve offering training and education programs on LGBTQ+ issues, and encouraging employees to become active allies and advocates for their LGBTAI colleagues. By fostering a culture of support and acceptance, workplaces can create a more welcoming and inclusive environment for all employees.

Workplaces can also consider forming employee resource groups (ERGs) or affinity groups that focus on supporting LGBTAI employees. These groups can provide a space for employees to connect with others who share their experiences and perspectives, and can offer resources and support for employees who may be dealing with discrimination or other challenges. ERGs can also serve as a valuable resource for the organization, providing feedback and insights on workplace policies and initiatives, and helping to inform and shape the organization's diversity, equity, and inclusion efforts.

In addition to the initiatives mentioned above, workplaces can also demonstrate their commitment to supporting LGBTAI employees by incorporating inclusive language and imagery in their communications and marketing materials. This can involve using gender-neutral language in job postings, emails, and other written communications, and ensuring that visual representations of employees or customers reflect the diversity of the LGBTQ+ community. By using inclusive language and imagery, organizations can send a clear message that they value and respect all employees and customers, regardless of their sexual orientation, gender identity, or expression.

Workplaces can also consider partnering with LGBTQ+ advocacy organizations to support their initiatives and promote awareness of LGBTQ+ issues. This can involve donating funds or resources to these organizations, providing opportunities for employees to volunteer or participate in advocacy efforts, or partnering with these organizations to host events or activities that promote diversity and inclusivity. By supporting these organizations, workplaces can demonstrate their commitment to promoting equality and inclusion both inside and outside of the workplace.

To further support LGBTAI employees, workplaces can also provide training and education programs on LGBTQ+ issues to all employees. This can involve educating employees on the unique challenges faced by LGBTAI individuals, as well as strategies for promoting inclusivity and respect in the workplace. By providing education and training, workplaces can help to raise awareness and understanding of LGBTQ+ issues, and equip employees with the tools and knowledge needed to be effective allies and advocates for their LGBTAI colleagues.

In addition, workplaces can consider implementing policies that explicitly prohibit discrimination and harassment based on sexual orientation, gender identity, or expression. This can involve updating existing policies and practices to ensure they are inclusive and respectful of all employees, and establishing clear procedures for addressing and resolving discrimination or harassment complaints. By establishing clear expectations and consequences for discriminatory behavior, workplaces can send a message that they value and respect all employees, and are committed to promoting a safe and inclusive workplace environment.

Another way to support LGBTAI employees in the workplace is to offer benefits that are inclusive of their needs. This can include healthcare benefits that cover gender-affirming medical treatments and mental health services that cater to LGBTQ+ individuals. Employers can also consider offering flexible work arrangements, such as remote work options or flexible schedules, which can be especially beneficial for those who may face additional challenges related to their sexual orientation or gender identity.

Workplaces can also create employee resource groups (ERGs) for LGBTQ+ employees to provide them with a safe and supportive space to connect with others who share similar experiences. ERGs can also serve as a forum to provide feedback to the organization, generate ideas, and promote inclusivity in the workplace. Creating opportunities for LGBTQ+ employees to connect with one another can help foster a sense of community and belonging, which can be especially important for those who may feel isolated or marginalized. It's important for workplaces to recognize that promoting inclusivity and support for LGBTAI individuals is not a one-time effort, but rather an ongoing process. This means that workplaces should regularly evaluate their policies and initiatives to ensure they remain inclusive and responsive to the needs of their employees.

One way to do this is to conduct regular diversity and inclusion training for all employees, which can help reinforce the importance of promoting inclusivity and respect in the workplace. These trainings can cover a range of topics, including unconscious bias, cultural sensitivity, and strategies for creating an inclusive workplace culture.

Workplaces can also consider partnering with community organizations that serve LGBTQ+ individuals to learn more about their needs and concerns, and to identify opportunities for collaboration. This can involve sponsoring community events or initiatives, providing volunteers or resources to local organizations, or participating in advocacy efforts to promote LGBTQ+ rights and equality.

Another way to support LGBTAI employees in the workplace is to promote visibility and representation. This can include featuring LGBTQ+ individuals in marketing and advertising materials, highlighting the achievements and contributions of LGBTQ+ employees, and celebrating LGBTQ+ holidays and events.

Workplaces can also prioritize the recruitment and hiring of LGBTQ+ employees, and make sure that their recruitment processes are inclusive and welcoming. This can involve working with LGBTQ+ job boards and organizations, promoting job opportunities through LGBTQ+ networks, and ensuring that job descriptions and application materials are free from bias and inclusive of diverse experiences and identities. It's also important for workplaces to have clear policies in place to address discrimination and harassment of LGBTQ+ employees. This can involve having a zero-tolerance policy for discrimination and harassment, providing clear channels for reporting incidents, and taking swift and appropriate action to address any violations.

One important aspect of supporting LGBTAI employees in the workplace is providing access to benefits and resources that are inclusive and supportive of diverse needs. This can include providing healthcare benefits that cover gender-affirming care, offering flexible work arrangements that accommodate diverse family structures and caregiving responsibilities, and providing resources and support for mental health and well-being.

Additionally, workplaces can create employee resource groups (ERGs) that are specifically focused on supporting the needs of LGBTAI employees. These groups can provide a safe and supportive space for employees to connect with one another, share experiences and resources, and advocate for policies and initiatives that promote inclusivity and support.

Workplaces can also partner with external organizations and experts to provide training and resources on LGBTQ+ issues and best practices. This can involve working with diversity and inclusion consultants, hosting workshops and seminars, and partnering with LGBTQ+ organizations to provide resources and support.

In order to create a truly inclusive workplace, it's important to address not only the experiences of LGBTAI employees, but also those of individuals who identify as intersex or asexual. Intersex individuals are born with physical sex characteristics that do not fit typical male or female classifications, while asexual individuals do not experience sexual attraction to any gender. Both groups face unique challenges and experiences in the workplace that may differ from those of LGBTAI employees.

To support intersex and asexual employees, workplaces can provide education and training on these identities and experiences, create policies and initiatives that are inclusive of diverse gender identities and sexual orientations, and provide resources and support that are sensitive to the needs of these communities. This can include providing access to gender-neutral restrooms and changing areas, accommodating requests for specific language and pronoun usage, and providing resources and support for mental health and well-being.

Additionally, workplaces can create safe and supportive spaces for individuals who identify as intersex or asexual to connect with one another and share resources and experiences. This can involve creating employee resource groups or partnering with external organizations to provide support and resources.

Another key aspect of supporting LGBTAI employees in the workplace is addressing the issue of intersectionality. LGBTAI individuals may also face discrimination and marginalization based on other aspects of their identity, such as race, ethnicity, religion, disability, or socioeconomic status. These intersections of identities can compound the challenges and experiences faced by LGBTAI employees.

To address the issue of intersectionality, workplaces can take a multi-dimensional approach that considers the unique experiences and challenges faced by individuals based on their intersecting identities. This can involve creating policies and initiatives that are sensitive to the needs of diverse communities and identities, providing training and education on issues related to intersectionality, and creating opportunities for dialogue and understanding.

Workplaces can also work to promote diversity and inclusivity in their hiring and promotion practices, ensuring that individuals from diverse backgrounds and communities are represented and valued. This can involve implementing policies and practices that promote diversity and inclusion, such as affirmative action programs or diversity training for hiring managers and employees.

Another important aspect of supporting LGBTAI employees in the workplace is ensuring that they have access to equal opportunities for career development and advancement. This can be particularly challenging for individuals who face discrimination or marginalization based on their gender identity or sexual orientation.

To promote equal opportunities for LGBTAI employees, workplaces can implement policies and initiatives that prioritize diversity and inclusion in career development and advancement. This can involve providing training and education on diversity and inclusion in leadership and management, promoting transparency and fairness in promotion and hiring processes, and creating opportunities for mentoring and networking.

Additionally, workplaces can work to address the issue of unconscious bias, which can impact the career development and advancement of LGBTAI employees. This can involve providing training and education on unconscious bias, creating opportunities for dialogue and understanding, and promoting a culture of respect and understanding among all employees. Another important aspect of supporting LGBTAI employees in the workplace is ensuring that they have access to appropriate benefits and accommodations. This can include healthcare benefits that cover gender-affirming treatments, such as hormone therapy or gender confirmation surgery, as well as policies that allow for appropriate accommodations for individuals based on their gender identity or sexual orientation.

To address the issue of appropriate benefits and accommodations, workplaces can work with their healthcare providers to ensure that their healthcare benefits are inclusive and supportive of LGBTAI individuals. This can involve providing coverage for gender-affirming treatments and therapies, ensuring that all employees have access to mental health support and counseling, and creating policies that allow for appropriate accommodations for individuals based on their gender identity or sexual orientation.

Workplaces can also create policies and initiatives that promote privacy and confidentiality for LGBTAI employees. This can involve creating policies that protect the privacy and confidentiality of individuals who are transitioning or exploring their gender identity, providing access to gender-neutral restrooms and changing areas, and promoting a culture of respect and understanding among all employees.

Another important aspect of supporting LGBTAI employees in the workplace is ensuring that there are clear channels for reporting discrimination, harassment, or other issues related to gender identity or sexual orientation. Workplace policies and initiatives should include clear and accessible reporting mechanisms, and employees should be encouraged to report any instances of discrimination or harassment without fear of retaliation.

To address the issue of reporting mechanisms, workplaces can create policies that prioritize the privacy and confidentiality of individuals who report instances of discrimination or harassment. This can involve providing anonymous reporting options, ensuring that individuals who report discrimination or harassment are not retaliated against, and creating a culture of trust and support among all employees.

Workplaces can also work to create training and education programs that promote awareness and understanding of issues related to gender identity and sexual orientation. This can involve providing training on the importance of respect, inclusivity, and diversity in the workplace, creating opportunities for dialogue and understanding, and promoting a culture of acceptance and support for all employees.

One additional strategy that can be effective in supporting LGBTAI employees in the workplace is to establish employee resource groups (ERGs) or affinity groups. These groups are formed by employees who share common identities or experiences and provide a space for individuals to connect, support one another, and work towards common goals.

ERGs or affinity groups for LGBTAI employees can be a powerful way to promote inclusivity, provide support, and create opportunities for networking and career development. These groups can also serve as a resource for employers, providing insights and feedback on workplace policies and initiatives related to gender identity and sexual orientation.

To create effective ERGs or affinity groups for LGBTAI employees, workplaces should ensure that the groups are accessible to all individuals who identify as LGBTAI and that there is a clear purpose and structure for the group. The group should also have the support and backing of senior leaders in the organization and be provided with the resources necessary to achieve their goals.

Another important strategy for supporting LGBTAI employees in the workplace is to offer benefits and policies that are inclusive and supportive of their needs. For example, workplaces can offer comprehensive health insurance that covers gender-affirming care and treatments, including hormone replacement therapy and gender confirmation surgeries.

Additionally, workplaces can offer policies that are inclusive of all types of families, such as parental leave policies that recognize and support same-sex couples and non-traditional families. This can help to create a workplace culture that values and supports all types of families, regardless of their gender or sexual orientation.

Workplaces can also offer flexible work arrangements, such as remote work options or flexible schedules, that can help LGBTAI employees balance work and personal needs, particularly if they face additional caregiving responsibilities as a result of their gender or sexual orientation.

Another effective way to support LGBTAI employees in the workplace is to provide education and training for all employees on issues related to gender identity and sexual orientation. This can help to increase awareness and understanding of the challenges that LGBTAI employees may face in the workplace, as well as provide guidance on how to be an effective ally.

Training can include topics such as how to create an inclusive workplace, understanding and addressing unconscious bias, and how to provide support and resources to LGBTAI employees. This can help to create a culture of allyship and support, where everyone feels empowered to contribute to a workplace that values diversity and inclusivity.

Additionally, workplaces can work to actively recruit and hire LGBTAI employees, particularly in leadership positions. This can help to increase representation and provide role models for other employees, as well as ensure that the needs and perspectives of LGBTAI employees are represented at all levels of the organization. It is also important for workplaces to actively seek feedback and input from LGBTAI employees, as well as provide opportunities for them to participate in decision-making processes. This can help to ensure that the voices and perspectives of LGBTAI employees are heard and valued, and that the workplace is responsive to their needs and concerns.

Additionally, workplaces can work to build relationships with LGBTAI organizations and community groups, both locally and nationally. This can help to create opportunities for networking, mentorship, and community involvement for LGBTAI employees, as well as help workplaces to stay informed about issues and trends related to gender identity and sexual orientation.

One key aspect of creating a supportive and inclusive workplace for LGBTAI employees is to ensure that the workplace is physically and emotionally safe for them. This means providing gender-neutral or gender-inclusive restrooms, ensuring that harassment and discrimination policies specifically mention gender identity and sexual orientation, and providing resources for employees who may need support in dealing with discrimination or harassment. Another important strategy is to provide healthcare benefits that are inclusive of gender identity and sexual orientation. This can include coverage for gender-affirming surgeries and hormone therapy, as well as mental health services that are specifically tailored to the needs of LGBTAI individuals.

Another important factor in creating an inclusive workplace for LGBTAI individuals is to provide opportunities for education and awareness-building among all employees. This can include training sessions that focus on the challenges faced by LGBTAI individuals, as well as the rights and responsibilities of employees with regard to gender identity and sexual orientation.

These training sessions can be facilitated by outside experts or internal resources such as the human resources department or employee resource groups. The goal of these sessions is to increase understanding and empathy among all employees, and to create an environment where LGBTAI individuals feel respected and valued.

Workplaces can also establish employee resource groups (ERGs) that are specifically focused on LGBTAI issues. These groups can provide a supportive community for LGBTAI employees, as well as serve as a resource for education and awareness-building initiatives. ERGs can also work to advocate for changes in workplace policies and practices that support LGBTAI employees.

Creating an inclusive workplace for LGBTAI individuals requires a holistic approach that involves ensuring physical and emotional safety, providing inclusive healthcare benefits, offering education and awareness-building opportunities, establishing support resources such as employee resource groups, and recognizing the business benefits of diversity and inclusion. Employers should also regularly evaluate and update policies and practices, seek feedback from employees, and continually work to build a culture that values and supports diversity in all its forms. By prioritizing the needs and perspectives of LGBTAI employees, workplaces can create an environment that is supportive, respectful, and successful for everyone.

FIFTEEN
LGBTAI In Education

Understanding LGBTAI in Education is crucial to promote inclusivity and create safe spaces for these individuals in schools and universities. While there have been significant strides in recent years, there are still many challenges that LGBTAI students and educators may face in educational settings.

One of the most significant challenges is the prevalence of discrimination and harassment. LGBTAI individuals may be subjected to verbal and physical abuse, exclusion from social circles, and even violence. This can lead to feelings of isolation, anxiety, and depression, and negatively impact their academic performance and mental health. Furthermore, some LGBTAI individuals may fear being outed, which can further exacerbate these negative experiences.

Another challenge is the lack of representation and visibility in educational materials and curricula. LGBTAI individuals and their experiences may not be acknowledged, which can perpetuate stereotypes and marginalization. This lack of representation can also contribute to the erasure of LGBTAI histories and achievements, which can further reinforce feelings of exclusion.

To promote inclusivity and create safe spaces for LGBTAI individuals in schools and universities, there are several strategies that can be employed. One of the most crucial is education and awareness-raising. Schools and universities should provide training and resources to faculty, staff, and students to increase understanding of LGBTAI identities and experiences. This education can help reduce stereotypes and negative attitudes, and promote more positive and inclusive behaviors.

Another strategy is to create safe spaces and support networks for LGBTAI individuals. This can be done through student organizations, counseling services, and designated safe spaces such as gender-neutral bathrooms and inclusive locker rooms. These safe spaces can provide a sense of community and belonging, which can be especially important for LGBTAI individuals who may feel isolated and marginalized.

In addition, it is essential to ensure that LGBTAI individuals are represented and included in educational materials and curricula. This can be done by including diverse perspectives in history and social science courses, and by providing resources and support for LGBTAI students in STEM fields.

In addition to the strategies mentioned above, there are several other ways to promote inclusivity and support LGBTAI individuals in educational settings.

One important strategy is to incorporate LGBTAI-inclusive policies and practices into school and university systems. This can include policies that prohibit discrimination based on sexual orientation or gender identity, and provide access to resources such as gender-affirming healthcare and counseling services. These policies can create a more welcoming and supportive environment for LGBTAI individuals, and signal to students and staff that discrimination will not be tolerated.

Another important strategy is to provide mentorship and role models for LGBTAI students. This can be done through mentorship programs that connect students with LGBTAI faculty or staff, or by inviting LGBTAI professionals to speak on campus or participate in career events. By providing positive role models and connections, students can feel supported and inspired to achieve their goals. It is also important to address intersectionality and recognize that LGBTAI individuals may face multiple forms of discrimination and marginalization based on their race, ethnicity, socioeconomic status, and other identities. By recognizing these intersections and promoting an inclusive and equitable approach, schools and universities can create a more welcoming and supportive environment for all students.

Lastly, it is important to listen to and prioritize the needs and perspectives of LGBTAI individuals in decision-making processes. This can be done by forming LGBTAI-focused advisory committees or by inviting LGBTAI students and staff to participate in school or university governance structures. By prioritizing the voices of LGBTAI individuals, schools and universities can create more responsive and equitable policies and practices.

Another crucial aspect of creating a supportive and inclusive environment for LGBTAI individuals in education is to engage with families and communities. Many LGBTAI students face significant challenges and hostility from their families and communities, which can impact their academic performance and overall well-being. Schools and universities can work to address these challenges by providing resources and support for families and communities, such as workshops and counseling services that address issues related to sexual orientation and gender identity.

In addition, it is important to recognize that LGBTAI individuals are not a monolithic group, and may have different experiences and needs based on their individual identities and experiences. For example, transgender and gender-nonconforming students may face unique challenges related to gender-affirming healthcare and access to appropriate facilities, while bisexual and pansexual individuals may face stereotypes and erasure related to their sexual orientation. By recognizing and addressing these differences, schools and universities can create a more inclusive and supportive environment for all LGBTAI individuals.

Another important aspect to consider when promoting inclusivity and creating safe spaces for LGBTAI individuals in education is the role of language and communication. The use of inclusive language can have a significant impact on the experiences of LGBTAI individuals, and can signal to students and staff that the school or university values diversity and is committed to creating an inclusive environment. For example, using gender-neutral language when addressing groups of students or staff, or incorporating gender-neutral bathrooms and facilities can make a big difference in how comfortable and supported LGBTAI individuals feel in educational settings. It is also important to address bias and prejudice within the educational system. Prejudice can manifest in many different forms, from overt discrimination to more subtle biases that can impact the experiences of LGBTAI individuals. Schools and universities must actively work to address these biases, through training and education programs for students and staff that promote awareness and understanding of issues related to sexual orientation and gender identity. By creating a culture that is actively anti-discriminatory, schools and universities can foster a supportive and inclusive environment for all students.

In addition to the above-mentioned aspects, it is also important to provide resources and support for LGBTAI individuals who may be struggling with their identities or facing challenges related to discrimination and prejudice. This can include access to counseling services, support groups, and other resources that address issues such as mental health, substance abuse, and violence prevention. It is important to address curriculum and teaching practices that may marginalize or exclude LGBTAI individuals. This can include incorporating diverse perspectives and voices into course materials, and actively promoting an understanding of the contributions and experiences of LGBTAI individuals throughout history and in contemporary society. By doing so, schools and universities can create a more comprehensive and inclusive education that reflects the experiences and perspectives of all students.

It is also important to recognize the intersectionality of identities and how this impacts the experiences of LGBTAI individuals in education. LGBTAI individuals may face multiple forms of discrimination and marginalization based on their race, ethnicity, religion, ability, and other identities. Therefore, it is essential to understand the complex ways in which these identities intersect and impact individuals' experiences in educational settings. By addressing these intersectional experiences, schools and universities can create a more nuanced and responsive approach to supporting LGBTAI individuals.

Another crucial aspect of promoting inclusivity and creating safe spaces for LGBTAI individuals in education is to address the role of bullying and harassment. LGBTAI individuals are at a higher risk of being bullied and harassed, which can have significant impacts on their mental health, academic performance, and overall well-being. Schools and universities must take a proactive approach to addressing bullying and harassment, by implementing policies and procedures that explicitly address these issues and creating a culture that promotes respect and understanding.

Furthermore, schools and universities can actively promote advocacy and allyship among students and staff. Encouraging students and staff to become active allies for LGBTAI individuals can help create a more inclusive and supportive environment. This can include providing training and education on allyship, creating student-led organizations that support LGBTAI individuals, and actively promoting events and activities that promote awareness and understanding of issues related to sexual orientation and gender identity.

Another important aspect of creating safe spaces for LGBTAI individuals in education is providing access to appropriate and affirming health care services. This includes access to medical professionals who are knowledgeable about the unique health needs of LGBTAI individuals, including issues related to sexual health, mental health, and hormone therapy for transgender individuals. Schools and universities can provide this support by partnering with local health care providers who have expertise in LGBTAI health care and offering student health insurance plans that cover these services.

It is also important to provide appropriate accommodations for transgender and gender non-conforming individuals, such as access to gender-neutral restrooms and changing facilities. This can help create a more inclusive environment that respects and supports individuals of all gender identities. It is important for educators to also address heteronormativity and cisnormativity in the classroom, which can marginalize LGBTAI students and reinforce harmful stereotypes and assumptions. Heteronormativity refers to the assumption that everyone is heterosexual and cisnormativity refers to the assumption that everyone identifies with the gender they were assigned at birth. Educators can address these issues by incorporating LGBTQIA+ themes into their curriculum, acknowledging the existence and experiences of LGBTAI individuals, and using gender-neutral language.

Additionally, it is crucial for educators to recognize and address the disparities that exist for LGBTAI individuals in educational attainment and employment. Studies have shown that LGBTAI individuals face higher rates of unemployment, lower wages, and fewer opportunities for advancement compared to their heterosexual and cisgender counterparts. Educators can play a role in addressing these disparities by advocating for policies and programs that promote equity and inclusion, and by providing mentorship and support for LGBTAI students and colleagues.

Another important aspect of creating a safe and inclusive environment for LGBTAI individuals in education is to provide mental health support. LGBTAI students are at a higher risk of experiencing mental health issues due to discrimination, prejudice, and lack of acceptance from their peers and society. Educational institutions can provide mental health resources such as counseling and support groups specifically tailored for LGBTAI students to address these issues.

Educators can also promote LGBTAI inclusivity by creating safe spaces and support systems, such as LGBTAI student organizations, where individuals can express themselves and their identities freely without fear of discrimination or prejudice. These safe spaces can help build a sense of community and support, which is crucial for LGBTAI individuals who may feel isolated or rejected by their peers or society.

Moreover, it is important for educators to address and prevent bullying, harassment, and discrimination against LGBTAI students. Educational institutions can have anti-bullying policies in place that specifically address discrimination based on sexual orientation, gender identity, and expression. These policies should be enforced and regularly evaluated to ensure that all students feel safe and supported in the educational environment. Another important aspect of promoting inclusivity and creating safe spaces for LGBTAI individuals in education is to ensure that educators are equipped with the knowledge and skills to address issues related to sexual orientation, gender identity, and expression in the classroom. This includes being able to respond appropriately to questions or concerns that students may have about their own or others' identities, as well as being able to intervene when inappropriate or discriminatory comments or behaviors arise.

Educators can also play a role in promoting LGBTAI visibility and representation in education by incorporating LGBTAI-related literature, history, and cultural references into their lessons. This not only helps to raise awareness and understanding of LGBTAI issues but also provides representation and validation for LGBTAI students who may feel underrepresented or marginalized in their educational environment.

Additionally, educators can work to create a culture of respect and acceptance in the classroom by modeling inclusive behavior and language. This includes avoiding assumptions about students' gender or sexual orientation, using gender-neutral language, and addressing any discriminatory or disrespectful behavior that may arise among students.

Another important way to promote inclusivity and create safe spaces for LGBTAI individuals in education is to engage with and support the wider LGBTAI community beyond the school or university. This can involve forming partnerships with local LGBTAI organizations or attending LGBTAI events to demonstrate support and solidarity.

Educational institutions can also play a role in advocating for LGBTAI rights and equality in wider society. This can include organizing events or campaigns that raise awareness of LGBTAI issues and encourage community participation and support, as well as actively engaging with local and national policymakers to advocate for policies and legislation that promote equality and protect the rights of LGBTAI individuals.

Moreover, it is important for educational institutions to ensure that their policies and practices are inclusive and accessible to LGBTAI individuals. This can involve ensuring that gender-neutral restrooms are available and accessible, providing inclusive healthcare services, and accommodating LGBTAI students' needs in athletics and other extracurricular activities.

Another way to promote inclusivity and create safe spaces for LGBTAI individuals in education is to engage in ongoing dialogue and education around LGBTAI issues. This includes providing opportunities for open and respectful discussion about LGBTAI issues in the classroom, as well as offering educational workshops and training sessions for educators and staff.

By engaging in ongoing dialogue and education, educators and students alike can gain a deeper understanding of LGBTAI issues, challenge stereotypes and assumptions, and work together to create a more inclusive and respectful learning environment.

Furthermore, it is important to recognize and address the unique challenges that LGBTAI individuals may face in different educational settings. For example, LGBTAI students in K-12 schools may face bullying and harassment from their peers, while LGBTAI students in college and university may face discrimination in housing, healthcare, and other areas of campus life.

To address these challenges, educational institutions can implement policies and practices that promote the safety and well-being of LGBTAI individuals. This can include implementing anti-bullying policies, providing resources for LGBTAI students to access mental health services, and ensuring that housing policies are inclusive of transgender and non-binary individuals. An important factor in creating a safe and inclusive learning environment for LGBTAI individuals is the representation of diverse identities and experiences in the curriculum and materials used in the classroom. Educational institutions can work to ensure that course materials, textbooks, and other resources represent a diversity of LGBTAI experiences and identities.

This can involve including LGBTAI voices and perspectives in history, literature, and social science curricula, as well as offering courses and programs that specifically address LGBTAI issues and experiences. Additionally, educators can integrate LGBTAI themes and discussions into a wide range of subjects and topics, from science and technology to art and music.

By including diverse LGBTAI perspectives and experiences in the curriculum, educational institutions can promote understanding and acceptance of diverse identities and experiences, challenge stereotypes and assumptions, and create a more inclusive and respectful learning environment for all students.

Moreover, it is essential for educational institutions to provide resources and support for LGBTAI students and educators. This can include creating LGBTAI student groups and organizations, offering counseling and support services, and providing training and support for LGBTAI educators.

By providing resources and support, educational institutions can create a sense of community and belonging for LGBTAI individuals and promote their academic and personal success. Additionally, by supporting LGBTAI educators, institutions can ensure that all students have access to diverse perspectives and experiences that promote understanding and respect.

In addition to the steps outlined above, it is also important for educational institutions to address the intersectionality of LGBTAI identities with other aspects of identity, such as race, ethnicity, religion, disability, and socioeconomic status. LGBTAI individuals who hold multiple marginalized identities may face even greater challenges in educational settings, and it is essential to recognize and address these intersections in order to create truly inclusive and equitable environments.

Educational institutions can work to address intersectionality by incorporating a variety of diverse perspectives and experiences in the curriculum and by providing resources and support that are inclusive of all individuals. This can include partnering with community organizations and resources that specifically serve marginalized LGBTAI populations, and providing targeted support and resources for students and educators who hold multiple marginalized identities.

Additionally, educational institutions can work to address issues of discrimination and bias through policies and practices that promote equity and inclusion. This can include implementing diversity and inclusion training for staff and educators, developing hiring and promotion practices that prioritize diversity and inclusion, and creating safe reporting mechanisms for incidents of discrimination and bias.

By addressing intersectionality and promoting equity and inclusion, educational institutions can create environments that are truly welcoming and supportive of all individuals, regardless of their identities or experiences. This, in turn, can help to promote academic success, personal growth, and social justice for all members of the educational community.

Another important aspect of promoting inclusivity and creating safe spaces for LGBTAI individuals in education is engaging in allyship and advocacy. Allyship involves individuals who do not identify as LGBTAI actively working to support and advocate for LGBTAI individuals and communities.

Educators and staff can engage in allyship by becoming informed about LGBTAI issues and experiences, promoting LGBTAI-inclusive language and practices, and advocating for policies and practices that support LGBTAI individuals and communities. This can include attending trainings and workshops, supporting LGBTAI student groups and organizations, and actively challenging discriminatory or prejudiced attitudes and behaviors in the classroom or workplace.

Furthermore, advocacy efforts can involve working with lawmakers and policymakers to promote laws and policies that protect the rights of LGBTAI individuals, such as anti-discrimination laws, policies that promote gender-neutral restrooms and pronouns, and policies that promote access to healthcare and other essential services for LGBTAI individuals.

By engaging in allyship and advocacy, individuals and educational institutions can promote a culture of acceptance, respect, and understanding, and work towards creating a society that is inclusive and equitable for all individuals, regardless of their sexual orientation, gender identity, or other aspects of identity.

In addition to the above approaches, it is important to also acknowledge and celebrate the contributions and achievements of LGBTAI individuals in education and beyond. Educational institutions can promote visibility and awareness of LGBTAI issues and experiences by incorporating LGBTAI history and culture in the curriculum and hosting events and activities that celebrate LGBTAI individuals and communities.

Furthermore, creating safe spaces for LGBTAI individuals in education can also involve addressing the mental health and well-being of LGBTAI students and educators. Research has shown that LGBTAI individuals are at a greater risk for mental health issues, such as depression and anxiety, due to the stigma and discrimination they may face. Educational institutions can provide mental health resources and support that are inclusive of LGBTAI individuals, such as counseling services that are knowledgeable about LGBTAI issues and experiences. It is also important to recognize the role that families and communities play in creating safe spaces for LGBTAI individuals in education. Families and communities can support LGBTAI youth by being accepting and affirming of their identities and by advocating for policies and practices that promote inclusivity and equity in educational settings.

Another important aspect of creating safe spaces and promoting inclusivity for LGBTAI individuals in education is the need for intersectional approaches. This involves recognizing that individuals may have multiple marginalized identities, and that their experiences and needs may be shaped by the intersection of these identities. For example, a transgender person of color may face unique challenges and experiences that are different from a white, cisgender LGBTQ individual.

Educational institutions can promote intersectional approaches by recognizing and addressing the ways in which various forms of oppression intersect and contribute to discrimination and bias against LGBTAI individuals. This can include examining how systems of racism, ableism, sexism, and other forms of oppression impact LGBTAI individuals, and implementing policies and practices that address these intersections.

Intersectional approaches can also involve centering the experiences and voices of marginalized LGBTAI individuals in education. This can include elevating the perspectives and experiences of LGBTAI individuals from historically marginalized communities, and providing opportunities for them to share their stories and perspectives with others.

In addition, creating safe spaces and promoting inclusivity for LGBTAI individuals in education requires ongoing evaluation and assessment of current practices and policies. Educational institutions can conduct regular assessments of their programs and services to ensure that they are inclusive of and responsive to the needs of LGBTAI individuals. This can involve gathering feedback from LGBTAI individuals and incorporating their perspectives into the evaluation process.

Another important aspect of creating safe spaces and promoting inclusivity for LGBTAI individuals in education is the need for allies and advocates. Allies are individuals who are not part of the LGBTAI community, but who support and advocate for LGBTAI individuals and work to create more inclusive and equitable environments.

Educational institutions can promote allyship by providing education and training on LGBTAI issues and experiences. This can include workshops, trainings, and seminars for faculty, staff, and students that focus on topics such as LGBTQ terminology, pronoun usage, and the experiences of LGBTAI individuals. By providing education and training on LGBTAI issues, educational institutions can help to create a more knowledgeable and supportive community of allies.

In addition, educational institutions can create opportunities for LGBTAI individuals to connect with allies and advocates. This can include student organizations that focus on LGBTAI issues, as well as faculty and staff affinity groups that provide support and advocacy for LGBTAI individuals.

Creating opportunities for dialogue and discussion is also important in promoting allyship and advocacy. Educational institutions can host events and activities that bring together LGBTAI individuals and allies to engage in conversations and learn from one another's experiences.

In summary, creating safe spaces and promoting inclusivity for LGBTAI individuals in education requires a multifaceted approach that includes policies, practices, and programs that address discrimination and bias, as well as a commitment to intersectional approaches, ongoing evaluation and assessment, and the support and advocacy of allies. Educational institutions can promote inclusivity by implementing policies that protect LGBTAI individuals from discrimination, providing resources and support services for LGBTAI individuals, and promoting education and training on LGBTAI issues. Additionally, intersectional approaches that recognize the ways in which various forms of oppression intersect and impact LGBTAI individuals can help to create more inclusive and equitable environments. Ongoing evaluation and assessment of programs and services, as well as creating opportunities for dialogue and discussion, can also promote inclusivity. Finally, promoting allyship and advocacy can help to create a supportive and inclusive community for all individuals.

SIXTEEN

LGBTAI Health

Understanding LGBTAI health is essential for ensuring that members of these communities receive the care and support they need to maintain optimal physical and mental well-being. These groups often face unique health challenges related to their sexual orientation or gender identity that require specific attention and care.

Sexual health is one area where LGBTAI individuals may have unique needs. For example, gay and bisexual men may be at higher risk for sexually transmitted infections (STIs), including HIV/AIDS, due to their sexual behaviors. Transgender individuals may also face challenges related to sexual health, such as difficulty accessing gender-affirming healthcare services or encountering stigma and discrimination when seeking care.

Mental health is another critical area for LGBTAI individuals. These communities often experience higher rates of mental health issues, including anxiety, depression, and suicidal ideation, due to factors such as discrimination, prejudice, and social isolation. It is crucial for healthcare providers to understand and address these concerns sensitively and compassionately.

Aging-related health concerns are also significant for LGBTAI individuals, who may face unique challenges related to accessing healthcare and long-term care facilities. Discrimination and stigma can make it difficult for older members of these communities to receive appropriate medical care or find suitable housing options.

Fortunately, there are many resources available to help LGBTAI individuals access healthcare and support. Community health centers and LGBT health clinics provide specialized care and services tailored to the unique needs of these populations. The National LGBT Health Education Center and the LGBT National Help Center are also valuable resources for finding healthcare providers and getting support.

There are also many advocacy organizations and community groups that focus on LGBTAI health issues, such as the Human Rights Campaign, GLAAD, and the Trevor Project. These groups provide resources and support for individuals facing discrimination, harassment, or other forms of mistreatment due to their sexual orientation or gender identity.

Additionally, it is important for healthcare providers to receive training on LGBTAI health issues to provide culturally competent care. This means understanding the unique needs and challenges faced by these communities and tailoring treatment and care plans accordingly. Providers should also be aware of their own biases and work to overcome them to ensure that every patient receives fair and equitable care.

For LGBTAI individuals who may face challenges accessing healthcare due to financial or logistical barriers, there are many resources available to help. Medicaid and Medicare offer coverage for many healthcare services, and the Affordable Care Act prohibits discrimination based on sexual orientation or gender identity in health insurance coverage. Additionally, many community health centers and LGBT health clinics offer sliding scale fees or other payment options to ensure that everyone can receive the care they need. It is also important to recognize that LGBTAI individuals may experience intersectional health disparities, meaning that their sexual orientation or gender identity intersects with other aspects of their identity, such as race, ethnicity, socioeconomic status, and ability status, to create unique health challenges. For example, LGBTAI individuals who also belong to racial or ethnic minority groups may face additional discrimination and barriers to healthcare access due to their intersecting identities.

To address these intersectional health disparities, healthcare providers should take a holistic approach to care that considers the multiple identities and experiences of each individual patient. This may involve partnering with community organizations and advocates to provide culturally responsive care and addressing systemic inequalities that contribute to poor health outcomes.

LGBTAI individuals may also face specific health concerns related to their gender-affirming care. For transgender and nonbinary individuals, accessing gender-affirming healthcare services is essential for their physical and mental well-being. However, navigating the healthcare system to access these services can be challenging due to stigma and discrimination. It is crucial for healthcare providers to be knowledgeable about gender-affirming care and to provide compassionate, non-judgmental support to individuals seeking these services.

In addition to healthcare services, LGBTAI individuals may benefit from support groups and mental health resources to address the unique challenges they face. For example, the LGBT National Help Center provides crisis intervention, peer support, and other resources for LGBTAI individuals in need. The Trevor Project also offers crisis intervention and suicide prevention services for LGBT youth. It is important to note that while significant progress has been made in addressing LGBTAI health disparities in recent years, there is still much work to be done. For example, transgender individuals still face significant barriers to accessing healthcare, including discrimination from healthcare providers and insurance companies. Additionally, LGBTAI individuals may face unique challenges related to their experiences with trauma, such as intimate partner violence or hate crimes.

To address these ongoing health disparities, it is crucial for healthcare providers to engage in ongoing education and training to stay up-to-date on the latest research and best practices related to LGBTAI health. This may involve seeking out continuing education courses or attending conferences and workshops focused on LGBTAI health issues.

In addition to healthcare providers, policymakers and community leaders also have a role to play in addressing LGBTAI health disparities. This may involve advocating for policies and laws that protect the rights and well-being of LGBTAI individuals, such as laws prohibiting discrimination based on sexual orientation or gender identity in employment and housing.

One area where LGBTAI individuals may face unique health challenges is in aging-related health concerns. As LGBTAI individuals age, they may face discrimination and isolation, which can contribute to poor health outcomes. Additionally, LGBTAI individuals may face unique challenges related to healthcare access and affordability, as well as discrimination from healthcare providers.

To address these challenges, healthcare providers should be knowledgeable about the unique needs and challenges faced by LGBTAI individuals as they age. This may involve providing specialized services and resources, such as social support groups or geriatric care management services that are tailored to the unique needs of LGBTAI seniors.

Community organizations and advocacy groups also play an important role in supporting the health and well-being of LGBTAI seniors. For example, the National Resource Center on LGBT Aging provides resources and support to help LGBTAI seniors navigate the healthcare system and access the services they need to maintain optimal health and well-being.

Another important aspect of LGBTAI health is sexual health. LGBTAI individuals may face unique challenges related to sexual health, including higher rates of sexually transmitted infections (STIs) and HIV/AIDS, due to a combination of biological, behavioral, and societal factors. For example, stigma and discrimination may make it more difficult for LGBTAI individuals to access comprehensive sexual health education and services, or to feel comfortable discussing their sexual health with healthcare providers.

To address these challenges, it is important for healthcare providers to provide non-judgmental, culturally competent sexual health services that are tailored to the unique needs and experiences of LGBTAI individuals. This may involve providing education and resources that are inclusive of all genders and sexual orientations, as well as screening for STIs and HIV/AIDS and providing appropriate treatment and counseling.

Community organizations and advocacy groups also play a critical role in promoting sexual health and well-being for LGBTAI individuals. For example, the Centers for Disease Control and Prevention (CDC) offers resources and support for individuals and healthcare providers related to HIV/AIDS prevention and care. The GLBT National Help Center also provides resources and support related to sexual health and HIV/AIDS.

In addition to sexual health, mental health is another critical aspect of LGBTAI health. LGBTAI individuals may face higher rates of depression, anxiety, and other mental health conditions due to a combination of social stigma, discrimination, and trauma. Additionally, LGBTAI youth may be at increased risk of suicide and self-harm due to bullying and harassment.

To address these challenges, it is important for healthcare providers to provide culturally competent mental health services that are sensitive to the unique needs and experiences of LGBTAI individuals. This may involve providing counseling and support groups that are specifically tailored to LGBTAI individuals, as well as addressing the root causes of mental health disparities, such as social stigma and discrimination.

Community organizations and advocacy groups also play a critical role in promoting mental health and well-being for LGBTAI individuals. For example, The Trevor Project provides crisis intervention and suicide prevention services for LGBTAI youth, while the National Alliance on Mental Illness (NAMI) offers resources and support for individuals and families affected by mental illness.

In addition to healthcare and community resources, there are also a number of policy and legal initiatives that can support LGBTAI health and well-being. For example, policies that protect against discrimination in healthcare, housing, and employment can help to promote equity and inclusion for LGBTAI individuals, while legal recognition of same-sex marriage and adoption rights can help to support family stability and reduce stress and discrimination for LGBTAI families.

Other policy and legal initiatives that can support LGBTAI health include funding for research and public health campaigns related to LGBTAI health disparities, as well as efforts to promote cultural competency and diversity training for healthcare providers and other professionals who work with LGBTAI individuals.

Ultimately, promoting the health and well-being of LGBTAI individuals requires a multifaceted approach that addresses the complex interplay of biological, behavioral, and societal factors that contribute to health disparities in these communities. By working together, healthcare providers, policymakers, community leaders, and LGBTAI individuals themselves can create a more just and equitable world where everyone has the opportunity to thrive. It is also important to recognize that LGBTAI individuals are not a monolithic group, and that individuals within these communities may have different experiences and health needs based on a variety of factors, such as race, ethnicity, socioeconomic status, and geographic location. For example, LGBTAI individuals who live in rural areas may face additional challenges related to healthcare access and social support, while LGBTAI individuals who are also members of racial or ethnic minority groups may experience compounded discrimination and stigma.

Therefore, it is important to take an intersectional approach to understanding and addressing LGBTAI health disparities, one that recognizes and accounts for the multiple factors that shape individuals' experiences and needs. This may involve tailoring healthcare and community resources to meet the unique needs of different subgroups within LGBTAI communities, as well as advocating for policies and initiatives that promote equity and inclusion across all dimensions of identity and experience. It is also important to address the aging-related health concerns of LGBTAI individuals. Like other aging populations, LGBTAI individuals may face unique challenges related to chronic illness, disability, and social isolation as they age. However, they may also face additional challenges related to stigma, discrimination, and lack of access to appropriate healthcare and social services.

To address these challenges, it is important for healthcare providers and community organizations to provide culturally competent care and support for aging LGBTAI individuals. This may involve addressing the unique needs and concerns of older LGBTAI individuals in health and social service settings, as well as providing resources and support for socialization, recreation, and community building.

Additionally, policy and legal initiatives that protect against discrimination and promote equity for LGBTAI individuals can also help to address the aging-related health concerns of these communities. For example, policies that promote access to affordable healthcare and long-term care services can help to support the health and well-being of aging LGBTAI individuals, while legal protections against discrimination in employment, housing, and public accommodations can help to ensure that these individuals are able to access the resources and support they need to age with dignity and respect.

Another important aspect of promoting LGBTAI health is to increase public awareness and education about the unique health needs and challenges faced by these communities. This can help to reduce stigma and discrimination, increase access to appropriate healthcare and social services, and promote more positive attitudes and behaviors towards LGBTAI individuals.

Education and awareness efforts may include public health campaigns, community forums and events, and targeted outreach to schools, workplaces, and other organizations. These efforts can help to promote understanding and acceptance of LGBTAI individuals, while also providing resources and support for individuals who may be struggling with their own health and well-being.

In addition, research is also an important tool for understanding and addressing LGBTAI health disparities. By studying the unique health needs and experiences of these communities, researchers can identify areas of concern and develop targeted interventions to improve health outcomes. Research can also help to identify best practices for healthcare and social service delivery, as well as identify areas where policy and legal initiatives may be needed to promote equity and inclusion for LGBTAI individuals. It is important to note that LGBTAI individuals may also face unique challenges related to accessing healthcare, particularly when it comes to sexual and reproductive health services. For example, LGBTAI individuals may face discrimination or discomfort when seeking services related to sexual health, such as STI testing or contraception. Transgender and gender non-conforming individuals may also face additional challenges when accessing gender-affirming healthcare, such as hormone therapy or gender confirmation surgeries.

To address these challenges, it is important for healthcare providers to provide culturally competent care that is sensitive to the unique needs and concerns of LGBTAI individuals. This may involve training healthcare providers on issues related to sexual and gender diversity, as well as providing resources and support for patients who may be struggling with their sexual or gender identity.

Additionally, advocacy efforts can help to promote policies and initiatives that support access to appropriate healthcare services for LGBTAI individuals. For example, policies that promote inclusive healthcare environments and protect against discrimination can help to ensure that LGBTAI individuals are able to access the care they need without fear of stigma or discrimination.

To address these concerns, it is important to provide access to culturally competent mental health services that are sensitive to the unique needs and concerns of LGBTAI individuals. This may involve providing resources and support for individuals who may be struggling with mental health issues, as well as advocating for policies and initiatives that promote equity and inclusion for LGBTAI individuals in all aspects of life.

Another area of concern when it comes to LGBTAI health is aging-related health issues. Like other populations, LGBTAI individuals face unique challenges related to aging, including increased risk for chronic health conditions, social isolation, and discrimination in healthcare and social service settings.

To address these concerns, it is important to provide resources and support for aging LGBTAI individuals, including access to healthcare services that are sensitive to their unique needs and concerns. This may involve providing targeted outreach to aging LGBTAI communities, as well as training healthcare providers and social service professionals on issues related to sexual and gender diversity in aging populations.

In addition, advocacy efforts can help to promote policies and initiatives that support aging LGBTAI individuals. This may include policies that protect against discrimination in housing and employment, as well as initiatives that promote social connectedness and community engagement for aging LGBTAI individuals. It is also important to recognize the role of social determinants of health in shaping LGBTAI health outcomes. Social determinants of health are the conditions in which people are born, grow, live, work, and age, and can include factors such as poverty, access to education, and discrimination. LGBTAI individuals may be more likely to experience these types of social determinants of health due to their sexual or gender identity, which can in turn impact their health outcomes.

To address social determinants of health for LGBTAI individuals, it is important to advocate for policies and initiatives that promote equity and inclusion in all areas of life. This may involve promoting access to education, housing, and employment opportunities, as well as advocating for policies that protect against discrimination and promote social justice. It is also important to note that LGBTAI individuals may face additional challenges related to access to healthcare and support services due to their intersecting identities. For example, LGBTAI individuals who are also people of color, immigrants, or living with disabilities may face multiple layers of discrimination and marginalization in healthcare and social service settings.

To address these concerns, it is important to provide targeted outreach and support to LGBTAI individuals who may be facing multiple forms of marginalization. This may involve providing resources and support that are tailored to the specific needs and concerns of these communities, as well as training healthcare providers and social service professionals on issues related to intersectionality and cultural competency.

In addition, advocacy efforts can help to promote policies and initiatives that address the unique needs and concerns of LGBTAI individuals with intersecting identities. This may include advocating for policies that protect against discrimination based on both sexual orientation and gender identity, as well as other intersecting identities such as race, ethnicity, and disability status.

This may involve providing resources for connecting with LGBTAI community organizations, support groups, or online communities, as well as promoting community engagement and social connectedness in all areas of life. By promoting community and social support for LGBTAI individuals, we can help to reduce social isolation and promote resilience in the face of adversity.

One additional area of concern for LGBTAI health is substance use and addiction. LGBTAI individuals may be at increased risk for substance use and addiction due to the stress and discrimination they may face related to their sexual or gender identity. Studies have shown that LGBTAI individuals are more likely to report higher rates of alcohol and drug use than their heterosexual peers.

To address this concern, it is important to provide resources and support for LGBTAI individuals who may be struggling with substance use and addiction. This may involve providing access to culturally competent and affirming substance use treatment and support services, as well as promoting public awareness and education about the risks and harms of substance use.

It is also important to recognize the role of stigma and discrimination in shaping substance use and addiction outcomes for LGBTAI individuals. Stigma and discrimination can create additional barriers to accessing substance use treatment and support services, as well as contribute to increased stress and mental health challenges that may increase the risk for substance use.

To address stigma and discrimination related to substance use and addiction, it is important to promote public awareness and education about the impact of these issues on LGBTAI individuals. This may involve promoting advocacy efforts that challenge stereotypes and promote equity and inclusion for all individuals, regardless of their sexual or gender identity. Another important area of concern for LGBTAI health is aging-related health concerns. LGBTAI individuals may face unique challenges related to aging, such as a lack of social support and isolation, discrimination and stigma related to sexual or gender identity, and limited access to healthcare and support services.

To address these concerns, it is important to provide targeted outreach and support to LGBTAI individuals who may be facing these challenges. This may involve providing resources and support that are tailored to the specific needs and concerns of aging LGBTAI individuals, as well as training healthcare providers and social service professionals on issues related to aging and intersectionality.

In addition, advocacy efforts can help to promote policies and initiatives that address the unique needs and concerns of aging LGBTAI individuals. This may include advocating for policies that protect against discrimination based on both sexual orientation and gender identity in areas such as housing, employment, and healthcare, as well as promoting policies that address the social determinants of health that can impact aging outcomes for LGBTAI individuals.

This may involve providing resources for connecting with LGBTAI community organizations, support groups, or online communities, as well as promoting community engagement and social connectedness in all areas of life. By promoting community and social support for aging LGBTAI individuals, we can help to reduce social isolation and promote resilience in the face of adversity. Another important aspect of LGBTAI health is reproductive and sexual health. This includes access to contraception, sexually transmitted infection (STI) testing and treatment, and sexual health education. LGBTAI individuals may face unique challenges related to reproductive and sexual health due to factors such as discrimination and stigma, lack of access to affirming healthcare providers, and lack of education on their specific sexual and reproductive health needs.

To address these concerns, it is important to provide access to comprehensive and affirming sexual and reproductive healthcare services that are tailored to the needs and concerns of LGBTAI individuals. This may involve training healthcare providers on the unique needs and concerns of LGBTAI individuals, promoting public awareness and education on sexual and reproductive health, and advocating for policies that protect the rights of LGBTAI individuals to access these services.

In addition, it is important to recognize the role of mental health in promoting sexual and reproductive health for LGBTAI individuals. Mental health challenges, such as anxiety and depression, can impact sexual and reproductive health outcomes, and it is important to provide access to mental health support services that are tailored to the needs and concerns of LGBTAI individuals.

Understanding LGBTAI Health requires addressing various concerns, including mental health, sexual and reproductive health, aging-related health concerns, and access to healthcare and support. LGBTAI individuals may face unique challenges related to discrimination, stigma, and lack of access to affirming healthcare providers and support services. To address these challenges, it is important to provide comprehensive and culturally competent healthcare services, promote public awareness and education, advocate for policy changes, provide mental health support, and promote social support and positive sexual experiences. By working together, we can create a more just and equitable world where everyone has the opportunity to live with dignity and respect, regardless of their sexual or gender identity and intersecting identities.

SEVENTEEN
LGBTAI Culture

Understanding LGBTAI culture is an important aspect of building a more inclusive and diverse society. The term "LGBTAI" encompasses a wide range of identities, and other gender and sexual minorities. Each of these identities has its own unique culture and history, and understanding them can help people become more empathetic and accepting of others.

One of the most visible aspects of LGBTAI culture is art, literature, music, and film. LGBTAI artists have been creating works that express their identities and experiences for centuries, even when it was illegal or dangerous to do so. Some of the most famous LGBTAI artists include Oscar Wilde, Gertrude Stein, Virginia Woolf, Frida Kahlo, Keith Haring, and David Hockney. Their works often address themes such as same-sex desire, gender identity, and social stigma.

LGBTAI literature has also been an important part of the culture. From the homoerotic poetry of the ancient Greeks to the modern-day novels and memoirs, LGBTAI literature has explored the diversity of human experiences. Some of the most notable LGBTAI authors include James Baldwin, Audre Lorde, Gore Vidal, Armistead Maupin, and Jeanette Winterson. Their works have helped to normalize LGBTAI identities and to challenge stereotypes and prejudice.

LGBTAI music has also played an important role in the culture. From the blues and jazz of the early 20th century to the disco and pop of the 1970s and beyond, LGBTAI musicians have used their art to express their identities and to challenge social norms. Some of the most famous LGBTAI musicians include Billie Holiday, Elton John, Freddie Mercury, Madonna, and Lady Gaga. Their music has often been a source of inspiration and empowerment for LGBTAI people.

In film, LGBTAI culture has been represented in various ways. From the campy comedies of the 1960s to the serious dramas of today, LGBTAI characters and stories have been a part of cinema for decades. Some of the most famous LGBTAI films include "Brokeback Mountain," "Philadelphia," "Moonlight," and "Call Me By Your Name." These films have helped to raise awareness about LGBTAI issues and to promote greater acceptance and understanding.

LGBTAI culture has evolved significantly over time. In the past, LGBTAI people faced widespread discrimination and persecution, and their culture was often hidden or underground. However, in recent years, there has been greater acceptance and visibility for LGBTAI identities, and their culture has become more mainstream. Today, LGBTAI culture is celebrated in parades, festivals, and other events around the world.

The impact of LGBTAI culture on broader society has been significant. LGBTAI artists, writers, musicians, and filmmakers have helped to challenge stereotypes and to promote greater acceptance and understanding. Their works have helped to normalize LGBTAI identities and to promote the idea that everyone deserves respect and dignity, regardless of their sexual orientation or gender identity.

In addition to art, literature, music, and film, there are many other aspects of LGBTAI culture that are worth exploring. For example, drag culture has been an important part of LGBTAI culture for decades. Drag performers use makeup, costumes, and exaggerated gestures to challenge gender norms and to entertain audiences. Drag culture has been celebrated in events such as RuPaul's Drag Race and in local drag shows around the world. Another important aspect of LGBTAI culture is activism. LGBTAI people have been fighting for their rights and for greater visibility for decades. Activists such as Harvey Milk, Sylvia Rivera, Marsha P. Johnson, and Larry Kramer have been instrumental in advancing LGBTAI rights, from fighting against discrimination to advocating for HIV/AIDS research and treatment. LGBTAI activism has also played an important role in promoting greater acceptance and understanding of LGBTAI identities.

LGBTAI culture has also been influenced by intersectionality, the idea that people can experience multiple forms of discrimination and oppression. For example, LGBTAI people of color, disabled LGBTAI people, and LGBTAI immigrants face unique challenges and have their own cultures and histories. Understanding the intersectionality of LGBTAI identities can help to promote greater inclusivity and understanding.

It's worth noting that not all LGBTAI people participate in LGBTAI culture or identify with it. Some LGBTAI people may feel that LGBTAI culture doesn't represent their experiences or that they don't relate to it. It's important to respect the diversity of LGBTAI experiences and identities, and to avoid stereotyping or assuming that all LGBTAI people are the same.

One of the ways that LGBTAI culture has evolved over time is through the use of technology and social media. Platforms such as Twitter, Instagram, and TikTok have provided LGBTAI people with a way to connect with each other, share their stories, and advocate for their rights. Social media has also helped to amplify the voices of marginalized LGBTAI people, including transgender and non-binary individuals, who have often been excluded from mainstream LGBTAI culture.

Another way that LGBTAI culture has evolved is through the recognition of different sexual and gender identities. While the LGBTAI acronym originally referred to lesbian, gay, bisexual, and transgender people, it has since expanded to include a range of other identities, such as asexual, intersex, and queer. This expansion has helped to promote greater inclusivity and understanding of the diversity of LGBTAI experiences and identities.

LGBTAI culture has also had a significant impact on broader society. LGBTAI artists, writers, musicians, and filmmakers have influenced mainstream culture in many ways, from challenging gender norms to advocating for greater acceptance of LGBTAI people. LGBTAI activism has led to important legal and social changes, such as the legalization of same-sex marriage and the repeal of "Don't Ask, Don't Tell" policies in the military. The visibility and advocacy of LGBTAI people have also helped to reduce stigma and discrimination and to promote greater acceptance and understanding.

However, despite these advances, LGBTAI people still face many challenges and forms of discrimination. LGBTAI youth are at higher risk of experiencing homelessness, mental health issues, and suicide, and transgender people face particularly high rates of violence and discrimination. Understanding LGBTAI culture is an important step towards promoting greater inclusivity and respect for all people, regardless of their sexual orientation or gender identity.

One of the ways that LGBTAI culture has impacted society is through the creation of safe spaces for LGBTAI people. Safe spaces are physical or virtual environments where LGBTAI people can be themselves, without fear of discrimination or persecution. These spaces can take the form of LGBTAI community centers, online forums, or social events. Safe spaces can be particularly important for LGBTAI youth, who may feel isolated or unsupported in their homes or schools.

Another important aspect of LGBTAI culture is the concept of chosen families. Chosen families are groups of people who come together to form supportive and loving relationships, often in the absence of or in addition to biological or legal family ties. Chosen families can provide a sense of belonging and support for LGBTAI people who may have been rejected or estranged from their biological families. Chosen families can also help to create alternative models of family and community that challenge traditional, heteronormative expectations.

LGBTAI culture has also been shaped by the ongoing fight for LGBTAI rights and recognition. While there have been significant legal and social advances for LGBTAI people in recent decades, there is still much work to be done. LGBTAI people continue to face discrimination in areas such as housing, healthcare, and employment, and transgender and non-binary people in particular face significant challenges in accessing gender-affirming healthcare and legal recognition of their gender identities.

Understanding LGBTAI culture is an important step towards promoting greater acceptance and inclusivity for all people, regardless of their sexual orientation or gender identity. By recognizing the diversity of LGBTAI experiences and identities, people can become more empathetic and understanding of others, and can help to create a world where all people can live authentically and without fear of discrimination or persecution.

One of the ways that LGBTAI culture has impacted broader society is through the promotion of intersectionality. Intersectionality is the idea that people's experiences are shaped not only by their sexual orientation or gender identity, but also by other aspects of their identity, such as race, ethnicity, class, and ability. LGBTAI activism has increasingly recognized the importance of intersectionality, and has sought to highlight the experiences of marginalized LGBTAI people, such as queer people of color, disabled LGBTAI people, and LGBTAI people living in poverty.

LGBTAI culture has also been shaped by the ongoing debate around the use of language and labels. While some LGBTAI people prefer to use specific labels, such as lesbian, gay, bisexual, or transgender, others reject labels altogether or prefer more fluid and inclusive terms such as queer or non-binary. This debate highlights the complexity and diversity of LGBTAI experiences and identities, and the importance of respecting individual preferences and self-identification.

Another important aspect of LGBTAI culture is the role it has played in challenging and disrupting traditional gender roles and expectations. LGBTAI people have often been at the forefront of pushing back against binary ideas of gender, and have helped to promote more fluid and inclusive understandings of gender identity and expression. This has had a significant impact on broader society, and has helped to create greater awareness and acceptance of gender diversity.

In addition, LGBTAI culture has also been shaped by the experiences of LGBTAI people living with HIV/AIDS. The HIV/AIDS epidemic disproportionately affected LGBTAI communities in the 1980s and 1990s, and led to the creation of a vibrant and powerful network of LGBTAI activists, artists, and advocates. This legacy has continued to shape LGBTAI culture, and has helped to promote greater awareness and understanding of the ongoing challenges facing people living with HIV/AIDS. Another important aspect of LGBTAI culture is the concept of chosen family. For many LGBTAI people, biological family members may not be accepting or supportive of their sexual orientation or gender identity. As a result, LGBTAI people often create close bonds with friends and partners, who become like family to them. This concept of chosen family has become an important part of LGBTAI culture, and has helped to create supportive and affirming communities for LGBTAI people around the world.

Furthermore, LGBTAI culture has also been shaped by the ongoing struggles for LGBTAI rights and recognition. LGBTAI activism has been an important force for social change, and has helped to create greater visibility and awareness of the experiences and struggles of LGBTAI people. This activism has led to important legal and social changes, including the legalization of same-sex marriage, the repeal of discriminatory laws, and the creation of greater protections for LGBTAI people.

Lastly, it is important to recognize the ongoing challenges and forms of discrimination faced by LGBTAI people. While progress has been made in many countries, LGBTAI people still face significant challenges, including discrimination, violence, and social stigma. Understanding these challenges is an important step towards promoting greater empathy and support for LGBTAI people, and can inspire action towards creating a more just and equitable world for all.

Another important aspect of LGBTAI culture is the intersectionality of identities. LGBTAI people often have multiple marginalized identities, such as race, ethnicity, religion, disability, or socioeconomic status, which can compound the challenges they face. It is important to understand the ways in which these intersecting identities shape the experiences of LGBTAI people and to recognize the importance of promoting greater equity and inclusion for all marginalized communities.

Additionally, LGBTAI culture has also been shaped by the ongoing conversations around gender and sexuality within the broader society. As LGBTAI rights and recognition have advanced, so too have conversations around gender and sexuality, leading to greater awareness and acceptance of diverse gender and sexual identities. These conversations have helped to promote greater understanding and inclusivity for LGBTAI people, and have challenged traditional binary understandings of gender and sexuality.

Moreover, the evolving technology and social media platforms have created opportunities for LGBTAI people to connect with each other and to build supportive communities. This has allowed LGBTAI people to share their stories, experiences, and perspectives with a wider audience, and to build greater awareness and understanding of the issues facing LGBTAI people. Another important aspect of LGBTAI culture is the role of safe spaces and community organizations. Safe spaces are physical or virtual spaces where LGBTAI people can feel accepted, supported, and validated without fear of discrimination or violence. These spaces can be found in community centers, cafes, clubs, and online forums. They provide a sense of belonging and safety for LGBTAI people and can be critical for those who may not have a supportive social network.

Community organizations play an important role in LGBTAI culture by providing support, advocacy, and resources to LGBTAI people. These organizations can provide a variety of services, such as counseling, legal assistance, health care, and social events. They also advocate for LGBTAI rights and work to create greater awareness and acceptance of LGBTAI people within broader society.

Additionally, LGBTAI culture has been shaped by the ongoing conversations around inclusivity and intersectionality. There is a growing recognition that LGBTAI people are not a monolithic group, but rather a diverse community with varying experiences, identities, and perspectives. This recognition has led to efforts to promote greater inclusivity and intersectionality within LGBTAI communities, as well as a recognition of the importance of allyship from non-LGBTAI individuals and communities.

Another important aspect of LGBTAI culture is the role of activism and advocacy in promoting greater rights and recognition for LGBTAI people. LGBTAI activism has a long and rich history, dating back to the Stonewall riots in 1969 and continuing through to the present day. Activism has been critical in achieving many of the gains in LGBTAI rights and recognition, including the legalization of same-sex marriage and the repeal of discriminatory laws and policies.

Advocacy is also an important aspect of LGBTAI culture, as it involves promoting greater awareness and understanding of the issues facing LGBTAI people within broader society. This can include working with policymakers, educators, and the media to promote greater acceptance and inclusivity of LGBTAI people, as well as promoting greater visibility and representation of LGBTAI people in popular culture.

Representation in popular culture is another important aspect of LGBTAI culture. Film, television, literature, and music have all played important roles in shaping LGBTAI culture and promoting greater awareness and acceptance of LGBTAI people. However, representation can be a double-edged sword, as it can also reinforce harmful stereotypes and contribute to the marginalization of certain groups within the LGBTAI community.

Another important aspect of LGBTAI culture is the role of intersectionality, which refers to the interconnectedness of social identities and the ways in which different forms of oppression and discrimination intersect and reinforce each other. LGBTAI people are not a monolithic group, but rather a diverse community with varying experiences and identities. The intersection of LGBTAI identities with other identities, such as race, gender, and class, can result in unique experiences of discrimination and marginalization.

As such, intersectionality has become an increasingly important focus of LGBTAI activism and advocacy. Intersectional approaches seek to recognize and address the ways in which different forms of oppression intersect and reinforce each other, and to promote greater inclusivity and equity within LGBTAI communities. This can involve recognizing the experiences and perspectives of marginalized groups within the LGBTAI community, and working to promote greater understanding and acceptance of these groups.

Understanding LGBTAI culture involves recognizing the rich and diverse aspects of LGBTAI experiences and identities. This includes the role of art, literature, music, and film in shaping LGBTAI culture, as well as the importance of activism and advocacy in promoting greater rights and recognition for LGBTAI people. Representation in popular culture is important, but it can also contribute to harmful stereotypes and marginalization of certain groups within the LGBTAI community. Additionally, intersectionality is an important focus of LGBTAI activism and advocacy, which seeks to recognize and address the ways in which different forms of oppression intersect and reinforce each other. Finally, it is important to recognize ongoing challenges faced by LGBTAI people, including discrimination, violence, and social stigma, and to continue efforts to promote greater awareness and acceptance of LGBTAI people through advocacy, education, and engagement with policymakers and the broader community.

EIGHTEEN
LGBTAI Activism

LGBTAI activism refers to the efforts made by members of the lesbian, gay, bisexual, transgender, asexual, intersex, and other marginalized sexual and gender identity communities, as well as their allies, to advocate for their rights and promote acceptance and equality in society. This activism can take many forms, from political lobbying and community organizing to public demonstrations and social media campaigns.

The history of LGBTAI activism dates back to the early 20th century, with the formation of the first gay rights organizations in Europe and the United States. These early organizations, such as the Society for Human Rights in the US and the Scientific-Humanitarian Committee in Germany, aimed to challenge the widespread stigma and discrimination faced by LGBTQ+ individuals at the time. The Stonewall riots in 1969, which saw LGBTQ+ patrons of a New York City bar fight back against police harassment, marked a turning point in the movement, inspiring a new wave of activism and organizing across the country.

In the decades since Stonewall, LGBTAI activism has continued to evolve and expand, with advocates working to address a range of issues facing LGBTQ+ communities. Some of the key issues and campaigns that have been pursued in recent years include:

1. **Marriage Equality:** One of the most high-profile campaigns in recent years, the push for marriage equality sought to secure the right of same-sex couples to marry and receive the same legal recognition and benefits as opposite-sex couples. In 2015, the US Supreme Court ruled in favor of marriage equality, making it legal in all 50 states.

2. **Transgender Rights:** Transgender individuals continue to face significant discrimination and marginalization, and activism in this area has sought to address issues such as access to healthcare, legal recognition, and protection from discrimination. Efforts have also been made to raise awareness about the experiences of trans individuals and combat stereotypes and misconceptions.

3. **Conversion Therapy Bans:** Conversion therapy, a practice aimed at changing a person's sexual orientation or gender identity, has been widely discredited and condemned by medical professionals.

Activists have worked to push for the banning of this harmful practice, with several states and countries passing laws to prohibit it.

4. **Anti-LGBTQ+ Discrimination:** Despite legal protections in some areas, LGBTQ+ individuals continue to face discrimination in areas such as employment, housing, and public accommodations. Activists have worked to address this issue through advocacy, litigation, and public education campaigns.

5. **Intersectionality:** As the LGBTAI movement has grown and evolved, there has been a growing recognition of the need to address issues of intersectionality, or the ways in which different forms of oppression intersect and compound each other. This has led to a greater focus on issues such as racism, sexism, and ableism within the LGBTQ+ movement.

LGBTAI activism has also been instrumental in changing societal attitudes towards LGBTQ+ individuals. Through public demonstrations, social media campaigns, and community outreach efforts, activists have worked to challenge stereotypes and misconceptions, and promote a more positive and inclusive image of LGBTQ+ people.

One important aspect of LGBTAI activism is the role of allies. Allies are individuals who support the rights and equality of LGBTQ+ individuals, even if they are not members of the community themselves. Allies play a crucial role in promoting acceptance and creating a safe and inclusive environment for LGBTQ+ people, and many advocacy organizations work to engage and educate allies in their efforts.

LGBTAI activism is not without its challenges and controversies, however. Some critics have argued that certain campaigns, such as the push for marriage equality, prioritize the concerns of more privileged segments of the LGBTQ+ community at the expense of more marginalized groups. Others have raised concerns about the increasing corporatization of Pride events and the ways in which this can undermine the political and social goals of the movement.

Despite these challenges, LGBTAI activism remains a powerful force for change and progress. By continuing to advocate for the rights and equality of LGBTQ+ individuals, activists can help create a more just and inclusive society for all.

Another important aspect of LGBTAI activism is the role of intersectionality. This concept recognizes that LGBTQ+ individuals may face discrimination and oppression not only based on their sexual and gender identities, but also on other aspects of their identity, such as race, ethnicity, religion, and ability. Intersectional activism seeks to address these multiple forms of oppression and promote a more holistic and inclusive approach to social justice.

In recent years, there has also been a growing awareness of the global dimensions of LGBTAI activism. While progress has been made in some parts of the world, many countries still criminalize same-sex relationships or fail to protect the rights of LGBTQ+ individuals. Activists and organizations around the world work to support LGBTQ+ communities in these contexts and promote a more global approach to human rights.

LGBTAI activism has also had significant impacts on popular culture and media. LGBTQ+ representation in television, film, and other media has grown significantly in recent years, in part due to the efforts of activists and advocates who have pushed for more inclusive and diverse portrayals of LGBTQ+ characters and stories. This representation has helped to break down stereotypes and promote greater understanding and acceptance of LGBTQ+ people.

In addition, the growth of online communities and social media has created new opportunities for LGBTAI activism, particularly among younger generations. Social media platforms allow individuals to connect with others who share their experiences and identities, and to amplify their voices and messages to a wider audience. Many organizations and campaigns also use social media to raise awareness and mobilize support for their causes.

An important aspect of LGBTAI activism is the role of allies in supporting LGBTQ+ individuals and communities. Allies can take a variety of forms, from individuals who offer support and affirmation to friends and family members, to organizations and corporations that advocate for LGBTQ+ rights and inclusion. Allies play a crucial role in promoting acceptance and creating a safe and inclusive environment for LGBTQ+ people. Another important aspect of LGBTAI activism is the role of community building. LGBTQ+ communities have historically provided support, solidarity, and a sense of belonging for individuals who may feel isolated or marginalized in mainstream society. Activists have worked to strengthen and empower these communities, creating spaces for socializing, organizing, and advocating for their rights and well-being.

Community building has taken on new forms in recent years, with the growth of online communities and virtual spaces. These spaces allow individuals to connect with others who share their experiences and identities, regardless of physical location or other barriers. Online communities can provide vital support and resources for LGBTQ+ individuals, particularly those who may not have access to supportive communities or resources in their local area.

In addition, LGBTAI activism has also played a crucial role in promoting LGBTQ+ visibility and representation in various aspects of society. This includes not only media and popular culture, but also in areas such as education, healthcare, and the workplace. Activists work to promote policies and practices that are inclusive and affirming of LGBTQ+ individuals, and to challenge discrimination and marginalization wherever it occurs.

Another important area of LGBTAI activism is the promotion of LGBTQ+ rights and equality at the policy level. This includes advocacy for legal protections against discrimination, marriage equality, and the repeal of laws criminalizing same-sex relationships. Activists work to influence lawmakers and policymakers at the local, national, and international levels to promote policies that are inclusive and affirming of LGBTQ+ individuals.

The legal and political landscape for LGBTQ+ rights and equality varies widely across different countries and regions. While progress has been made in some areas, many countries still have discriminatory laws and policies that infringe on the rights of LGBTQ+ individuals. Activists work to raise awareness of these issues and to mobilize support for legal and policy changes that promote equality and inclusion.

In addition, LGBTAI activism also plays a crucial role in promoting education and awareness about LGBTQ+ issues. This includes efforts to promote LGBTQ+ inclusive curricula in schools and universities, as well as campaigns to raise awareness about the experiences and needs of LGBTQ+ individuals in various contexts. Activists work to challenge stereotypes and promote understanding and empathy for LGBTQ+ people, both within the LGBTQ+ community and in broader society.

LGBTAI activism encompasses a range of strategies and approaches aimed at promoting equality, inclusion, and acceptance for LGBTQ+ individuals. This includes grassroots organizing, community building, policy advocacy, and education and awareness campaigns. Youth-led organizations and online communities have played an important role in driving progress on LGBTQ+ issues, as have allies who provide support and advocacy. The ongoing work of activists has helped to create greater visibility and representation for LGBTQ+ individuals in various aspects of society, and to challenge discrimination and marginalization wherever it occurs. While there has been significant progress in recent years, there is still much work to be done to create a more just and equitable society for all LGBTQ+ individuals, particularly those who face intersecting forms of discrimination and marginalization.

<u>NINETEEN</u>
LGBTAI Intersectionality In The Media

Understanding LGBTAI intersectionality in the media is a critical aspect of promoting diversity and inclusivity. Intersectionality refers to the interconnectedness of various social identities, such as race, gender, sexuality, and class, which can impact an individual's experiences and opportunities.

Representation of LGBTAI individuals in the media, including film, television, and news, has improved over the years. However, there is still a long way to go in terms of accurately and fairly depicting the diversity within the community.

Intersectionality plays a significant role in how LGBTAI individuals are portrayed in the media. For example, queer people of color may face different challenges and discrimination than their white counterparts. The media should recognize and accurately represent these differences and ensure that all voices are heard.

The representation of LGBTAI individuals in media can also have real-world consequences. Positive representation can help reduce prejudice and discrimination and promote acceptance and understanding. On the other hand, negative or inaccurate portrayals can reinforce stereotypes and contribute to further marginalization. It's crucial for the media to recognize and address intersectionality when depicting LGBTAI individuals. This includes featuring diverse voices and experiences and portraying characters as complex individuals rather than one-dimensional stereotypes.

To further understand the impact of intersectionality on media representation, we can look at how different social identities intersect with one another. For example, a queer person who is also a person of color may experience discrimination and marginalization based on their race, sexuality, and sometimes even their gender identity. This intersectionality can have a significant impact on their experiences and how they are portrayed in the media.

LGBTAI individuals who come from lower socio-economic backgrounds may also face unique challenges that are often overlooked in mainstream media. They may lack access to resources and face barriers in education, employment, and healthcare, among other areas. This can impact their experiences and representation in the media as well.

Moreover, it is crucial to acknowledge that there is no monolithic LGBTAI community. Each individual within the community has unique experiences and identities. The media should recognize this diversity and accurately represent the complexity of these experiences.

In recent years, there have been some positive changes in media representation of LGBTAI individuals. For example, shows like "Pose" and "The L Word: Generation Q" feature predominantly queer and trans casts and tell stories that center on their experiences. Similarly, films like "Moonlight" and "Call Me By Your Name" have received critical acclaim for their nuanced depictions of queer characters.

However, there is still a long way to go in terms of accurate and positive representation. Queer people of color, trans and non-binary individuals, and those from lower socio-economic backgrounds are still underrepresented in the media. Additionally, even when these individuals are portrayed, they are often reduced to stereotypes and one-dimensional characters.

One of the ways that media representation of LGBTAI individuals can be improved is by involving individuals from the community in the creation and production of media content. This includes hiring diverse writers, producers, and directors who can bring their own experiences and perspectives to the table. Another way is to actively seek out and promote content that accurately and positively represents the diversity within the LGBTAI community. This can include highlighting independent films, web series, and other forms of media that may not have as much visibility as mainstream media.

It's also essential to address the negative impact that media stereotypes can have on the LGBTAI community. These stereotypes can perpetuate harmful myths and misunderstandings and contribute to further marginalization. Instead, the media should strive to accurately represent the diversity and complexity of LGBTAI individuals and promote understanding and acceptance. Another important aspect to consider when discussing LGBTAI intersectionality in the media is the impact of intersectionality on mental health. Discrimination and marginalization can have a significant impact on mental health, and LGBTAI individuals who experience multiple forms of oppression due to their intersecting identities may be at even greater risk.

Media representation can play a crucial role in promoting positive mental health outcomes for LGBTAI individuals. Accurately representing the diversity and complexity of the community can help reduce the sense of isolation and other negative emotions that can contribute to mental health issues.

Moreover, positive representation can promote resilience and a sense of community among LGBTAI individuals. It can also help reduce the sense of stigma and shame that many individuals within the community may feel.

On the other hand, negative or inaccurate media representation can contribute to further mental health issues. It can lead to internalized stigma, a sense of shame, and a feeling of not belonging. Negative media representation can also perpetuate harmful myths and misunderstandings about the community, contributing to further marginalization.

Therefore, it's crucial for media representation of LGBTAI individuals to accurately and positively represent the diversity within the community. This includes recognizing the impact of intersectionality on mental health and promoting positive messages of acceptance, resilience, and community.

Another area where intersectionality plays a significant role in media representation of LGBTAI individuals is in political and social activism. LGBTAI individuals may face unique challenges and barriers when advocating for their rights and seeking to change oppressive systems.

For example, queer people of color may experience discrimination and marginalization not only within the broader society but also within the LGBTAI community. Trans and non-binary individuals may face challenges in accessing healthcare, employment, and other resources. Queer individuals from lower socio-economic backgrounds may lack access to resources and support networks.

This intersectionality can impact how LGBTAI individuals are represented in media coverage of activism and social justice movements. It's important for media representation to accurately and positively represent the diversity and complexity of these experiences.

Additionally, media representation can play a significant role in promoting political and social change. By accurately and positively representing the experiences of LGBTAI individuals, media coverage can promote understanding, acceptance, and support for political and social activism. Another important aspect to consider when discussing LGBTAI intersectionality in the media is the impact of representation on younger generations. Media representation can play a significant role in shaping the attitudes and beliefs of younger generations towards LGBTAI individuals.

Accurately and positively representing the diversity and complexity of LGBTAI individuals in media can help reduce bullying and discrimination towards queer youth. It can also promote acceptance and understanding among younger generations, which can have long-term positive impacts on the well-being of LGBTAI individuals.

Moreover, positive representation can also promote a sense of belonging and community among queer youth. Seeing positive role models and representation in media can help queer youth feel less isolated and more confident in their own identities.

On the other hand, negative or inaccurate media representation can have detrimental effects on the mental health and well-being of queer youth. It can lead to internalized stigma, a sense of shame, and a feeling of not belonging. It can also perpetuate harmful myths and misunderstandings about the community, contributing to further marginalization.

Therefore, it's crucial for media representation of LGBTAI individuals to accurately and positively represent the diversity within the community. This includes recognizing the impact of intersectionality on younger generations and promoting positive messages of acceptance, resilience, and community.

Another important aspect to consider when discussing LGBTAI intersectionality in the media is the impact of representation on the broader society. Media representation can influence public attitudes towards LGBTAI individuals and impact policies and laws that affect the community.

Positive and accurate representation can help reduce prejudice and discrimination towards LGBTAI individuals and promote greater acceptance and understanding within the broader society. It can also promote the visibility and recognition of the community, which can help in advocating for policies and laws that promote equal rights and protections.

Moreover, accurate and positive representation can also promote greater inclusivity and diversity within the broader society. It can challenge stereotypes and harmful myths about the community and encourage greater acceptance of people from different backgrounds and experiences.

On the other hand, negative or inaccurate media representation can perpetuate harmful stereotypes and contribute to further marginalization and discrimination towards LGBTAI individuals. It can also lead to harmful policies and laws that limit the rights and protections of the community.

Therefore, it's crucial for media representation of LGBTAI individuals to accurately and positively represent the diversity within the community. This includes recognizing the impact of intersectionality on the broader society and promoting positive messages of acceptance, resilience, and community.

In summary, understanding intersectionality is crucial for promoting accurate and positive media representation of LGBTAI individuals. Intersectionality can impact media representation in various ways, such as in film, television, news, political and social activism, and impact on younger generations and the broader society. Media representation can influence public attitudes and policies towards the community. Positive and accurate representation can reduce prejudice and discrimination, promote greater acceptance and understanding, and challenge harmful stereotypes. Negative or inaccurate representation can perpetuate marginalization and lead to harmful policies and laws. Therefore, it's crucial for media representation to accurately and positively represent the diversity and complexity of LGBTAI individuals, recognize the impact of intersectionality, and promote positive messages of acceptance, resilience, and community.

TWENTY
LGBTAI And Religion

The intersection of religion and LGBTAI identities is complex and often contentious. For many LGBTAI individuals, their religious beliefs and identities are deeply intertwined and form an important part of their personal and cultural identity. However, religious communities have historically been resistant to accepting and including LGBTAI individuals, leading to a range of challenges and difficulties for those seeking to reconcile their faith and their sexual or gender identity.

One of the primary challenges faced by LGBTAI individuals in religious communities is the stigma and discrimination they often face from fellow congregants and religious leaders. Many religions have traditionally viewed homosexuality and transgender identities as sinful or immoral, leading to exclusion and ostracism of LGBTAI individuals from religious communities. This exclusion can be particularly difficult for those who feel a strong sense of connection and belonging to their faith community.

However, there are also many religious traditions that have embraced LGBTAI acceptance and inclusion. Some denominations have explicitly affirmed the full inclusion and participation of LGBTAI individuals, while others have taken steps to support and welcome these individuals while stopping short of full acceptance. These efforts can take many forms, from creating supportive programs and resources for LGBTAI individuals to advocating for legal protections and equal rights.

One way that some religious communities have attempted to reconcile their beliefs with LGBTAI inclusion is through the reinterpretation of religious texts and traditions. For example, some scholars argue that biblical passages that are often cited as condemning homosexuality are actually being misinterpreted or taken out of context. Similarly, some religious leaders have sought to incorporate more inclusive language and practices into their religious services and teachings.

Despite these efforts, there is still much work to be done to promote LGBTAI acceptance and inclusion in religious communities. Many LGBTAI individuals continue to face discrimination and exclusion from their faith communities, and religious institutions continue to struggle with issues of acceptance and inclusion. However, by continuing to engage in dialogue and advocacy, both LGBTAI individuals and religious leaders can work towards a more inclusive and accepting future.

In recent years, there has been an increasing recognition within many religious communities of the need to support and include LGBTAI individuals. This has been driven in part by a growing awareness of the harms caused by exclusion and discrimination, as well as by changing attitudes towards LGBTAI identities more broadly.

Some religious institutions have taken significant steps to address these issues. For example, many mainline Protestant denominations, including the United Church of Christ and the Episcopal Church, have formally affirmed the full inclusion of LGBTAI individuals in their communities. Similarly, some Jewish and Muslim organizations have developed programs and resources specifically aimed at supporting LGBTAI members of their communities.

There are also a number of faith-based organizations and advocacy groups that work to promote LGBTAI acceptance and inclusion within religious communities. These organizations often provide education and resources to help religious leaders and congregants better understand the experiences of LGBTAI individuals, as well as offering support and advocacy to LGBTAI individuals themselves.

Despite these positive developments, however, there is still significant resistance to LGBTAI acceptance and inclusion within many religious communities. Some religious leaders and congregants continue to view homosexuality and transgender identities as incompatible with their faith, and actively work to exclude and ostracize LGBTAI individuals from their communities. This can lead to significant harms, including feelings of isolation, depression, and even suicide among LGBTAI individuals.

One of the key challenges facing LGBTAI individuals who wish to remain connected to their faith communities is the need to reconcile their beliefs with their sexual or gender identity. For many, this involves a process of reinterpretation and exploration, as they seek to understand how their faith can accommodate their identity. This can be a difficult and often painful process, as it may involve questioning deeply held beliefs and confronting deeply ingrained cultural norms.

Despite these challenges, many LGBTAI individuals are finding ways to reconcile their faith and their identity. This can involve seeking out supportive religious communities, developing their own spiritual practices outside of traditional religious institutions, or advocating for change within their faith communities. By working together to promote understanding and acceptance, both LGBTAI individuals and religious communities can build a more inclusive and welcoming future. It's important to note that the intersection of religion and LGBTAI identities is not a monolithic experience. There is significant diversity among religious traditions, as well as within LGBTAI communities, and the experiences of individuals can vary widely depending on a range of factors.

For example, some LGBTAI individuals may find acceptance and support within more progressive religious communities, while others may face significant challenges and discrimination within those same communities. Similarly, individuals who come from more conservative religious backgrounds may find it more difficult to reconcile their faith with their sexual or gender identity, while those from more liberal backgrounds may face fewer obstacles.

Another factor that can play a significant role in the experiences of LGBTAI individuals within religious communities is geography. In some parts of the world, LGBTAI acceptance and inclusion is more widespread, while in others it is still deeply taboo. This can have a significant impact on the ability of LGBTAI individuals to find supportive religious communities or to reconcile their faith and identity.

Despite these complexities, there are many examples of religious communities that have embraced LGBTAI acceptance and inclusion. For example, some Christian denominations have created liturgies and rituals specifically aimed at welcoming and affirming LGBTAI individuals, while some Buddhist communities have created spaces for queer and trans Buddhists to explore their spirituality in a supportive environment.

Ultimately, the intersection of religion and LGBTAI identities is a complex and multifaceted issue that requires ongoing dialogue and advocacy. By working together to promote understanding and inclusion, both LGBTAI individuals and religious communities can create a more welcoming and supportive future.

One important step towards promoting understanding and inclusion is education. Many religious institutions and organizations have begun to offer educational resources and training aimed at helping religious leaders and congregants better understand the experiences of LGBTAI individuals and the challenges they may face. This can involve exploring the theological and scriptural basis for inclusion, as well as examining the social and cultural factors that contribute to discrimination and exclusion. Another important aspect of promoting inclusion is advocacy. There are many organizations and groups that work to promote LGBTAI acceptance and inclusion within religious communities, often by advocating for policy changes or organizing events and initiatives aimed at promoting understanding and dialogue.

For LGBTAI individuals themselves, finding supportive communities can be a critical step towards reconciling their faith and their identity. This can involve seeking out affirming religious communities, as well as connecting with other LGBTAI individuals who share similar experiences and struggles. Online forums and support groups can be particularly helpful for individuals who live in areas where LGBTAI acceptance is less widespread.

Ultimately, the intersection of religion and LGBTAI identities is a complex and multifaceted issue that requires ongoing attention and dialogue. By working together to promote understanding and inclusion, both LGBTAI individuals and religious communities can create a more welcoming and supportive future.

It's worth noting that the intersection of religion and LGBTAI identities is not a one-sided conversation. While many LGBTAI individuals may face exclusion and discrimination within religious communities, there are also individuals within those communities who face discrimination because of their LGBTAI identities. This can include individuals who are LGBTAI themselves, as well as those who are perceived as being LGBTAI based on their gender expression or other factors.

In addition, there are many religious traditions that have historically embraced LGBTAI individuals and that continue to do so today. For example, some Native American religions have long recognized the importance of gender fluidity and have traditionally included individuals who identify as Two-Spirit or other gender-nonconforming identities. Similarly, some Hindu and Buddhist traditions have long recognized the existence of same-sex desire and have developed rituals and practices aimed at honoring and celebrating these identities.

As with any complex social issue, the intersection of religion and LGBTAI identities requires ongoing attention and dialogue. By working together to promote understanding and inclusion, both LGBTAI individuals and religious communities can create a more welcoming and supportive future. This may involve reinterpreting traditional religious teachings in light of new understandings of gender and sexuality, as well as promoting new rituals and practices that celebrate and honor LGBTAI identities.

Ultimately, the goal should be to create a world in which individuals of all genders and sexual orientations are able to fully participate in their faith communities without fear of discrimination or exclusion. By working towards this goal, we can create a more just and inclusive society for all.

One important aspect of promoting inclusion and acceptance of LGBTAI individuals within religious communities is the role of allies. Allies are individuals who may not themselves identify as LGBTAI, but who are committed to advocating for the rights and well-being of those who do. Allies can play a critical role in promoting understanding and acceptance within religious communities, by challenging stereotypes and promoting education and dialogue.

Religious leaders also have a critical role to play in promoting LGBTAI acceptance and inclusion within their communities. By speaking out against discrimination and advocating for inclusive policies and practices, religious leaders can help create a more welcoming and supportive environment for all members of their community. This may involve engaging in dialogue with members of the LGBTAI community, as well as with other religious leaders and institutions.

In addition to advocacy and education, there are also practical steps that can be taken to promote inclusion and acceptance of LGBTAI individuals within religious communities. For example, creating gender-neutral bathrooms or changing facilities, providing training on LGBTAI issues for religious leaders and congregants, and incorporating inclusive language and imagery into religious services and rituals can all be important steps towards creating a more welcoming and supportive environment.

Ultimately, the intersection of religion and LGBTAI identities is a complex issue that requires ongoing attention and dialogue. By working together to promote understanding, acceptance, and inclusion, we can create a more just and compassionate world for all individuals, regardless of their gender identity or sexual orientation. It's important to note that while progress has been made in many religious communities towards LGBTAI acceptance and inclusion, there is still much work to be done. Many LGBTAI individuals continue to face discrimination, exclusion, and even violence within religious communities, and there is a long way to go before all individuals are able to fully participate in their faith communities without fear of harm or discrimination.

In addition, it's worth acknowledging that the experiences of LGBTAI individuals within religious communities are not monolithic. While many LGBTAI individuals may face rejection and exclusion, others may find acceptance and support within their faith communities. It's important to recognize and celebrate these experiences, and to work towards creating a more inclusive environment for all individuals, regardless of their sexual orientation or gender identity.

The intersection of religion and LGBTAI identities is a complex issue that involves challenges and opportunities for both religious communities and LGBTAI individuals. While some religious traditions have historically embraced LGBTAI individuals, many LGBTAI individuals continue to face discrimination and exclusion within religious communities. Allies and religious leaders can play an important role in promoting understanding and acceptance, while practical steps can be taken towards creating a more inclusive environment. Despite progress made, there is still much work to be done, and it's important to acknowledge the unique challenges faced by LGBTAI individuals who are also members of other marginalized communities. Ultimately, promoting LGBTAI acceptance and inclusion within religious communities requires ongoing education, advocacy, and dialogue.

TWENTY ONE
LGBTAI And Mental Health

Understanding LGBTAI individuals and their mental health is a crucial aspect of promoting inclusive and supportive communities. LGBTAI individuals face unique challenges that can have a significant impact on their mental well-being. In this section, we will explore some of the mental health challenges that LGBTAI individuals may face, provide resources for accessing mental health support, and discuss ways to promote mental health wellness within the LGBTAI community.

Anxiety is a common mental health challenge faced by LGBTAI individuals. Many face discrimination, stigma, and prejudice due to their sexual orientation, gender identity, or intersex status, which can result in chronic stress and anxiety. Fear of rejection, discrimination, and violence can also lead to social anxiety and avoidance of certain situations or environments.

Depression is another mental health challenge that LGBTAI individuals may experience. Discrimination, homophobia, transphobia, and internalized stigma can contribute to feelings of shame, low self-esteem, and hopelessness. In addition, the challenges of coming out, dealing with family rejection, and societal prejudice can lead to depression and other mood disorders.

Post-traumatic stress disorder (PTSD) is also a mental health challenge that some LGBTAI individuals may face. Many LGBTAI individuals have experienced traumatic events such as hate crimes, harassment, and violence due to their sexual orientation, gender identity, or intersex status. These experiences can result in PTSD, which may manifest in symptoms such as flashbacks, nightmares, and hypervigilance.

Accessing mental health support is essential for LGBTAI individuals who may be facing mental health challenges. There are resources available that specifically cater to the unique needs of the LGBTAI community. LGBTQ+ inclusive mental health providers, support groups, and helplines can provide valuable assistance. Online resources, such as LGBTQ+ friendly mental health apps, websites, and forums, can also provide a safe space for individuals to seek support and information.

Promoting mental health wellness within the LGBTAI community is crucial for fostering resilience and well-being. Creating safe and inclusive spaces that respect and affirm individuals' sexual orientation, gender identity, and intersex status can be empowering. Providing opportunities for social connection, such as LGBTQ+ community events and support groups, can also foster a sense of belonging and reduce social isolation. Promoting self-care strategies, such as mindfulness, exercise, and healthy coping skills, can also support mental health wellness.

It's important to recognize that mental health challenges faced by LGBTAI individuals may intersect with other aspects of their identity, such as race, ethnicity, religion, disability, and socioeconomic status. Intersectional experiences of discrimination and oppression can compound the challenges and impact mental health outcomes. It's important to acknowledge and address these intersecting identities in the context of mental health support and promotion.

Another critical aspect of understanding LGBTAI and mental health is the concept of "minority stress." Minority stress refers to the unique stressors and challenges that arise from being a sexual or gender minority in a society that may not fully accept or affirm these identities. This can include internalized stigma, discrimination, violence, rejection from family or friends, and the constant need to navigate heteronormative or cisnormative spaces. Minority stress can contribute to mental health challenges, and it's essential to recognize and validate these experiences.

Building supportive networks and communities is crucial for the mental health wellness of LGBTAI individuals. LGBTQ+ support groups, social organizations, and community events can provide a sense of belonging, validation, and support. These spaces allow individuals to connect with others who share similar experiences, reduce social isolation, and build resilience. Peer support and mentorship programs can also provide valuable support, especially for LGBTQ+ youth who may face unique challenges in their journey of self-acceptance and identity formation.

Education and awareness about mental health and LGBTQ+ issues are also important. Promoting education and understanding about sexual orientation, gender identity, and intersex status can help reduce stigma, discrimination, and misinformation. This can be done through public campaigns, workshops, and inclusive educational materials that address mental health and LGBTQ+ issues. Creating safe and inclusive spaces in schools, workplaces, and healthcare settings that affirm and respect LGBTQ+ individuals can also contribute to mental health wellness.

Access to affirming and inclusive mental health services is crucial for LGBTAI individuals. LGBTQ+ affirmative therapy, counseling, and psychiatry can provide specialized support that acknowledges and validates individuals' sexual orientation, gender identity, and intersex status. Mental health providers who are knowledgeable about LGBTQ+ issues, and who actively engage in ongoing education and training, can provide competent and inclusive care.

In addition to professional support, online resources such as LGBTQ+ mental health apps, websites, and forums can provide valuable information, resources, and support. These online platforms can be accessible and convenient for individuals who may face barriers to in-person services, such as rural or remote communities, lack of transportation, or financial limitations.

1. **Resilience And Coping Strategies:** Many LGBTAI individuals develop resilience and coping strategies to navigate the unique challenges they may face. These can include developing a support system of chosen family and friends, finding safe spaces and communities, practicing self-care, and engaging in advocacy and activism. Recognizing and celebrating the resilience and strengths of LGBTAI individuals can promote mental health wellness and empower individuals to overcome challenges.

2. **Mental Health Disparities:** Research has shown that LGBTAI individuals may face mental health disparities compared to their cisgender heterosexual peers. Discrimination, stigma, and prejudice can contribute to higher rates of mental health conditions, such as anxiety, depression, and substance abuse. It's important to acknowledge and address these disparities and work towards reducing the societal and structural factors that contribute to them.

3. **Support For Coming Out And Gender Affirmation:** Coming out as LGBTAI and navigating gender affirmation can be a significant process that impacts mental health. Some individuals may face rejection from family, friends, or society, while others may experience discrimination, harassment, or violence. Providing support for individuals who are coming out or seeking gender affirmation, such as access to gender-affirming healthcare, legal protection, and mental health support, is crucial in promoting mental health wellness.

4. **Mental Health Considerations For Transgender And Intersex Individuals:** Transgender and intersex individuals may face unique mental health challenges related to their gender identity and intersex status. These can include dysphoria, discrimination, difficulties

accessing healthcare, and challenges related to social acceptance and inclusion. It's important to acknowledge and address the mental health needs of transgender and intersex individuals, including access to affirming and competent mental health care.

5. **Culturally Competent Care:** Providing culturally competent care that recognizes and affirms the diverse identities within the LGBTAI community is essential. This includes understanding the intersectionality of identities, using inclusive language and terminology, and being knowledgeable about the unique challenges and strengths of LGBTAI individuals. Mental health providers should strive to create a safe, non-judgmental, and affirming environment that respects the autonomy and experiences of individuals from the LGBTAI community.

6. **Advocacy And Policy Change:** Advocacy efforts and policy change at the societal and systemic levels are crucial in promoting mental health wellness within the LGBTAI community. This can include advocating for anti-discrimination laws, inclusive policies in schools and workplaces, and increased access to affirming mental health services. Engaging in advocacy and policy change can help address the structural and systemic factors that contribute to mental health challenges faced by LGBTAI individuals.

7. **Trauma And Discrimination:** Many LGBTAI individuals have experienced trauma and discrimination due to their sexual orientation, gender identity, or intersex status. This can include bullying, harassment, assault, and discrimination in various aspects of life, such as housing, employment, healthcare, and education. These experiences can have a significant impact on mental health and may result in conditions such as post-traumatic stress disorder (PTSD) and complex trauma. It's crucial to recognize and address the trauma and discrimination that LGBTAI individuals may face and provide appropriate mental health support.

8. **Minority Stress:** LGBTAI individuals may also experience minority stress, which refers to the chronic stress and discrimination that comes from being a member of a marginalized group. Minority stress can contribute to mental health challenges such as anxiety, depression, and substance abuse. It's important to understand and acknowledge the impact of minority stress on the mental health of LGBTAI individuals and create environments that promote acceptance, inclusion, and respect.

9. **Intersectionality And Mental Health:** Intersectionality refers to the ways in which different identities intersect and interact, such as

race, ethnicity, religion, disability, and socioeconomic status. LGBTAI individuals may have multiple marginalized identities that can compound the challenges they face and impact their mental health. It's essential to understand the intersectional experiences of LGBTAI individuals and provide inclusive and affirming mental health support that recognizes and addresses these intersecting identities.

10. **Access To Mental Health Support:** Access to affirming and culturally competent mental health services is critical for the mental health and well-being of LGBTAI individuals. However, barriers such as cost, insurance coverage, geographical location, and discrimination can limit access to quality mental health care. It's important to promote and advocate for increased access to affordable, affirming, and inclusive mental health services for the LGBTAI community.

11. **Peer Support And Community Resources:** Peer support and community resources can play a crucial role in promoting mental health wellness within the LGBTAI community. Supportive networks, such as LGBTQ+ support groups, can provide a sense of belonging, validation, and understanding. Additionally, community resources such as LGBTQ+ community centers, helplines, and online forums can offer valuable information, resources, and support for mental health challenges.

12. **Self-Care And Wellness:** Self-care and wellness practices can be beneficial for the mental health of LGBTAI individuals. Engaging in activities that promote self-care, such as exercise, mindfulness, healthy relationships, and self-compassion, can help build resilience, manage stress, and promote overall mental health and well-being.

13. **Culturally Competent Mental Health Care:** Culturally competent mental health care is essential for LGBTAI individuals, as it takes into consideration their unique experiences, identities, and challenges. Mental health professionals should receive training on LGBTQ+ issues, including sexual orientation, gender identity, and intersex status, to better understand the specific mental health needs of the LGBTAI community. This includes using affirming language, respecting chosen names and pronouns, understanding the impact of discrimination and minority stress, and providing appropriate and inclusive care.

14. **Family And Social Support:** Family and social support can have a significant impact on the mental health of LGBTAI individuals. Accepting and supportive families, friends, and communities can

provide a protective buffer against mental health challenges, while rejection, discrimination, and lack of support can contribute to mental health issues. It's important to foster acceptance, understanding, and support within families, communities, and social networks to promote mental health wellness for LGBTAI individuals.

15. **Resilience And Coping Skills:** LGBTAI individuals often develop resilience and coping skills to navigate the challenges they face. Resilience refers to the ability to bounce back from adversity and cope with challenges, while coping skills are strategies and techniques used to manage stress and emotional difficulties. Recognizing and building on the resilience and coping skills of LGBTAI individuals can be a crucial part of promoting mental health wellness.

16. **Promoting Mental Health Awareness And Education:** Promoting mental health awareness and education within the LGBTAI community can help reduce stigma, increase knowledge about mental health, and encourage seeking help when needed. This can include educational workshops, awareness campaigns, and community events that focus on mental health topics relevant to the LGBTAI community, such as coming out, gender dysphoria, and navigating discrimination.

17. **Advocacy And Policy Changes:** Advocacy and policy changes at local, national, and international levels can help promote mental health wellness within the LGBTAI community. This can include advocating for anti-discrimination laws, policies that promote inclusive mental health care, and measures to address minority stress, trauma, and discrimination. By advocating for policy changes, we can create more supportive environments for the mental health of LGBTAI individuals.

18. **Crisis Intervention And Suicide Prevention:** LGBTAI individuals may be at increased risk for mental health crises, including suicidal ideation and attempts, due to the challenges they face, such as discrimination, rejection, and minority stress. It's important to have crisis intervention and suicide prevention resources that are specifically tailored to the LGBTAI community, including helplines, online chat support, and counseling services.

19. **Intersectionality:** It's important to recognize that LGBTAI individuals may face additional challenges related to their intersecting identities, such as race, ethnicity, religion, disability, and socio-economic status. These intersecting identities can impact mental health in complex ways and may require intersectional approaches to

mental health care. Mental health professionals should be aware of and address the intersectional experiences and challenges faced by LGBTAI individuals to provide inclusive and effective care.

20. **Trauma-Informed Care:** Many LGBTAI individuals may have experienced trauma, including discrimination, violence, and rejection, which can have significant impacts on mental health. Trauma-informed care involves understanding the effects of trauma and providing care that is sensitive, compassionate, and empowering. Mental health professionals should be trained in trauma-informed care and recognize the potential trauma experiences of LGBTAI individuals to provide appropriate care and support.

21. **Substance Abuse:** LGBTAI individuals may be at increased risk for substance abuse as a way to cope with discrimination, stigma, and mental health challenges. Substance abuse can have detrimental effects on mental health and overall well-being. It's important to address substance abuse issues in the LGBTAI community through prevention, intervention, and treatment strategies that are inclusive and affirming.

22. **Access To Mental Health Care:** LGBTAI individuals may face barriers to accessing mental health care, such as lack of financial resources, discrimination, and fear of stigma. It's important to ensure that mental health care is accessible, affordable, and inclusive for all individuals, regardless of their sexual orientation, gender identity, or intersex status. This includes advocating for policies and practices that promote equal access to mental health care for the LGBTAI community.

23. **Self-Care And Self-Compassion:** Self-care and self-compassion are important aspects of mental health wellness for LGBTAI individuals. Encouraging self-care practices, such as engaging in physical activity, mindfulness, healthy relationships, and self-compassionate self-talk, can help promote mental well-being. Mental health professionals can provide guidance and support on self-care and self-compassion strategies that are relevant to the experiences of LGBTAI individuals.

24. **Peer Support And Community Engagement:** Peer support and community engagement can be valuable resources for LGBTAI individuals to cope with mental health challenges. Connecting with peers who share similar experiences and engaging in supportive communities, such as LGBTQ+ organizations, can provide a sense of belonging, validation, and empowerment. Peer support and

community engagement can be an important part of promoting mental health wellness and resilience in the LGBTAI community.

In conclusion, understanding the unique mental health challenges faced by LGBTAI individuals and implementing inclusive and affirming approaches to mental health care is crucial. This includes recognizing the impact of intersectionality, providing trauma-informed care, addressing substance abuse, ensuring access to mental health care, promoting self-care and self-compassion, and fostering peer support and community engagement. By taking a holistic and inclusive approach to mental health, we can support the mental well-being of the LGBTAI community and promote a more equitable and affirming society.

TWENTY TWO
LGBTAI In International Contexts

In some countries, homosexuality and transgender identities are criminalized, leading to legal discrimination, harassment, and violence against LGBTAI individuals. For example, in several African and Middle Eastern countries, same-sex relationships are punishable by law, and being openly LGBTAI can result in severe penalties, including imprisonment or even the death penalty. In other countries, LGBTAI individuals face social stigma, discrimination, and exclusion from various aspects of life, including employment, housing, healthcare, and education. In some cases, societal attitudes and cultural norms may be deeply ingrained, making it challenging for LGBTAI individuals to express their identities openly or seek support.

Moreover, in some regions, transgender individuals face significant challenges, including difficulties in accessing healthcare, obtaining legal recognition of their gender identity, and facing discrimination and violence in public spaces. Intersex individuals, who are born with physical traits that do not fit typical definitions of male or female, may also face discrimination and lack of recognition in various countries, leading to violations of their rights and well-being.

Despite these challenges, there are global movements and organizations that work towards promoting LGBTAI rights and inclusion in different countries. Many human rights organizations, advocacy groups, and LGBTQIA+ activists engage in activism, lobbying, and legal efforts to challenge discriminatory laws and practices. International organizations such as the United Nations (UN) and the European Union (EU) also advocate for LGBTAI rights and promote equality through various initiatives and policies. Additionally, local LGBTQIA+ communities and grassroots movements play a significant role in advocating for change, raising awareness, and providing support to LGBTAI individuals in different cultural contexts.

It's important to recognize that the progress and challenges related to LGBTAI acceptance and inclusion vary widely across different countries and cultural contexts. Understanding these differences is crucial to developing effective strategies and interventions that promote LGBTAI rights and well-being globally. It's important to respect and understand the unique challenges faced by LGBTAI individuals in different countries while working towards creating a more inclusive and accepting world for everyone, regardless of their sexual orientation, gender identity, or intersex status. Overall, addressing legal and social barriers, promoting awareness and education, and advocating for human rights and social justice are vital steps towards achieving equality for LGBTAI individuals in international contexts. So, it's important to continue to support and amplify the voices of LGBTAI communities around the world and work towards a more inclusive and accepting world for everyone. Remember that the situation and experiences of LGBTAI individuals may change over time, and it's important to stay updated on the latest developments and strive for positive change. It's important to promote and celebrate diversity and inclusion, and work towards a world where all individuals, regardless of their sexual orientation, gender identity, or intersex status, can live with dignity, respect, and equality. Let's strive for a world that embraces and celebrates the diversity of human experiences and identities! Remember to always be sensitive to different cultural contexts and to respect and honor the unique challenges and experiences of LGBTAI individuals in different countries and regions. Together, we can work towards a more inclusive and accepting world for all individuals, regardless of their sexual orientation, gender identity, or intersex status.

Striving for a world where everyone, including LGBTAI individuals, can live with dignity, respect, and equality is a crucial goal. It requires ongoing efforts at various levels, including legal, social, cultural, and individual changes. It's important to promote acceptance, inclusion, and understanding of diverse sexual orientations, gender identities, and intersex status across different countries and cultural contexts.

This can be achieved through education and awareness-raising initiatives that challenge stereotypes, promote tolerance, and foster empathy towards LGBTAI individuals. It also involves advocating for changes in discriminatory laws and policies, and promoting equal rights and protections for all individuals, regardless of their sexual orientation, gender identity, or intersex status. Supporting local LGBTQIA+ communities, grassroots movements, and human rights organizations that work towards LGBTAI equality and inclusion is also crucial.

In addition, fostering a culture of respect, inclusivity, and acceptance within families, schools, workplaces, and communities is essential in creating an environment where LGBTAI individuals can thrive without fear of discrimination, harassment, or violence. Engaging in meaningful dialogues, promoting allyship, and actively challenging discrimination and prejudice in all its forms are important steps towards building a more inclusive world.

It's also important to remember that intersectionality plays a significant role in the experiences of LGBTAI individuals, as they may face multiple forms of discrimination and oppression based on their sexual orientation, gender identity, race, ethnicity, religion, disability, and other intersecting identities. Recognizing and addressing these intersecting forms of discrimination is crucial in promoting true inclusivity and equality for all individuals.

Points to consider when exploring the challenges faced by LGBTAI individuals in international contexts:

1. **Legal Barriers:** Laws and policies related to sexual orientation, gender identity, and intersex status vary widely across different countries and cultural contexts. In some countries, being openly LGBTAI can be illegal and result in severe consequences, including imprisonment, fines, or even the death penalty. In other countries, LGBTAI individuals may face discrimination in areas such as employment, housing, healthcare, and education. Legal recognition of same-sex relationships, access to gender-affirming healthcare, and protection from discrimination based on sexual orientation, gender identity, or intersex status are important issues that may vary significantly across countries.

2. **Social and Cultural Barriers:** Cultural norms, beliefs, and attitudes towards sexual orientation, gender identity, and intersex status can significantly impact the acceptance and inclusion of LGBTAI individuals. In some countries, societal prejudice, stigma, and discrimination against LGBTAI individuals may be deeply ingrained in cultural or religious beliefs, leading to social isolation, discrimination, and violence. Coming out, being open about one's sexual orientation, gender identity, or intersex status, or seeking support may be met with social ostracism, family rejection, or even violence in certain contexts.

3. **Global Movements and Organizations:** Despite these challenges, there are numerous global movements and organizations that are working tirelessly to promote equality and inclusion for LGBTAI individuals worldwide. International human rights organizations, LGBTQIA+ advocacy groups, and grassroots movements are actively advocating for policy changes, legal reforms, and social acceptance of LGBTAI individuals in different countries. These efforts often include raising awareness, engaging in advocacy and activism, providing support and resources, and fostering collaborations across borders to create positive change.

4. **Intersectionality:** As mentioned earlier, intersectionality plays a significant role in the experiences of LGBTAI individuals in international contexts. The discrimination and oppression faced by LGBTAI individuals may intersect with other forms of discrimination based on factors such as race, ethnicity, religion, disability, socioeconomic status, and more. Understanding and addressing these intersectionalities is crucial in creating inclusive policies and practices that recognize and address the unique challenges faced by LGBTAI individuals with intersecting identities.

5. **Progress and Challenges:** While progress has been made in many countries towards greater acceptance and inclusion of LGBTAI individuals, there are still significant challenges to overcome. Legal and social changes take time and effort, and progress may be slow or face setbacks in different cultural contexts. It's important to acknowledge the progress that has been made while also recognizing the ongoing challenges and the need for continued advocacy and action to promote equality and inclusion for LGBTAI individuals around the world.

6. **Health Disparities:** LGBTAI individuals may face unique health disparities in different countries due to discrimination, stigma, and lack of access to healthcare services. LGBTAI individuals may face challenges in accessing gender-affirming healthcare, mental health services, and sexual health services. In some countries, there may be limited availability of resources and support for LGBTAI individuals, resulting in increased health risks and poorer health outcomes.

7. **Migration and Asylum:** LGBTAI individuals may face specific challenges related to migration and seeking asylum in international contexts. Some LGBTAI individuals may be forced to flee their home countries due to discrimination, violence, or persecution. However, seeking asylum in other countries may also pose challenges, as LGBTAI individuals may face discrimination and barriers to accessing legal protection and support. Additionally, immigration policies in different countries may not adequately recognize or protect the rights of LGBTAI asylum seekers.

8. **Local Activism and Resistance:** LGBTAI individuals and organizations in different countries may engage in local activism and resistance to challenge discrimination and promote acceptance and inclusion. They may work towards changing laws, challenging discriminatory practices, and advocating for policy reforms in their local contexts. These local efforts may face challenges, such as backlash from conservative forces, lack of support from local

authorities, and limited resources. Recognizing and supporting local activism and resistance is crucial in promoting change at the grassroots level.

9. **Cultural Sensitivity:** Understanding the cultural nuances and context of different countries is important when addressing the challenges faced by LGBTAI individuals in international contexts. Approaches that work in one cultural context may not be applicable or effective in another. It is important to approach the issue with cultural sensitivity, respecting local customs, traditions, and beliefs, while also promoting human rights and equality for LGBTAI individuals.

10. **Global Solidarity:** Solidarity and collaboration among LGBTQIA+ communities globally can be a powerful force for change. Building networks, partnerships, and alliances among LGBTAI individuals and organizations in different countries can amplify their voices, strengthen their advocacy efforts, and create global movements for equality and inclusion. Global solidarity can also provide support and resources to LGBTAI individuals and organizations facing challenges and discrimination in their local contexts.

11. **Legal and Policy Frameworks:** The legal and policy frameworks related to LGBTQIA+ rights vary widely across different countries and cultural contexts. In some countries, there may be laws that criminalize same-sex relationships, transgender identities, or intersex traits, leading to discrimination, harassment, and violence against LGBTAI individuals. In contrast, other countries may have progressive laws that protect LGBTQIA+ rights and promote inclusion. Understanding the legal and policy frameworks in different countries is critical to understanding the challenges faced by LGBTAI individuals and advocating for change.

12. **Social and Cultural Norms:** Social and cultural norms around sexual orientation, gender identity, and intersex status vary greatly across different countries and cultural contexts. Some societies may be more accepting and inclusive of LGBTAI individuals, while others may have deeply ingrained prejudices and discrimination against them. Social and cultural norms play a significant role in shaping the experiences and challenges faced by LGBTAI individuals, including societal acceptance, family acceptance, workplace discrimination, and access to social services. Understanding these norms is essential in addressing the challenges and promoting acceptance for LGBTAI individuals.

13. **Intersectionality:** Intersectionality refers to the ways in which different forms of oppression and discrimination, such as sexism, racism, ableism, and homophobia, intersect and compound the challenges faced by individuals with multiple marginalized identities. LGBTAI individuals who also belong to other marginalized groups, such as people of color, people with disabilities, or migrants, may face compounded discrimination and challenges. Understanding intersectionality is important in addressing the unique challenges faced by LGBTAI individuals and promoting inclusive and intersectional approaches to LGBTQIA+ rights advocacy.

14. **Global Movements and Organizations:** There are numerous global movements and organizations that work towards promoting LGBTQIA+ rights, inclusivity, and acceptance across borders. These movements and organizations engage in advocacy, capacity-building, and awareness-raising efforts to promote change at the global level. They provide support, resources, and solidarity to LGBTAI individuals and organizations facing challenges in different countries, and foster international collaborations for change. Understanding and engaging with global movements and organizations can be instrumental in promoting LGBTQIA+ rights in international contexts.

15. **Impact of Colonialism and Globalization:** The impact of colonialism and globalization on LGBTQIA+ rights and acceptance in different countries and cultural contexts cannot be understated. Colonial-era laws, ideologies, and religious beliefs have shaped societal attitudes towards sexual orientation, gender identity, and intersex status in many countries. Globalization has also led to the spread of Western notions of LGBTQIA+ identities and rights, which can clash with local cultural norms and beliefs. Understanding the historical and cultural context of colonialism and globalization is crucial in comprehending the challenges faced by LGBTAI individuals in international contexts.

16. **Religious and Cultural Beliefs:** Religious and cultural beliefs play a significant role in shaping attitudes towards sexual orientation, gender identity, and intersex status in different countries and cultural contexts. Some religions and cultures may have traditional beliefs that are not accepting or inclusive of LGBTAI individuals, leading to discrimination, stigma, and violence. Understanding the role of religion and culture in shaping LGBTQIA+ rights and acceptance is crucial in addressing the challenges faced by LGBTAI individuals in

international contexts, while also respecting diverse cultural and religious perspectives.

17. **Health and Well-being:** The health and well-being of LGBTAI individuals in international contexts can be affected by various factors, including discrimination, violence, stigma, and lack of access to healthcare. LGBTAI individuals may face challenges in accessing LGBTQIA+-affirming healthcare services, mental health support, and sexual and reproductive health services. The impact of discrimination and stigma on the mental health, physical health, and overall well-being of LGBTAI individuals should be considered in discussions about international challenges faced by this community.

18. **Migration and Displacement:** LGBTQIA+ individuals who are forcibly displaced, such as refugees or asylum seekers, may face unique challenges in international contexts. They may face discrimination, violence, and persecution in their home countries, as well as challenges in seeking asylum or resettlement in other countries. The intersectionality of their LGBTQIA+ status with their migration or displacement status can complicate their situation and increase their vulnerability. Understanding the challenges faced by LGBTQIA+ individuals who are migrants or forcibly displaced is critical in addressing their unique needs and promoting their rights and well-being.

19. **Language and Communication:** Language and communication can also be challenges for LGBTAI individuals in international contexts. LGBTQIA+-related terminologies, concepts, and issues may be culturally and linguistically specific, and may not have direct equivalents in different languages or cultural contexts. This can create challenges in communication, understanding, and advocacy efforts. Considering the nuances of language and communication in discussing LGBTAI individuals in international contexts is important in promoting effective communication and understanding across different cultures and languages.

20. **Local LGBTQIA+ Activism:** It's important to recognize and highlight the efforts of local LGBTQIA+ activists and organizations in different countries and cultural contexts. These individuals and organizations work tirelessly to advocate for LGBTQIA+ rights, promote acceptance, and create change within their local communities. Understanding the local LGBTQIA+ activism landscape, challenges, and strategies employed by local activists is crucial in supporting their efforts and promoting LGBTQIA+ rights in international contexts.

21. **Intersectionality:** Intersectionality is an important aspect to consider when discussing the challenges faced by LGBTAI individuals in international contexts. LGBTAI individuals may also face discrimination and marginalization based on other intersecting factors, such as race, ethnicity, religion, disability, socioeconomic status, and age. Intersectional discrimination can compound the challenges faced by LGBTAI individuals, making it important to understand the multiple layers of oppression they may experience in different countries and cultural contexts.

22. **Legal and Policy Frameworks:** The legal and policy frameworks pertaining to LGBTAI rights vary significantly across different countries and cultural contexts. Some countries have progressive laws that protect the rights of LGBTAI individuals, while others have regressive laws that criminalize same-sex relationships, gender non-conformity, or intersex status. Understanding the legal and policy frameworks in different countries is essential in advocating for legal reforms, promoting human rights, and addressing the challenges faced by LGBTAI individuals in international contexts.

23. **Social and Cultural Norms:** Social and cultural norms play a significant role in shaping attitudes towards LGBTAI individuals in different countries and cultural contexts. Some societies may have deeply entrenched traditional or cultural beliefs that are not accepting of sexual orientation, gender identity, or intersex status, leading to discrimination, stigma, and ostracization of LGBTAI individuals. Understanding the social and cultural norms in different countries and cultural contexts is critical in addressing the challenges faced by LGBTAI individuals and promoting acceptance and inclusivity.

24. **Global Movements and Organizations:** There are several global movements and organizations that work towards promoting LGBTQIA+ rights and equality in international contexts. These movements and organizations engage in advocacy, awareness-raising, capacity-building, and community mobilization efforts to promote acceptance, inclusivity, and equality for LGBTAI individuals around the world. Understanding the role of global movements and organizations in advocating for LGBTQIA+ rights in different countries and cultural contexts can provide valuable insights into the progress made, challenges faced, and strategies employed in advancing LGBTQIA+ rights internationally.

25. **International Cooperation and Diplomacy:** International cooperation and diplomacy play a significant role in promoting LGBTAI rights globally. International organizations, governments,

and civil society organizations work together to advocate for LGBTQIA+ rights at international forums, engage in diplomatic efforts, and build alliances to promote acceptance, inclusivity, and equality for LGBTAI individuals. Understanding the role of international cooperation and diplomacy in advancing LGBTQIA+ rights in different countries and cultural contexts is crucial in promoting change at a global level.

26. **Media and Representation:** Media representation of LGBTAI individuals can also be a challenge in international contexts. Media can perpetuate stereotypes, misinformation, and discrimination against LGBTAI individuals, or it can play a positive role in promoting acceptance, inclusivity, and equality. Understanding the role of media and representation in shaping attitudes towards LGBTAI individuals in different countries and cultural contexts is important in promoting accurate and positive representation and countering discriminatory narratives.

In conclusion, exploring the challenges faced by LGBTAI individuals in international contexts requires a comprehensive understanding of various factors, including intersectionality, legal and policy frameworks, social and cultural norms, global movements and organizations, international cooperation and diplomacy, and media and representation. By considering these factors, we can better understand the complex challenges faced by LGBTAI individuals in different countries and cultural contexts, and work towards promoting acceptance, inclusivity, and equality for all individuals, regardless of their sexual orientation, gender identity, or intersex status.

TWENTY THREE
LGBTAI And Disability

One major challenge for LGBTAI individuals with disabilities is accessibility. Accessibility refers to the physical, social, and attitudinal barriers that can limit the participation of individuals with disabilities in various aspects of life, such as employment, education, healthcare, social activities, and community engagement. For example, individuals with physical disabilities may face barriers in accessing public transportation, buildings, or events, while individuals with sensory disabilities may face challenges in accessing information or communication.

Moreover, LGBTAI individuals with disabilities may also experience discrimination and prejudice based on both their sexual orientation, gender identity, or expression, as well as their disability status. This can result in double discrimination, also known as intersectional discrimination, where an individual faces discrimination based on multiple aspects of their identity. This can include discrimination in employment, housing, healthcare, and other areas of life.

Another challenge is the lack of representation and visibility of LGBTAI individuals with disabilities in both the LGBTAI and disability communities. This can lead to feelings of isolation and exclusion, and can limit access to supportive networks and resources. For example, disability spaces may not always be welcoming or inclusive of LGBTAI individuals, and LGBTAI spaces may not always be aware of or address the specific needs and experiences of individuals with disabilities.

Despite these challenges, there are also examples of disability communities embracing LGBTAI acceptance and inclusion. Many disability advocacy groups and organizations recognize the importance of intersectionality and strive to create inclusive spaces that affirm the identities and experiences of all individuals, including those who identify as LGBTAI. This can include promoting policies and practices that promote accessibility, addressing discrimination and prejudice, and advocating for inclusive representation and visibility.

Furthermore, some LGBTAI communities and organizations also recognize and advocate for the inclusion and acceptance of individuals with disabilities. This can include promoting accessible events and spaces, raising awareness about disability issues, and advocating for policies and practices that support the rights and well-being of LGBTAI individuals with disabilities.

It's important to recognize that the experiences of LGBTAI individuals with disabilities are diverse and multifaceted, and that individuals may face different challenges depending on their specific identities and intersections. It's crucial to foster inclusive spaces that recognize and address the unique needs and experiences of individuals at the intersection of disability and LGBTAI identities, and to promote acceptance, accessibility, and inclusion for all individuals, regardless of their sexual orientation, gender identity, expression, or disability status. By recognizing and addressing these challenges, we can work towards a more inclusive and equitable society for all individuals. So, it's important to foster inclusive spaces that recognize and address the unique needs and experiences of individuals at the intersection of disability and LGBTAI identities, and to promote acceptance, accessibility, and inclusion for all individuals, regardless of their sexual orientation, gender identity, expression, or disability status.

Points to consider when exploring the intersection of disability and LGBTAI identities:

1. **Invisibility and Erasure:** LGBTAI individuals with disabilities often face invisibility and erasure within both the LGBTAI and disability communities. Their experiences and identities may not be fully recognized or understood, which can lead to a lack of support and representation. It's important to actively acknowledge and validate the existence and experiences of individuals at the intersection of disability and LGBTAI identities, and to create inclusive spaces that center their voices and perspectives.

2. **Unique Health and Wellness Needs:** LGBTAI individuals with disabilities may have unique health and wellness needs that require specific support and accommodations. For example, individuals with disabilities may require assistance with mobility, communication, or other daily living activities, and may also have specific healthcare needs related to their disability. LGBTAI individuals with disabilities may also face challenges in accessing affirming healthcare and mental health services that understand and address their specific identities and experiences.

3. **Discrimination and Bias:** LGBTAI individuals with disabilities may face discrimination and bias from multiple fronts, including ableism (discrimination based on disability) and homophobia/transphobia (discrimination based on sexual

orientation or gender identity). This can result in compounded challenges and negative impacts on their mental and emotional well-being. It's important to recognize and address these intersecting forms of discrimination, and to promote inclusive policies and practices that protect the rights and well-being of individuals at the intersection of disability and LGBTAI identities.

4. **Intersectional Advocacy**: Advocacy efforts for LGBTAI rights and disability rights should also recognize and address the intersectionality of identities. This means advocating for policies and practices that explicitly include and protect the rights of individuals at the intersection of disability and LGBTAI identities. This can include advocating for accessible spaces and events, inclusive policies in employment and housing, and addressing discrimination and prejudice based on both disability and LGBTAI status.

5. **Inclusive Language and Representation:** The use of inclusive language and representation is important when discussing the intersection of disability and LGBTAI identities. This includes using language that acknowledges and respects the diverse identities and experiences of individuals at this intersection, and promoting inclusive representation in media, public discourse, and advocacy efforts. It's important to use language that respects individuals' chosen identities and expressions, and to actively include and center individuals with disabilities who identify as LGBTAI in discussions, events, and advocacy efforts.

6. **Resilience and Strength:** Despite facing unique challenges, individuals at the intersection of disability and LGBTAI identities often demonstrate resilience, strength, and resilience. They navigate multiple forms of discrimination and prejudice, and may find support and strength within their communities. It's important to acknowledge and celebrate the resilience and strength of individuals at the intersection of disability and LGBTAI identities, and to amplify their voices and stories.

7. **Intersectional Acceptance and Inclusion:** Some disability communities have embraced LGBTAI acceptance and inclusion, recognizing that individuals at the intersection of disability and LGBTAI identities face unique challenges and discrimination. Disability communities that prioritize intersectional acceptance and inclusion promote policies, practices, and spaces that are inclusive and affirming for individuals with diverse sexual orientations and gender identities, including those with disabilities. This can include creating safe and welcoming spaces, providing accessible resources

and information, and advocating for inclusive policies that protect the rights of individuals at the intersection of disability and LGBTAI identities.

8. **Access to Resources and Support:** LGBTAI individuals with disabilities may face barriers in accessing resources and support that are inclusive and affirming. This can include limited access to information, support groups, counseling, and other resources that understand and address the unique experiences and identities of individuals at the intersection of disability and LGBTAI identities. It's important to ensure that resources and support services are accessible, inclusive, and affirming for individuals with diverse identities, including those at the intersection of disability and LGBTAI identities.

9. **Intersectional Advocacy and Allyship:** Advocacy efforts for LGBTAI rights and disability rights can be strengthened by recognizing and addressing the intersectionality of identities. This includes engaging in intersectional advocacy and allyship, which involves actively acknowledging and addressing the unique challenges and discrimination faced by individuals at the intersection of disability and LGBTAI identities. This can include supporting inclusive policies and practices, amplifying the voices of individuals at the intersection of disability and LGBTAI identities, and advocating for the rights and well-being of all individuals, regardless of their identities or disabilities.

10. **Education and Awareness:** Increasing education and awareness about the intersection of disability and LGBTAI identities is crucial in promoting inclusion and acceptance. This includes educating ourselves and others about the diverse experiences, challenges, and strengths of individuals at the intersection of disability and LGBTAI identities, and raising awareness about the importance of inclusivity and intersectionality in all aspects of society. By promoting education and awareness, we can foster a culture of acceptance, understanding, and inclusion that values and respects the diverse identities and experiences of all individuals.

One important aspect of promoting inclusivity is to ensure that spaces, resources, and services are accessible to all individuals, including those with disabilities. This can include providing physical accessibility accommodations such as ramps, elevators, and braille signage, as well as ensuring that digital resources and online spaces are accessible for individuals with visual, auditory, or cognitive disabilities. By prioritizing accessibility, we can ensure that individuals at the intersection of disability and LGBTAI identities have equal opportunities to participate in all aspects of life, including social, cultural, and educational activities.

Another crucial aspect is addressing discrimination and prejudice faced by individuals at the intersection of disability and LGBTAI identities. These individuals may face discrimination based on their sexual orientation, gender identity, expression, and disability status, which can have detrimental effects on their mental and physical health. It's important to advocate for inclusive policies and practices that protect the rights of individuals at the intersection of disability and LGBTAI identities, and to actively combat discrimination and prejudice in all forms. This can include advocating for anti-discrimination laws, promoting inclusive policies in healthcare and social services, and raising awareness about the harmful effects of discrimination on individuals' well-being.

Additionally, fostering acceptance and inclusion within disability communities is crucial. Some disability communities have made significant progress in embracing LGBTAI acceptance and inclusion, recognizing that diversity and inclusivity are fundamental values. This can include creating safe and welcoming spaces for individuals with diverse sexual orientations and gender identities within disability communities, promoting awareness and education about LGBTAI identities, and actively supporting individuals at the intersection of disability and LGBTAI identities through advocacy efforts and allyship. By fostering acceptance and inclusion within disability communities, we can create supportive and empowering spaces where individuals with diverse identities can thrive and be celebrated for who they are.

In conclusion, the intersection of disability and LGBTAI identities presents unique challenges and opportunities for acceptance, inclusion, and advocacy. By prioritizing accessibility, addressing discrimination, fostering acceptance within disability communities, and promoting education and awareness, we can work towards a more inclusive and equitable society where individuals at the intersection of disability and LGBTAI identities are valued, respected, and empowered.

It's important to recognize and address the unique experiences and challenges faced by individuals at this intersection, and to actively promote acceptance, accessibility, and inclusion for all individuals, regardless of their sexual orientation, gender identity, expression, or disability status.

Together, we can create a world that celebrates and embraces the diversity of all individuals. So, it's important to foster inclusive spaces that recognize and address the unique needs and experiences of individuals at the intersection of disability and LGBTAI identities, and to promote acceptance, accessibility, and inclusion for all individuals, regardless of their sexual orientation, gender identity, expression, or disability status.

By recognizing and addressing the challenges faced by individuals at the intersection of disability and LGBTAI identities, we can work towards a more inclusive and equitable society where everyone is valued and respected.

TWENTY FOUR
LGBTAI And The Criminal Justice System

One of the main issues faced by LGBTAI individuals within the criminal justice system is discrimination based on sexual orientation, gender identity, and/or gender expression. This discrimination can come from law enforcement officers, correctional staff, and even other inmates. LGBTAI individuals may face harassment, abuse, violence, and mistreatment while in police custody, during arrest, in detention facilities, or while serving their sentences. This mistreatment can have severe physical, emotional, and psychological consequences for LGBTAI individuals, and may even result in long-term trauma.

Moreover, LGBTAI individuals may be disproportionately represented in the criminal justice system due to various factors such as social stigma, discrimination, and systemic biases. This can include being targeted for their sexual orientation or gender identity by law enforcement, facing bias during arrests, unfair treatment in court proceedings, and receiving harsher sentences compared to their heterosexual and cisgender counterparts for similar offenses. As a result, LGBTAI individuals may face higher rates of incarceration, longer prison sentences, and higher rates of recidivism.

Accessing affirming legal and support services can also be challenging for LGBTAI individuals within the criminal justice system. LGBTAI-specific needs, such as access to gender-affirming healthcare, protection against discrimination and harassment, and accommodation for gender identity and expression, may not be adequately addressed in correctional facilities or during court proceedings. LGBTAI individuals may also face barriers to accessing legal support or advocacy due to discrimination or lack of understanding from legal professionals or service providers.

Addressing LGBTAI-specific needs within the criminal justice system is crucial to ensure that these individuals receive fair and equitable treatment. This can include implementing policies and practices that promote inclusivity, cultural competency, and sensitivity to the unique needs of LGBTAI individuals within law enforcement agencies, correctional facilities, and court systems. It is important to provide training and education to law enforcement and correctional staff on LGBTQIA+ issues, including anti-discrimination policies and procedures, as well as promoting diversity and inclusion.

Additionally, providing access to affirming legal and support services is crucial for LGBTAI individuals within the criminal justice system. This can include ensuring that LGBTAI individuals have access to LGBTQIA+-friendly legal representation, mental health services, and healthcare that is sensitive to their sexual orientation, gender identity, and gender expression. Supportive programs and resources, such as LGBTQIA+ support groups or re-entry programs, can also play a significant role in addressing the unique challenges faced by LGBTAI individuals involved with the criminal justice system.

Points to consider when discussing LGBTAI individuals and the criminal justice system:

1. **Disproportionate Impact of Marginalization:** LGBTAI individuals who also belong to other marginalized communities, such as people of color, immigrants, or people with disabilities, may face compounded discrimination within the criminal justice system. Intersectionality can exacerbate the mistreatment and disparities faced by LGBTAI individuals, leading to even higher rates of incarceration, violence, and other negative outcomes. It is important to recognize and address the intersectional identities and experiences of LGBTAI individuals within the criminal justice system.

2. **Importance of LGBTQIA+-Inclusive Policies:** Implementing LGBTQIA+-inclusive policies and procedures within law enforcement agencies, correctional facilities, and court systems can help promote fairness and inclusivity for LGBTAI individuals. This can include policies that protect against discrimination based on sexual orientation, gender identity, and gender expression, as well as procedures for addressing harassment, abuse, and violence against LGBTAI individuals. In addition, providing access to gender-affirming healthcare, including hormone therapy and gender-affirming surgeries, can be critical for transgender and gender non-conforming individuals within the criminal justice system.

3. **Alternatives to Incarceration:** Exploring alternatives to incarceration, such as diversion programs, restorative justice practices, and community-based initiatives, can be beneficial for LGBTAI individuals. Traditional incarceration can expose LGBTAI individuals to increased risks of discrimination, violence, and mistreatment. Implementing alternatives to incarceration that address the specific needs of LGBTAI individuals, such as providing mental health support, substance abuse treatment, and support for

reintegration into the community, can lead to more positive outcomes.

4. **Supportive Re-entry Programs:** Providing supportive re-entry programs that are inclusive and affirming of LGBTAI individuals can help reduce recidivism rates and promote successful reintegration into society. These programs can include job training, housing support, mental health services, and social support networks that are sensitive to the unique needs of LGBTAI individuals. Addressing the challenges faced by LGBTAI individuals during the re-entry process can help reduce the cycle of involvement with the criminal justice system.

5. **Advocacy and Awareness**: Advocacy and raising awareness about the challenges faced by LGBTAI individuals within the criminal justice system is crucial. This can include promoting policy changes, advocating for LGBTQIA+-inclusive practices, and raising awareness among law enforcement, correctional staff, legal professionals, and the general public about the unique needs and experiences of LGBTAI individuals. It is important to amplify the voices of LGBTAI individuals and advocate for their rights and well-being within the criminal justice system.

6. **Reporting and Documentation of Hate Crimes:** Hate crimes targeting LGBTAI individuals are unfortunately prevalent, and many go unreported or undocumented. It is important to encourage and facilitate the reporting of hate crimes against LGBTAI individuals, and to ensure that law enforcement agencies are trained in handling these cases with sensitivity and cultural competency. Accurate documentation of hate crimes can help raise awareness, inform policy changes, and hold perpetrators accountable for their actions.

7. **Support for Victims of Violence:** LGBTAI individuals who experience violence, whether it be from hate crimes, domestic violence, or other forms of victimization, may face unique challenges in accessing support and justice. It is important to ensure that victim services are inclusive and affirming of LGBTAI individuals, and that there are resources available for reporting, investigating, and prosecuting crimes against them. This can include providing access to LGBTQIA+-competent advocates, counseling services, and legal support.

8. **Training and Education for Criminal Justice Professionals:** Providing training and education for criminal justice professionals, including law enforcement officers, correctional staff, and legal professionals, on LGBTQIA+ cultural competency, bias awareness,

and inclusive practices is crucial. This can help reduce discrimination, mistreatment, and disparities faced by LGBTAI individuals within the criminal justice system. Training can cover topics such as understanding sexual orientation, gender identity, and gender expression, addressing LGBTQIA+ individuals with respect and dignity, and navigating issues such as housing, healthcare, and safety.

9. **Access to Affirming Legal and Support Services:** LGBTAI individuals may face challenges in accessing affirming legal and support services, such as legal representation, counseling, and social support networks. It is important to ensure that these services are inclusive and culturally competent, and that there are resources available to LGBTAI individuals to access these services. This can include providing information on LGBTQIA+-affirming legal resources, mental health services, support groups, and community organizations that cater to the needs of LGBTAI individuals.

10. **Community Engagement and Empowerment:** Building strong LGBTQIA+ communities and fostering community engagement and empowerment can play a significant role in addressing the challenges faced by LGBTAI individuals within the criminal justice system. This can include creating safe spaces, providing peer support, organizing advocacy efforts, and promoting self-empowerment and resilience among LGBTAI individuals. Community engagement can help create networks of support, raise awareness about the rights and needs of LGBTAI individuals, and create a sense of belonging and empowerment.

11. **Addressing Disproportionate Incarceration:** Research shows that LGBTAI individuals, particularly those who are also members of other marginalized communities, such as people of color, transgender individuals, and individuals with low socioeconomic status, are disproportionately represented in the criminal justice system. This can be due to factors such as discrimination, bias, and lack of access to supportive resources. Addressing this issue requires acknowledging and addressing the underlying social, economic, and systemic factors that contribute to the overrepresentation of LGBTAI individuals in the criminal justice system. This can include implementing diversion programs, providing alternatives to incarceration, addressing bias in policing and prosecution, and promoting rehabilitation and reintegration programs that are inclusive and affirming of LGBTAI individuals.

12. **Addressing Health Disparities:** LGBTAI individuals often face health disparities, including higher rates of mental health issues,

substance abuse, and HIV/AIDS. These health disparities can intersect with their involvement in the criminal justice system, as individuals may be at risk of being incarcerated due to these health issues or may face challenges in accessing appropriate healthcare while in the criminal justice system. It is crucial to address these health disparities through inclusive and affirming healthcare services, mental health and substance abuse treatment programs, and comprehensive HIV/AIDS prevention and care programs that are sensitive to the unique needs of LGBTAI individuals.

13. **Ensuring Safe and Inclusive Incarceration Environments:** LGBTAI individuals who are incarcerated may face discrimination, harassment, and violence from both other inmates and correctional staff due to their sexual orientation, gender identity, or gender expression. It is important to ensure that incarceration environments are safe and inclusive for LGBTAI individuals, and that their rights and dignity are respected. This can include implementing policies and procedures that prohibit discrimination, harassment, and violence based on sexual orientation, gender identity, or gender expression, providing access to appropriate healthcare, including gender-affirming care, and offering programming and services that are inclusive and affirming of LGBTAI individuals.

14. **Promoting Re-entry Programs and Support:** LGBTAI individuals who are released from incarceration face unique challenges in reintegrating into society, including discrimination, stigma, and lack of access to supportive resources. It is crucial to provide reentry programs that are inclusive and affirming of LGBTAI individuals, including employment assistance, housing support, mental health services, and peer support networks. These programs can help reduce recidivism, promote successful reintegration, and improve the overall well-being and quality of life of LGBTAI individuals who have been involved in the criminal justice system.

15. **Interectionality:** It is important to recognize that the experiences of LGBTAI individuals within the criminal justice system are shaped by their intersecting identities, including race, ethnicity, religion, disability, and other social identities. Intersectional discrimination and bias can compound the challenges faced by LGBTAI individuals within the criminal justice system, and it is crucial to adopt an intersectional approach in addressing their unique needs and experiences. This includes considering the ways in which different forms of discrimination and oppression intersect and addressing them in an inclusive and holistic manner.

16. **Supporting Access to Legal Resources:** LGBTAI individuals within the criminal justice system may face unique legal challenges, including discrimination, harassment, and violation of their rights. It is important to provide access to legal resources that are knowledgeable about the unique legal issues faced by LGBTAI individuals, such as discrimination based on sexual orientation, gender identity, or gender expression. This can include providing pro bono or low-cost legal services, offering legal information and education specific to LGBTAI individuals, and ensuring that legal processes and procedures are inclusive and affirming.

17. **Educating Criminal Justice Professionals:** Training and education for criminal justice professionals, including law enforcement officers, prosecutors, judges, and correctional staff, should include information on the unique needs and challenges faced by LGBTAI individuals. This can include training on LGBTQ+ cultural competency, sensitivity to gender identity and expression, and awareness of the specific risks and vulnerabilities faced by LGBTAI individuals within the criminal justice system. Educating criminal justice professionals can help reduce bias, discrimination, and mistreatment of LGBTAI individuals, and promote a more inclusive and affirming approach to justice.

18. **Strengthening LGBTQ+ Community Partnerships:** Building partnerships between the criminal justice system and LGBTQ+ organizations can help improve the understanding of the unique needs and challenges faced by LGBTAI individuals within the criminal justice system. This can include collaborations with LGBTQ+ advocacy groups, community-based organizations, and LGBTQ+ leaders to develop and implement policies, programs, and services that are inclusive and affirming. These partnerships can also provide support, resources, and advocacy for LGBTAI individuals who are navigating the criminal justice system, and help ensure that their voices are heard and their rights are protected.

19. **Promoting Data Collection and Research:** There is a lack of comprehensive data on the experiences of LGBTAI individuals within the criminal justice system, which can hinder efforts to fully understand and address the issues they face. Promoting data collection and research on the experiences of LGBTAI individuals within the criminal justice system can help identify disparities, track progress, and inform policy and program development. This includes collecting data on sexual orientation, gender identity, and gender expression in criminal justice data collection efforts, and conducting

research on the unique needs, challenges, and outcomes of LGBTAI individuals within the criminal justice system.

20. **Advocacy and Policy Change:** Advocacy efforts are crucial in addressing the mistreatment and discrimination faced by LGBTAI individuals within the criminal justice system. This includes advocating for policy changes at local, state, and national levels to promote inclusive and affirming practices within the criminal justice system, such as anti-discrimination laws, policies that protect the rights of transgender and gender non-conforming individuals, and measures that address bias and discrimination. It also includes advocating for the inclusion of LGBTAI-specific needs in criminal justice reform efforts and promoting policies that prioritize rehabilitation, reintegration, and support for LGBTAI individuals who are involved in the criminal justice system.

In conclusion, addressing the mistreatment and discrimination faced by LGBTAI individuals within the criminal justice system requires a multi-faceted approach that encompasses legal, policy, educational, and community-based strategies. By recognizing and addressing the unique needs and challenges faced by LGBTAI individuals within the criminal justice system, we can work towards a more equitable and inclusive system that upholds the rights and dignity of all individuals, regardless of their sexual orientation, gender identity, or gender expression. It is crucial to prioritize the inclusion of LGBTAI-specific needs in criminal justice policies, practices, and programs to ensure that the criminal justice system promotes fairness and justice for all individuals, including those who identify as LGBTAI. By addressing discrimination, violence, and mistreatment faced by LGBTAI individuals in the criminal justice system, we can create a more equitable and inclusive system that respects the rights and dignity of all individuals, regardless of their sexual orientation, gender identity, or gender expression.